—— Revealing Lives ——

Prepared under the auspices of
The Institute for Research on Women and Gender,
Stanford University

◆

SUNY Series in Feminist Criticism and Theory
Michelle A. Massé, Editor

Revealing Lives

Autobiography, Biography, and Gender

Editors
Susan Groag Bell
and
Marilyn Yalom

Consulting Editors
Diane Wood Middlebrook
and Peter Stansky

State University of New York Press

Published by
State University of New York Press, Albany

© 1990 State University of New York

All rights reserved

Printed in the United States of America

For information, address State University of New York
Press, State University Plaza, Albany, N.Y., 12246

Library of Congress Cataloging-in-Publication Data

Revealing lives: autobiography, biography, and gender / edited by
    Susan Groag Bell and Marilyn Yalom.
        p.   cm.
    Papers from a conference on autobiography and biography: gender,
text, and context, 1986, sponsored by the Center for Research on
Women at Stanford University.
    Includes bibliographical references.
    ISBN 0–7914–0435—8. — ISBN 0–7914–0436–6 (pbk.)
    1. Biography (as a literary form)—Congresses. 2. Autobiography–
–Congresses. 3. Identity (Psychology)—Congresses. 4. Sex role in
literature—Congresses. 5. Self in literature—Congresses.
I. Bell, Susan Groag II. Yalom, Marilyn. III. Stanford University.
Institute for Research on Women and Gender
CT21.R47 1990
809'.93592—dc20   89–26285
                                                                          CIP

10 9 8 7 6 5 4 3 2 1

Contents

Foreword

Why sex? According to the *Honolulu Advertiser*, this provocative question was to be addressed by the Citizens' Professor of English Literature at the University of Hawaii's Center for Biographical Study. As the announced speaker, I had explained earlier that, unlike the other weekly speakers, I had no work of my own in progress on the theory or practice of life-writing. Perhaps I could raise some issues that had arisen in the course of my teaching certain American autobiographies? But the director of the Center had a more specific assignment in mind. I might, he hoped, shed light on something that had long perplexed him: "Why do you feminists go on so much about sex, class, and race?"

Although "why not?" and "because," as well as " 'cuz that's what people *have*" readily occurred as responses, I agreed to undertake a more thoughtful discussion of the question in its implications for the writing and reading of biography. The talk was listed as "Why Sex, Class, and Race in Biography?" and the local press saw fit to abridge this mouthful as described.

I began, that day, by violating a longstanding resolution against use of the barbarism "to problematize." For, if I was to do more than simply preach to those already convinced of the centrality of large social categories for the analysis of individual lives, my approach had to focus on the consequences to intellectual activity of rendering problematic what had previously been considered entirely *un*problematic, even natural.

To explore some of these consequences, I chose three classic pieces of autobiographical writing by American men that had raised troubling questions in the classroom: the *Autobiographies* of Malcolm X and Benjamin Franklin and Thoreau's *Walden*. For Malcolm, of course, race is the social force that is foregrounded; I set out to examine what happens when we also problematize gender in his writing. Class, specifically the reflection of mercantile values on a man's inner life and consciousness, is salient for Franklin; I looked at how the image shifts when we problematize race and posit Franklin as a *white* man. Throeau is usually considered outside of those (inferentially reductive) categories; but I had recently had the experience of teaching *Walden* against my own hero-worship of its author to street-wise students who tended to dismiss Thoreau and his text as privileged, white, and male.

Although the historical operations of class or race have attracted a certain amount of attention both from biographers and from those who endeavor to make sense of the biographical phenomenon, gender, which is even more universally acknowledged as a factor in individual human development, remained a neglected area in biography studies until quite recently. It is of particular interest, therefore, that the essays in *Revealing Lives,* varied as their subjects are in class, ethnic, and national background, all concentrate on the meanings of gender in the telling of a life story.

It is not only to avoid misunderstandings like the one into which the local newspaper precipitated me that I have been following editors Susan Bell and Marilyn Yalom in their preference for "gender" over "sex" to characterize their volume's focus. Specifically sexual motives and behavior have been a matter of biographical interest rather longer than the more comprehensive questions of gender. The result is that we still have more biographies and even autobiographies that tell us about, say, a male subject's homosexuality or a female subject's pathological repression than we have investigations of the many other ways that experiencing life as a male or a female informs consciousness or events.

Interest in the factors that may shape a woman's life differently from a man's begins, of course, with the influence of feminism on the reading of both lives and texts. Feminist criticism focused attention onto such questions of difference, as well as asserting that what happens in *women's* lives is a legitimate and significant object of intellectual inquiry. Feminists also attributed new importance to the private sphere that defined women's lives for so long and to the private genres of writing—diaries, letters, personal memoirs—that that sphere fostered.

At first, gender-oriented criticism focused almost exclusively on women. Only the marked variant in the gender universe was assumed to possess a gender identity that was biographically significant—perhaps even to possess one at all. (In much the same way, race is too often presumed to function only for people of color, class for working people or the poor.) But some of the most interesting applications of a gender studies approach to biography are those that recognize how problematic maleness and masculinity are in a highly gendered social and intellectual context.

It is not surprising, therefore, that the majority of essays included in *Revealing Lives*, like the majority of contributions to the conference at which they were originally presented, should be about the workings of gender in the lives of women—*particular* women, though representing different historic moments, cultures, and relations to social power. But some of the collection's most exciting conceptual breakthroughs occur in those contributions that problematize male gender experience or that explicitly contrast male and female identity and attitudes.

Nor are these breakthroughs restricted to academic discourse. The way we understand the text of a biography is directly related to the way we understand a life. It also intersects with our apprehension of society itself and social movements, and hence with the way we imagine the possibilities for change in our *common* life story. In this sense, *Revealing Lives* does more than reveal the lives, in gendered terms, of the specific individuals and groups the contributors study. Through the revelation of gendered biographical strategies, the book reveals something about the process of revealing *life*—eventually including our own.

Lillian S. Robinson
University of Hawaii at Manoa

Acknowledgments

We wish to thank the Center for Research on Women, now re-named the Institute for Research on Women and Gender, at Stanford University for sponsoring the 1986 conference on "Autobiography and Biography: Gender, Text, and Context." Most of the papers in this collection were initially prepared for that memorable event. We are particularly indebted to Professors Diane Wood Middlebrook and Peter Stansky of Stanford University for acting as consulting editors for this book. Grateful acknowledgment is made to the following authors, publishers, and journals for permission to reprint previously published materials:

Cid Corman, Literary Executor of Lorine Niedecker's works, for quotations from her poems and letters.

Peter Dent and Kenneth Cox for quotations from Lorine Niedecker's letters to Kenneth Cox.

The Poetry/Rare Books Collection, University Libraries, SUNY at Buffalo for quotations from Lorine Niedecker's material.

The Harry Ransom Humanities Research Center at the University of Texas at Austin for quotations from Lorine Niedecker's manuscripts.

Duke University Press for quotations from *Between Your House and Mine: The Letters of Lorine Niedecker to Cid Corman* (1986).

Biography for permission to reprint Barbara Babcock's "Reconstructing the Person: the Case of Clara Shortridge Foltz," (Winter 1989). This essay was originally presented at the 1986 Stanford Center for Research on Women Conference.

Routledge for permission to reprint from *Textual Practice* (Spring 1989) Regenia Gagnier's "The Literary Standard, Working-Class Life-writing, and Gender." This essay was originally presented at the 1986 Stanford Center for Research on Women Conference.

xii   *Acknowledgments*

Cambridge University Press for reuse of material from Anna Kuhn's *Christa Wolf's Utopian Vision: From Marxism to Feminism* (1988).

AMS Press for reuse of material from Carol Hanbery MacKay's introduction to a new edition of Anne Thackeray Ritchie's introductions (1988).

Introduction

Susan Groag Bell and Marilyn Yalom

In an age of daunting machines and awesome bureaucracies, when family, work, and community patterns are undergoing dizzying transformations, it is reassuring to look into a human face. Portraits and self-portraits in art and literature; life stories told by their protagonists or recorded by more distant chroniclers; even life-writing with plural subjects or a strong sense of group identity effect an affirmation of individual worth. As readers entering into the experiential world of another consciousness, we move once more within the human dimension where it is still possible to believe in the meaning of a personal identity. The impersonality, fragmentation, and alienation of the postmodern world seem less overwhelming as we follow the vicissitudes of a real person—a brother or sister creature from whom we grasp vicarious validation of our own lives. Perhaps this is one reason why autobiographies and biographies are proliferating as never before.[1]

Similarly, the production of scholarly works devoted to the study of autobiography and biography has risen dramatically during the past two decades. Our book reflects this burgeoning interest and joins the ongoing debate at the intersection of gender. This discourse on life-writing has produced a number of important theoretical works, especially in the area of women's autobiography—among them books by Estelle Jelinek, Domna Stanton, Sidonie Smith, Shari Benstock, Celeste Schenck and Bella Brodzki, Valerie Sanders and Carolyn Heilbrun. These scholars have raised an undeniable challenge to the history of literary criticism as previously written from an androcentric bias. They have protested the exclusion of women from the autobiographical canon, questioned the paradigm of "singular" or "exemplary" lives based on men's experience, explored the differences between men's and women's forms

1

of self-representation, and proposed several new woman-centered literary models.[2]

The contemporary debate on autobiography is frequently grounded in various post-structuralist theories that deconstruct texts and decenter subjects so as to deny or at least question the familiar concept of a mimetic relationship between literature and life. As editors of this collection, we, on the contrary, reclaim that relationship. Yes, we believe like Philippe Lejeune that the autobiographical "I," however fugitive, partial, and unreliable, is indeed the privileged textual double of a real person, as well as a self-evident textual construct.[3] And because that real person has selected from his or her past those kernels of experience which appear, in retrospect, to be the most formative and the most enduring, autobiography can offer a significantly "historical" form of self-expression. As Herbert Leibowitz concedes in his recent book on American autobiography, recalling a citation from the earlier work of Albert Stone: "Life is the more inclusive sign—not *Literature*—which deserves to be placed above the gateway to the house of autobiography."[4] Clearly, before they acquired celebrity status, autobiographers were once people like the rest of us, connected to a certain birthdate, birthplace, and a set of existential realities into which (*pace* Heidegger) they were thrown. This much maligned referentiality gives autobiographical and biographical writing its particular tension and flavor. Whatever their differences, autobiography and biography presuppose the factual data of a lived existence, if only to provide the nest from which the author's imagination and interpretation may then take flight.

Both autobiography and biography, linguistically united by their common roots in the Greek words *bios* (life) and *graphe* (writing), are fundamentally hybrid creations of historicity and textuality. How the life inflects the text, how the text inflects the life are proper subjects of theoretical speculation, but for most readers, the appeal of life-writing is its evocation of a human being, dead or alive, and the mythologizing (or demythologizing) power inherent in a written account of that life.

Libraries and bookstores usually group biography and autobiography together, making no distinction between the life history written about another person or about oneself. Not so with literary critics or historians. Historians have traditionally distinguished between these terms, writing biography themselves and skeptically using autobiographical material as their source. Literary scholars have until very recently also treated autobiography and biography as distinct from one another, although the attempt to define the former as a genre has been abandoned decisively by influential critics, such as Paul Jay and Paul de Man, who formulate the discourse in terms of "self-reflexive" texts or "self-presentation" in the text.[5] Many feminist literary scholars have taken over this deconstructionist mode in order to create, in the words of Domna Stanton, "a more generous and dynamic space for the exploration of women's texts."[6] The only thing most literary scholars seem to agree upon is that autobiography is *not* biography.

Our work questions even this basic assumption. We have found that the boundaries between autobiography and biography are not always so distinct as their definitions imply. Biography is generally defined as the story of a person's life written by another, and autobiography as the story of one's life written by oneself. Most theoreticians by now agree that biography—reputedly the more objective of the two—is commonly colored by the subjective world of the biographer; indeed, as Blanche Wiesen Cook succinctly puts it: "For biographers. . . . all choices are autobiographical."[7] Biographers often have special affinities with their subjects, not the least of which is gender, and they sometimes discover further confirmation of what attracted their interest in the first place—i.e., the distinctive characteristics of appropriate role models, alter egos, foremothers, forefathers, or even explanations for their own personal problems. It is not surprising that they develop in the course of their research and writing a strong sense of identification with the chosen subject, one that sometimes leads them to imitate personal mannerisms, linguistic patterns, and even illnesses. Paul Mariani, the biographer of poet William Carlos Williams, notes that some "biographers have taken to wearing their subjects' clothes or hats or shoes, others find their smoking habits and diets and tastes . . . changing to conform to their subjects'. . . ." Describing his own biographical breakthrough when, after eight years of research, he began to be able to guess the contents of Williams's letters before reading them, Mariani concluded: "In a sense, then, the biographer had finally managed to become his subject."[8] Belle Gale Chevigny calls this a "mirroring self" and suggests that it is often reciprocal—that the subject provides a sanctioning parent for the biographer and that the biographer in turn validates the life under scrutiny. She argues further that this is especially common when women write about other women.[9] Michèle Sarde's biography of Colette provides a pointed example of this phenomenon. Sarde calls her work "a wished-for

encounter" through which Colette's life illuminated her own "existence as a woman." What emerged was "the history of a particular
subjectivity"—Colette's—"filtered through another subjectivity."
Biography, as Sarde construes it, becomes an interactive venture
between sister lives.[10]

Sometimes biography provides the means for a person to enter
into recorded history through the life of a more celebrated relative
or friend. This was particularly true for women in the past, who,
limited in their access to the public sphere, often seized the opportunity of writing their lives "obliquely" through the biographies of
their famous husbands, fathers, brothers, lovers, or employers.
Autobiography masquerading as biography is one of the central
discoveries of this book.

As for autobiography, historians and literary critics have different ideas concerning the constitution of this corpus. Historians
approach all types of first-person documents as valid sources and
tend to consider diaries, journals, letters, and travel memoirs—as
well as narrative autobiography—as "autobiographical material,"
as in the French catch-all words "mémoires" and "témoignages."
Literary critics, on the other hand, wedded as they are to esthetics,
have until recently examined only high-culture avatars of autobiography proper—e.g., Augustine, Rousseau, Mill and Sartre—thus
distinguishing this category of prose recollections from the form-
lessness of "autobiographical material." In *Fictions in Autobiography,* Paul John Eakin summarizes these two major approaches,
perhaps contrasting them too starkly: "Historians and social sci-
entists attempt to isolate the factual content of autobiography
from its narrative matrix, while literary critics, seeking to approach the appreciation of autobiography as an imaginative act,
have been willing to treat such texts as though they were indistinguishable from novels."[11] Eakin's own approach accepts and extends the model of Philippe Lejeune's "autobiographical pact,"
which proposes as the decisive generic criteria the writer's stated
intention to produce a work based upon one's personal history,
with the presence of one's real name in the text and on the title
page as guarantee of its authenticity.[12]

We find it useful to think of autobiographical material according to the model of the fan proposed by Georges May. This model
lays out a full spectrum of autobiographical possibilities, ranging
from the more realistic accounts of diaries and letters, at one end
of the spectrum, to the more imaginative forms of autobiographical
fiction and poetry on the other.[13] The central area of the fan is

claimed by the genre of narrative autobiography, as traditionally
defined by literary critics. But even so catholic an approach to self-
reflexive literature may suggest lines of demarcation between the
genres that are not so evident when one examines individual texts.
Many of the essays in this collection highlight the overlap between
autobiography, autobiographical fiction, and biography, namely in
the works of Bettina von Arnim and Christa Wolf, Adèle Hugo, Anne
Thackeray Ritchie, Charles and Mary Lamb, Nadezhda Durova,
and the children of German fascist fathers. In each of these, the
literary work in question is revealed to be an amalgamation of autobiography and/or biography and/or fiction and/or chronicle, thus
defying traditional generic classification. And how should one clas-
sify the personal narratives dictated to historians by nineteenth-
century Mexican women, or the autobiography in the paintings
accompanied by verbal citations created by the twentieth-century
German artist Charlotte Salomon? We have welcomed these singular examples of self-expression in a conscious attempt to broaden
the arena of life-writing, not only for the sake of abolishing arbitrary boundaries, but also and especially so as to include the texts
of those whose gender and/or class and/or ethnicity would, in the
past, have provided unconscious criteria for exclusion.

What unites all the pieces in this book—keeping it from
becoming a mere kaleidoscope of heterogeneous chapters is the
central insistence upon gender as the lens through which autobiography and biography are scrutinized. We ask what is revealed
when we magnify the gendered aspects of both men's and women's
life-writing—when we "overread" gender, to use Nancy Miller's
phrase.[14] In examples taken from Europe, Britain and the New
World during the past two centuries, the eternal human questions
of identity, choice, responsibility, happiness, tragedy, even death
are interpreted in terms of a gender analysis.

Gender, as we understand and use it, is that deep imprinting
of cultural beliefs, values, and expectations on one's biological
sex, forming a fundamental component in a person's sense of identity. When viewed collectively, it is a system of difference between
men and women, and a system of relations between the two
groups, with males almost universally in a position of dominance.
While the physical distinctions between men and women can be
enumerated with relative economy and ease, the psycho-
social-political ramifications of gender are far more varied and difficult to assess. Contemporary feminists, breaking loose from a
Freudian belief system that gave primacy to genital awareness in

human development, have focused instead on the socio-cultural constructs that are imposed upon biological differences and on the systems of meaning in which sex and gender are embedded. Yet there is by no means consensus even among feminists about such issues as the definition of gender; its relation to anatomical difference; how gender arrangements are constituted and sustained; or the role of differences *within* each gender (such as lesbian and gay identities within the categories of "female" and "male").[15] Some feminist theoreticians, demonstrating a postmodern scepticism toward all dualisms, have attempted to erode the notion of gender salience by giving equal weight to other social categories such as race, age, and class. In a recent collection of essays on sexual difference, the attempt of anthropologists Jane Collier and Sylvia Yanagisako, for example, to reduce the biological and physiological differences between the sexes to one set of factors no more nor less important than many others has been contested by historians Karen Offen and Estelle Freedman, who continue to claim the need and the value for asserting gender difference as a critical stance for feminist scholarship and politics.[16]

Other American and French theorists from developmental psychology and psychiatry focussing upon the early acquisition of gender identity in children have provided empirical and clinical evidence to support the view that gender is essentially determined by culture, rather than genital difference, and intricately bound up with the acquisition of language.[17] The child who identifies itself as "girl" or "boy" in its second year has already begun the ongoing task of processing interpersonal cues about the meaning of those words. And even if that child develops a core gender identity at so early an age, he or she will constantly be subject to reinforcement or revision of ideas about the mandates of gender throughout a lifetime.[17] As they experience the vicissitudes of puberty, adolescence, young adulthood, work, family, mid-life and aging, human beings are constantly negotiating gender issues, whether they do so consciously or not.

The subjects of autobiographies and biographies, especially those written prior to the feminist revolution, have often been unaware of gender imperatives in their personal development. In contrast, the scholarly detective work necessary for a more accurate understanding of any individual life must recognize that gender is an overarching category of human identity, similar to race in its immutability, and contestably more primary than class. A gender analysis may take the form of a close reading designed to illuminate not only the written word but also the loaded associations and unspoken thoughts and feelings contained within the text. Alternatively, moving from text to context, it may investigate the society surrounding the subject itself—on the one hand, close relationships with family members, friends, teachers, employers, or subordinates; on the other, the wider political, religious, and economic circumstances occurring in a specific time and place. Special attention to the prevailing ideological infra-structure and its system of signification often provides a fruitful method with which to isolate the sexual and sexist threads of the cultural fabric enveloping these scripted lives.

The authors of the chapters in this book use varying techniques, according to their scholarly disciplines and personal interests, to analyze the place of gender in the construction of lives and texts. They also illuminate the complex interrelations of gender and other aspects of identity such as nationality, ethnicity, class divisions between "mental" and "manual" labor, religion, colonization, and even cross-dressing.

Individuals writing about themselves have traditionally been prone to take their gender as a given, usually conflating it with sex, and to reflect upon it less than they do on their race, class, religious or political affiliation, which have appeared to them as more idiosyncratic. Men rarely make an issue of their gender because the generic masculine has been the norm in Western society for at least three millenia, with woman conceptualized as derivative from and secondary to man. A few women in the past wrote their autobiographies with some consciousness of gender significance—Elizabeth Cady Stanton understood that being born female was the determining fact in her life, and George Sand pointedly acknowledged a crucial maternal influence at a time when mothers were rarely present in autobiographies and biographies. For the most part, however, women and men alike had to await the twentieth century for a feminist perspective that would highlight gender and declare it problematic. Autobiographies written during the nineteen-seventies and eighties from the vantage of a heightened sensitivity to women's issues often also underscore the prominence of race, ethnicity and class (for example, Maya Angelou's *I Know Why the Caged Bird Sings*, Maxine Hong Kingston's *The Woman Warrior*, and Kim Chernin's *In My Mother's House*).[18]

If autobiographers have tended to take gender for granted, so too have biographers. In the nineteenth century, if they considered it at all, most assumed an essentialist division between a masculine and a feminine "nature," observing how the biographical subject did or did not deviate from so-called feminine virtues, such · as modesty and intuitiveness, or so-called masculine qualities, such as courage and rationality. Most nineteenth-century biographies and dictionaries of biography have privileged the subject's father and ignored the mother, and in the mid-twentieth century this bias often turned toward an outright denigration of the mother. This was frequently the case when biographers and literary critics, influenced by the pseudo-psychoanalytic notion of mothers as a "generation of vipers,"[19] examined the lives of men such as Hemingway and Rimbaud. Even with the increased attention to women that has marked Western publishing during the past decade, and, ironically, despite an almost prurient insistence on sexual acts and orientations, most biographers have continued to ignore the deep implications of gender in their subjects' life histories. This is particularly true of literary biography and its related scholarly discourse.[20] However, a few biographers grounded in feminist theory have demonstrated how the gender system informs basic aspects of private lives. Among these are Jean Strouse's brilliant study of Alice James and Phyllis Rose's innovative account of the parallel lives of four famous Victorian couples.[21]

We have yet to see the autobiographies and biographies of men give to gender its due, perhaps because, as suggested earlier, this concern is less obvious to them. White men tend to look at themselves with a normative eye, conflating the masculine viewpoint with universal vision, as if it were the eye of God. As Simone de Beauvoir so pointedly wrote in The Second Sex: "Representation of the world like the world itself is the work of men; they describe it from their own point of view, which they confuse with absolute truth."[22] A feminist vision has begun to challenge this hegemonic view.

By turning the camera back upon men, by assuming the position of the one who sees and records rather than the one who is seen and recorded, writers may be able to give to the biography of men and even to men's self-portraits what they have already begun to establish in the biographies and autobiographies of women— that is, a vision of a world that is gendered to the core and where no life story can be told without decoding the sexual politics of one's time and place.

Exploding myths about gender and genre is by now a given for scholars who approach literary and historical documents with a feminist awareness. As editors we have refused to be pigeon-holed into traditional generic categories; so too we have particularly welcomed those studies that refuse to accept a conventional monolithic conception of gender. In this volume we encounter sex role mergence in the writings of Charles and Mary Lamb, as examined by Jane Aaron; a remarkable case of military cross-dressing in Mary Zirin's account of the memoirs of the Russian woman soldier Nadezhda Durova; and John Stuart Mill's attempt to incorporate values seen traditionally as "feminine" into a masculinist rational ethos in Susan Bell's study of his autobiography. These three essays demonstrate that even in the nineteenth century—a time when European men and women were assigned distinctly separate spheres—a binary system is inadequate as a mode of approach to actual life stories.

Three other studies of nineteenth-century life-writing investigate the subversion of prevailing gender ideologies by women narrators in both Europe and the New World. Without official voice in the public domain, enjoined to domesticity and silence, these women must be seen as uneasy transgressors, as Sidonie Smith so lucidly argues in her work on women's autobiography.[23] Applying this thesis to biography, Marilyn Yalom writing on Adèle Hugo, and Carol MacKay on Anne Thackeray Ritchie, demonstrate the strategies by which women inscribed their lives surreptitiously into the biographies of the famous men to whom they were related, and thus entered the "male" arena not only of authorship, but also, more dramatically, of self-authorship.

Genaro Padilla found another form of subversion among the women narrators who contributed to a collection of oral Native Hispano-Mexican stories edited by the historian Hubert H. Bancroft in the 1870s. Padilla discovered that these women had in fact told their stories in a much broader context than Bancroft's edition reveals, since he attended only to the domestic domain. Retranslation informed by a feminist sensibility discloses how the women described, both overtly and covertly, their own participation in the major transformation of California in the 1840s.

Like Padilla, Regenia Gagnier is concerned with a group analysis that raises questions of gender alongside those of class. In her study of nineteenth-century British working-class autobiographies, she argues that the literary conventions and individualist esthetics of the period were at odds with the material and emotional lives of working-class men and women. This disjunction has engendered a lack of appreciation for much working-class life-writing while contributing to problems of personal identity for others who tried to write their lives according to European middle-class male models.

Another group of essays examines specific problems encountered by the biographers of three highly diverse American women—Clara Foltz, Lorine Niedecker, and Anne Sexton. Barbara Babcock researches the history of the first woman lawyer in California, Clara Foltz. Willing to challenge the professional sexual division of her era, Foltz was, however, reluctant to abandon a personal claim to those attributes deemed by her contemporaries as "feminine." Babcock's approach to her subject through an investigation of Foltz's mysterious divorce from her husband reveals many contradictions in the psyche of a notoriously successful public figure who had nonetheless internalized many late nineteenth- and early twentieth-century ideas as to what was appropriate for women.

Glenna Breslin documents similarly engendered constraints in the life of the poet Lorine Niedecker. In Breslin's view, Niedecker "made choices at odds with her culture's expectations of her as a woman" for the sake of her development as a poet. Her decision to have an abortion in the midst of her relationship with the poet Louis Zukofsky was characteristic of that feminine dilemma: she never had another child (whereas he went on to become a father). The much-discussed conflict between creation and procreation was indeed a simmering subtext in Niedecker's life script.

Diane Middlebrook focuses on biographical methods, the relationship between biographer and subject, and problems of postmodernism in the production of biography. She invokes a feminist challenge to the traditional humanistic position that the biographer "speaks from a secure center of culture" where "he" provides a trustworthy, civilizing view of reality. Instead, there is "the acknowledgement that the personal is political, that the objective representation of a person in a book is not now and has never been possible."

The last cluster of essays is linked primarily by their common World War II German context. Given the enormity of the Holocaust, gender differences might be dismissed as trivial. Yet even here biographers, historians, and literary critics confront significant issues wrought by sexual difference.[24]

John Felstiner presents the Romanian German Jewish poet Paul Celan—a life profoundly seared by Nazi brutality. Felstiner illuminates the complex role of language in Celan's development, and especially the significance of the mother tongue, transmitted by his own mother and constituting a female influence in his life and poetry. In Felstiner's work, translation becomes a biographical tool, drawing the critic close to the poet in a linguistic embrace.

Mary Felstiner brings to life the remarkable pictorial autobiography of a German Jewish woman artist, whose existence was threatened both by Nazi persecution and by the suicidal tendencies of the women in her family. Salomon painted her life story in a desperate effort to pursue her artistic profession *and* hold onto her sanity. At the same time, she fulfilled the traditional female nurturing role in her relationship to her grandmother, whom she encouraged to resist suicide by writing her own autobiography.

Susan Figge's essay on the memoirs of fascist fathers, like Padilla's on Mexican women's narratives and Gagnier's on British working-class autobiographies, places the accent on the phenomenon of group identity: how sex and gender inform the life-writing of groups or communities with a common heritage or culture. Figge asserts that "narrative power was an important feature in the transmission of psycho-social patterns in the German family"; she finds that sons locate narrative authority in the father, buttressed by German patriarchal politics and culture, while daughters explicitly contrast the fathers' overriding voice with the mothers' silence and verbal disenfranchisement.

Since our book encompasses a time frame from the early nineteenth to the late twentieth century, Anna Kuhn's introductory chapter on Bettina von Arnim and Christa Wolf could well have been either the first or the last chapter. Her study demonstrates how two German authors from vastly different eras slipped through the cracks of autobiography, biography, and fiction to create highly original hybrid texts that illuminate women's use of other women to validate and inspire their own writing.

This collection of predominantly historico-literary essays illuminates the omnipresence of gender in the unfolding of lives. At a time of transition and uncertainty in our aspirations for women and men, attention to individual journeys through the life cycle—often into stages and situations we have not personally encountered—opens new vistas, offers unexpected precedents, provides a sense of continuity and connection. The ever growing interest in women and previously ignored groups has found expression in autobiography, biography and the corresponding research on life-writing, thus opening the curtain a little wider on that stage where men and women script new destinies and enact their changing roles by accepting, rejecting, and often transforming traditional gender expectations.

Chapter One

The "Failure" of Biography and the Triumph of Women's Writing: Bettina von Arnim's *Die Günderode* and Christa Wolf's *The Quest for Christa T.*

——————————— *Anna K. Kuhn*

Conventional biography—a third-person narration of the life of a public figure—has traditionally been a male domain. Autobiography, on the other hand, while sometimes defined as a subcategory of biography, is increasingly viewed as a prototypically female enterprise. It is true that far more biographies of men than of women exist, just as it is true that women, relegated to the private sphere, have produced an abundance of autobiographical writings that have reached an unprecedented richness in the twentieth century.[1] The publication of these autobiographical texts by women has, moreover, blurred the boundaries between the traditionally separate spheres: it has made the private public.

Expectations concerning biographical and autobiographical writing are currently a topic of intense debate among literary scholars. It is a commonplace that both genres are in a state of flux. Few critics today would subscribe to the long-held belief in the dichotomy between the inherent "objectivity" of biography and autobiography's innate subjectivity. Scholars now generally concede, for example, that a biographer's choice of subject matter and his or her attitude toward the material chosen reveals as much about the biographer as s/he seeks to reveal about the subject. Thus, instead of classifying autobiography as a subcategory of biography, one could argue for an inversion of these categories and call for a reading of biography as a subcategory of autobiography.

Recent postmodern critical theory, furthermore, has called into question the concept of the unified subject, for so long considered the informing principle of (auto)biographical writing. It has

13

made us aware that in writing lives, (self)representation entails various degrees of (self)invention,[2] that in writing we create (our)-selves. In the following I examine Bettina von Arnim's *Die Günderode* and Christa Wolf's *The Quest for Christa T.*, two texts by German women writers which invoke traditional generic expectations of both biography and autobiography only to disappoint those expectations. The strategies employed by these writers allow them to create new structures through which to express a highly differentiated, complex, and changing sense of self, and simultaneously to dismantle common generic categories within the dominant literary tradition.

Although separated by one hundred and twenty-nine years, Bettina von Arnim's *Die Günderode* (1839), a work written in the spirit of early German Romanticism, and *The Quest for Christa T.* (1968), by the contemporary East German writer Christa Wolf, show striking similarities.[3] These texts present us with successful examples of the praxis of women's (auto)biography and can be read as literary counterparts to recent theoretical reflections,[4] reflections that have led to a destabilization and reassessment of these genres. Von Arnim's and Wolf's challenge to traditional generic norms results in the creation of a unique, hybrid form: the auto/biographical novel, a form that amalgamates the biographical and the autobiographical novel, two extant hybrid forms of biography and autobiography. Ultimately, however, they render attempts at generic categorization meaningless by defying generic classification.

Both *Die Günderode* and *The Quest for Christa T.* represent a woman writer's attempt to come to terms with the premature death of a beloved female friend. Karoline von Günderode committed suicide in 1806 at the age of twenty-six; Christa T. died of leukemia in 1963 at the age of thirty-five.[5] While both von Arnim and Wolf seek to immortalize their friends, the traditional goal of biography, their works explode expectations of this genre. *Die Günderode* and *Christa T.* are as much autobiographical[6] as they are biographical. In addition, both authors call upon the imagination to augment their narratives. By consciously fictionalizing their authentic material,[7] they undermine a fundamental claim of both biography and autobiography, namely verifiability. These texts therefore exemplify precisely the problematic issues in the vanguard of current theoretical discussions of (auto)biography.

The uniqueness of *Die Günderode* and *The Quest for Christa T.* lies in the reciprocity they establish between writer and subject and between reader and text. Both texts establish a dialogue between the writing subject (the "I" narrator of *Die Günderode* and *Christa T.*), who at times appears to be identical with the author (Bettina von Arnim and Christa Wolf), and the subject of narration, Karoline von Günderode (but also Bettina von Arnim) and Christa T. (but also the first-person narrator). This dialogue is then extended to include the reader as well, either through direct address[8] or through the active involvement of the reader in the reading process (*Die Günderode* and *Christa T.*). In creating works whose theme is intersubjectivity, these women writers circumvent the objectification inherent in Western hegemonic discourse. They conscientiously resist asserting authorial supremacy over their subject matter and consequently avoid making objects out of their human material. By shifting the emphasis away from the outcome of narration, that is, a self-contained story, to the process of narrating or writing itself, these women also undermine traditional generic concepts of biography and autobiography. Indeed, they call into question traditional notions of narration itself, conceived as the product of an author's skillful mastery over his material.

Both *Die Günderode* and *Christa T.* lack closure. These intentionally open-ended narratives seek to duplicate for readers the process of relationship experienced by their writers by inviting them to share in that process through active interaction with the text. The narrative strategies employed by Bettina von Arnim and Christa Wolf thus conform to those employed by other women writers, for, as recent feminist scholarship reveals, women's narrative strategies often circumvent the closure endemic to conventional romance plots.[9] To the extent that both Bettina von Arnim and Christa Wolf devise narrative strategies reflective of specifically female interaction, strategies that challenge traditional norms and present alternative forms, their works can also be considered a "writing beyond the ending."[10] In their endeavors to articulate their experiences, they devise writing techniques that enable them to subvert some of the limitations of conventional (male) literary structures. By transcending traditional norms of canonical genres, von Arnim and Wolf create new literary forms that substitute a dialogic structure for phallocentric discourse: a conversation between two women replaces the single authoritative (and authoritarian) narrative voice.

In keeping with the noncanonical focus of my study, I will abandon the chronological sequencing literary critics traditionally favor for an experiential one. Since my reading of *Die Günderode* is clearly influenced by my reading of *Christa T.* and by Wolf's essays

on the women romantics, both of which predate my acquaintance
with von Arnim's text, I will deal with the texts in the order I
encountered them.

At the time of its publication in 1968, Christa Wolf's *The
Quest for Christa T.*, was considered one of the most politically controversial works to emerge from the German Democratic Republic
(GDR).[11] Critics in both the East and West read the text in the
context of GDR politics and Christa T., a nonconformist who cham-
pioned the rights of the individual in the communist collective, as
a statement of Wolf's disenchantment with the GDR. Thus East
German (male) critics tended to be defensive, whereas their West
German counterparts tended to be smugly satisfied about what
they perceived to be Wolf's criticism of repression in the East.
Feminists in the West, often overlooking the text's overt political
context, heralded *Christa T.* as a milestone of women's writing. In
so doing they recognized the subtler, more pervasive subversive
power of Wolf's text, which lies not in its content but its form.

Originally conceived as a posthumous biography of her friend,
Wolf's narrative changed its focus as she was writing the text. In
"Interview with Myself," Wolf describes this shift:

> Later on, I noticed that the object of my story was not at all, or did
> not remain so clearly herself, Christa T. I suddenly faced myself. I
> had not foreseen this. The relations between "us"—Christa T. and
> the narrator "I"—shifted of themselves into the center; the differ-
> ences in character and the points at which they touched, the ten-
> sions between "us" and the way they dissolved or failed to dissolve.
> If I were a mathematician I should probably speak of a "function"—
> nothing tangible, visible, material, but extraordinarily effective.[12]

In what amounts to a classic description of female mirroring, Wolf
distinguishes her text from phallocentric ones in which woman is
posited as other. Since Christa T. and the narrator are both
women, their experience of themselves and each other is not
marked by the alterity[13] that is characteristic of male-female interaction in Western culture.

Wolf's description also distinguishes her undertaking from
those autobiographies in which the narrator indulges in endless
self-reflection and self-absorption. In her text, the narrator's act of
mourning[14] (that is, the writing of the text of *Christa T.*) serves as
a catalyst for reviewing her own past and enables her to reach a
new understanding of both her friend and herself. *Christa T.*, a

turning point in Christa Wolf's artistic development, marks the breakthrough to her own unique style. Wolf describes the process of writing that informs the text of *Christa T.* as a dialectic between the writer and people, events, and things she has encountered that affect or change her, enabling her to perceive everything differently, resulting in a breakdown of subject/object boundaries and in a sense of interconnectedness and interrelationship.[15] According to Wolf:

> one sees a different reality than before. Suddenly everything is interrelated and in flux, objects perceived as immutable; "givens" become soluble and disclose social relationships objectified in them; we are no longer dealing with that hierarchically ordered social cosmos in which human particles either move according to sociologically or ideologically dictated paths or diverge from this expected movement.[16]

Wolf's unorthodox attitude toward her subject matter reveals the aesthetic ramifications of the dissolution of hierarchical structures in what she calls the writer's "appropriation of reality."[17] The author/narrator[18] sees Christa T. not as an object of investigation, to be mastered and shaped at will, but rather as living material, as capable of changing the writer as the writer is capable of changing her. This notion of transformative subjectivity, which informs all of Wolf's writing, causes her to be scrupulous about sustaining Christa T. as an autonomous subject, rather than as a "miniature," that is, as the object of Wolf's own reified memory of her.

Christa Wolf's description of "miniatures," essential for an understanding of *Christa T.*, has far-reaching implications for the theory of autobiography as well. An articulate description of the notion of self-creation, it implicates memory in the fashioning of (fictions of) the self. According to Wolf:

> we seem to need the help and approval of the imagination in our lives; it means playing with the possibilities open to us. But something else goes on inside us at the same time, daily, hourly, a furtive process hard to avoid, a hardening, petrifying, habituating, that attacks the memory in particular.
>
> We all carry with us a collection of miniatures with captions, some quaint, some gruesome. These we occasionally bring out and show round, because we need confirmation of our own reassuringly clear feelings: beautiful or ugly, good or evil. These miniatures are

for the memory what the calcified cavities are for people with tu-
berculosis, what prejudices are for morals: patches of once active
life now shut off. At one time one was afraid to touch them, afraid
of burning one's fingers on them; now they are cool and smooth,
some of them artistically polished, some especially valuable bits
have cost years of work, for one must forget a great deal and re-
think and re-interpret a great deal before one can see oneself in the
best light everywhere and at all times. That is what we need them
for, the miniatures. You will know what I mean.

But we are in the habit of calling it "remembering" when we
show people these prettily made pieces of arts and crafts and call
them genuine, so that they can show their market value and measure up with the other pieces on show; and the more like these others they are the more genuine they are said to be.[19]

In crafting miniatures we dispense with ambiguity and contradiction and replace painful memories with flattering and unproblem-
atic memories, ones that conform with our images and
understanding of self. Wolf's suspicion of memory, her consciousness of the distortions wrought by a remembering ego which seeks
to (re)create its own past, reveals a level of (self)-awareness that
most autobiographers lack. By consciously writing against her own
"miniatures," she resists the propensity to "recreate the past in
the image of the present" that, according to James Olney, is endemic to "every autobiographer who tries to recapture his personal
history."[20] She is therefore able to bridge the "gap between the
avowed plan of autobiography, which is simply to retrace the history of a life, and its deepest intentions, which are directed toward
a kind of apologetics or theodicy of the individual being."[21]

The Quest for Christa T., in no way an apology for either
Christa T. or the narrator/author, is perhaps best viewed from the
theoretical perspective of women's autobiography. As Mary G. Mason
has noted, "the self-discovery of female identity seems to acknowledge the real presence and recognition of another consciousness,
and the disclosure of female self is linked to the identification of
some 'other.' This recognition of another consciousness . . . this
grounding of identity through relation to the chosen other,
seems . . . to enable women to write openly about themselves."[22]

In both *The Quest for Christa T.* and *Die Günderode* the self-
discovery of female identity is attained through female bonding
and mirroring, through the dynamics of friendship between members of the same sex.[23] In these texts the quest for the other also

becomes a quest for the self. Thus *Christa T.*, as biography *manqué*, is not presented as a consistent third-person narrative but rather as an interweaving of first-person and third-person narration, with the subjective first-person voice given precedence.

Christa Wolf considers herself a spokesperson of her generation—the generation that grew up during the Third Reich and experienced the war, the defeat of Germany, and the establishment of the socialist state. In *Christa T.* she recalls the traumatic events of her transitional generation. In (re)constructing her friend's life story, Wolf's narrator (re)assesses her own life. The text, which is interspersed with "authentic"[24] documents—such as Christa T's diary entries, letters, and literary sketches—that prompt the narrator to call into question her memories of her friend, articulates the process of revision and reassessment set in motion by the act of writing. She recognizes that during the Stalin era she and her compatriots devoted themselves to building up the GDR with a singleness of purpose that bordered on monomania. Christa T., on the other hand, troubled by the personal toll exacted by blind obedience to the collective will, did not join in this endeavor; instead, she sustained her call for individual self-actualization within the socialist collective. Throughout her life, Christa T. uncompromisingly refused to abandon her humanistic ideals. Consequently she was relegated to the position of outsider in postwar East Germany— a society that as recent events in Central Europe have made palpably clear, had foresaken the humanistic Marxist social vision on which it was ostensibly founded. In (re)creating Christa T's life, the narrator is forced to reassess her own behavior and her assumptions about the "really existing socialism"[25] as manifested in the German Democratic Republic (GDR), specifically about its potential to realize the nonalienated community envisioned by Marx. Written for a GDR audience, the structure of *Christa T.* calls upon the reader to question these assumptions as well.

Critics have pointed out the utopian dimensions of *Christa T.*, arguing that the mere existence of this woman who quests for self-actualization is an expression of hope that keeps alive in both narrator and reader what the Marxist philosopher Ernst Bloch calls the "memory of the future." Andreas Huyssen has discussed the similarities between *Christa T.* and Bloch's concept of a "concrete utopia," as elucidated in his *Principle of Hope.*[26] In contrast to purely speculative utopian thought, Bloch's "concrete utopia" is based on the past and present and envisions the actualization of a utopian society in the future. For Bloch, the possibility of realizing

utopia is inextricably connected with Marxism, which he considers
to be the "praxis of concrete utopia."[27]

   The Quest for Christa T. also deviates from traditional biography by breaking down the distinction between life and art. The narrator freely invents the details surrounding the most important
events of Christa T.'s life. Pointing self-consciously to her own inven-
tions, she often reflects on, revises, or repudiates her imaginative
constructs, at times calling upon the reader to choose from among
different possible variants. Linear chronology is abandoned in favor
of an associative, multitemporal structure in which the boundaries
between author, narrator and Christa T. become fluid as their
lives intermesh.[28] By means of this sophisticated, complex narrative structure, Christa T.'s significance, her capacity to transform
the author/narrator, even from beyond the grave, becomes clear.

   The text of *Christa T.*, rich in complexity, ambiguity, and contradiction, initially frustrated critics who failed to recognize Wolf's
challenge to the reader. As an analysis of *Christa T.* based on
reader-response theory reveals,[29] Wolf, by calling upon readers to
unravel the book's complex narrative and chronological structure
and fill in the lacunae of the text, encourages them to duplicate
the process of reassessment undertaken by the narrator, a liberating process resulting in heightened self-awareness.

   The most revolutionary reading of *Christa T.*, however,
has come not from Wolf's intended reader (i.e., the citizen of the
GDR), but from American feminists. In her groundbreaking essay,
"Christa Wolf and Feminism: Breaking the Patriarchal Connection,"[30] Myra Love advocates reading *Christa T.* as a process of de-
constructing the system of dichotomous oppositions that informs
the patriarchal model of perception and discourse. Implicit in
Love's argument is a critique of the concept of phallogocentricity,
derived from deconstructionist and French feminist theory.[31] In
Christa T., Love maintains, the patriarchal model of experience is
subverted and overcome through the interweaving of two oppositions: presence/absence and speech/writing. If Wolf's purpose in
Christa T. is to make her absent (dead) friend present in the text
through reflection, then the presence of Wolf in "the text which
constitutes itself in relation [not in opposition] to the absence
which is Christa T." signifies a "process of self-constitution in in-
tersubjective relationship" and represents the "coming into being
of subjectivity free of domination."[32]

   The second deconstructive strategy of the text is seen to be
the subversion of the oppositions literature/communication and

speech/writing. Citing Roland Barthes's juxtapositions of written and spoken language and his assertion that the "closed" structure of written language militates against communication: "writing is anticommunication, it is intimidating,"[33] Love argues persuasively that *Christa T.*, in contrast, through its use of nonlinear, self-interrupting mode of discourse, through its use of the familiar "you" (*du*) and the inclusive "we," creates the aura of conversation between narrator and reader and in so doing overcomes the polarity between writing and speech.

While Love's monolithic use of the term "patriarchal" seems problematic to me today (as does Barthes's valorization of speech as opposed to writing)[34] the insights gleaned from Love's reading remain fundamentally unchanged: Wolf's writing strategies in *Christa T.* elude closure, and the text's dialogic structure substitutes multivocality for the authoritative narrative voice of hegemonic biographical and autobiographical discourse.[35]

Like *Christa T.*, the narrative strategies of *Die Günderode*[36] lead to dialogicism and intersubjectivity and undermine conventional expectations of both biography and autobiography. Bettina von Arnim (1785–1859) was a member of the generation that experienced the French Revolution, the Napoleonic Wars, and the Restoration. She was raised by her grandmother, Sophie La Roche, Germany's first woman novelist. She was also the sister of the early romantic poet Clemens Brentano and the wife of the romantic writer Achim von Arnim. Thus, by virtue of her family situation, she was intimately associated with the Jena circle, that group of early romantics which—in contrast to the later Heidelberg and Berlin groups—was socially, politically, philosophically, and aesthetically revolutionary.

The Jena romantics democraticized the salon, which had been an aristocratic institution in the eighteenth century. Romantic salons were led by women—Rahel Varnhagen and Bettina von Arnim, to name the two best known. Composed of members of the aristocracy and middle classes, they welcomed Jews into their midst. Informed by the principle of *Geselligkeit* (sociability or gregariousness),[37] the belief that individual subjectivity could be realized only through communication with others, the salons furnished intellectuals with a community: they were the locus of social and intellectual life, providing a forum for the discussion of literature, art and politics.

For the Jena romantics, who were firmly committed to the democratic ideals of the French Revolution, the reactionary out-

come of the Revolution, with its oppressive consequences for all
of Europe—censorship and political oppression under the restor-
ative Metternich system—was a blow from which they never
recovered.[38] In Prussia, a perfectly functioning state machinery
oversaw effective enforcement of Restoration policies, such as the
repressive Carlsbad Degrees,[39] and severely curtailed the personal
liberties of its citizens. Politically disillusioned, the early romantics found their alienation compounded by the rise of a new bourgeois class with a crassly materialistic ethos. Christa Wolf has
described the generation of 1800, Bettina's generation, as follows:

> A small group of intellectuals (avant-garde without a hinterland, as
> so often the case in German history since the peasant wars),
> equipped with a worthless ideal, differentiated sensibility, an un-
> controllable desire to apply their newly developed consciousness,
> encounters the narrowmindedness of an underdeveloped class—
> without self-esteem but full of blissful subservience—which has ap-
> propriated for itself from the bourgeois catechism only the
> commandment: Enrich yourself.[40]

Clearly, the romantic ideal of "differentiated sensibility," the
attempt to bridge the mind/body dichotomy by infusing the sensuous with the rational and the rational with the sensuous, was
doomed to frustration in the age of instrumental rationality being
ushered in by capitalism. It was against this narrow one-
dimensionality that the romantics protested—both aesthetically,
by invoking the imagination in an attempt to counteract the limitations they experienced, and politically, by embracing egalitarian
ideals. Unfortunately, many did not sustain their oppositional consciousness. Unlike many of her male compatriots from the Jena
circle, however, who later became politically reactionary or sought
refuge in Catholic mysticism, (these included August Wilhelm and
Friedrich Schlegel, as well as her brother, Clemens Brentano) Bettina von Arnim remained committed to the progressive, democratic ideals of her youth. Strongly opposed to Restoration politics,
she actively strove for social reform, and often came under suspicion for her dangerously progressive sentiments. Thus in 1844 she
was forced to curtail work on *Das Armenbuch* (Book of the Poor), a
sociological study of proletarian living conditions in Prussia with
special consideration of the plight of the Silesian weavers, when
she was accused of having incited the weavers to revolt. Much of
Bettina's *oeuvre,* such as the *Armenbuch* and *Dies Buch gehört*

dem König (This Book Belongs to the King), shares the politically engaged stance of Young German revolutionary literature. Like the writing of the Young Germans (*das junge Deutschland*), a radical group comprised mainly of journalists[41] who wrote between the aborted revolutions of 1830 and 1848 (the *Vormärz* ["Pre-March"] period) these von Arnim texts protest political, social, and economic oppression and agitated for reform.

In contrast, *Die Günderode*, also written during the conservative backlash of the Restoration, is fundamentally an early romantic work. As Edith Waldstein has persuasively argued,[42] *Die Günderode* replicates the *Geselligkeit* of the romantic salon through its use of conversational tone. Its revolutionary import is more covert than von Arnim's later *Vormärz* texts. It is also more far-reaching. For what is at stake in *Die Günderode* is nothing less than a repudiation of hierarchical social structures, a pervasive undermining of societal expectations, and a reaffirmation of the egalitarian ideals of 1789. In lieu of the Revolution's "fraternity," however, von Arnim's text explores the liberating "sorority" experienced by the characters Bettine and Karoline.

Let us examine the genesis and development of the *Günderode* text. The historical Bettina von Arnim was devastated by Karoline von Günderode's death. She had passionately courted Günderode, her senior by five years, and felt abandoned and betrayed by her suicide. Written thirty-three years after her friend's death, *Die Günderode* is structured as an epistolary novel, based on letters exchanged between the two women between 1804 and 1806. The long hiatus between Günderode's death and von Arnim's literary tribute to their friendship may well testify to the traumatic impact of Günderode's suicide on Bettina. There were, however, more immediate and practical reasons for Bettina's long silence. In the thirty-three years between Günderode's death in 1806 and the appearance of *Die Günderode* in 1839, Bettina von Arnim fulfilled the role expectations placed on women by her society: she married and bore seven children. Not until Achim von Arnim's death in 1831 did Bettina start to write. Significantly, *Die Günderode* was not Bettina's first literary endeavor. *Goethes Briefwechsel mit einem Kinde* (Goethe's Correspondence With A Child), which appeared in 1835, documents her relationship with the German poet, a relationship in which she was clearly subservient. Only after her effusive and sentimentalized portrayal of that relationship did Bettina depict her more egalitarian relationship with Karoline von Günderode.

Although based on authentic material, the Günderode–
Bettina correspondence merely serves as the basis for Bettina's
auto/biography. Freely editing, Bettina synthesizes letters, inter-
polates excerpts from other correspondences and, like Christa Wolf
after her, freely invents. For years critics castigated *Die Günderode* as a "forgery,"[43] judging it on its lack of historical accuracy,
the traditional criterion of biography.

It is easy to see why *Die Günderode* daunted critics. An amal-
gam of fact and fiction, it incorporates conversations and reflections on poetry, religion, history, and philosophy. Panegyrics to an
empathetic union with nature stand side by side with lyrical poems
and with mundane details of the everyday life of these women.

It is also understandable why Christa Wolf would defend *Die
Günderode*, which in many ways is a precursor of her *Quest for
Christa T.* The characterizations of both Bettina and Günderode
are not simply epistolary self-revelations. Both figures exist in the
text in relation to each other, that is, each constantly defines the
other. Although Wolf did not read *Die Günderode* until some ten
years after completing *Christa T.*,[44] she must have been struck by
the affinity between the two texts. Calling *Die Günderode* authentic in a poetic sense, Wolf reads it as a text that successfully combines the personal and the political. In her view it is a "testimony
of a lasting friendship between these two . . . an illustration also of
the life styles and mores of a specific time . . . and a critique of
these mores that is unafraid of going to the root of things."[45]

Thus for Christa Wolf, *Die Günderode* is radical (in the literal
sense of the word). What then precisely constitutes the radicality
of this text? It is radical first of all in its analysis of the social
malaise of its time, in its critique of the bourgeois ideology of incipient capitalism, that is, in its rejection of the notion that human life can be quantified. Bettina in particular, thoroughly
antiauthoritarian by nature, rejects the straitjacket of convention
and conformity, and repudiates the instrumental rationality prop-
agated by the "philistines," as she calls those who have internalized the materialistic values of the day.

Die Günderode is also revolutionary in its presentation of an
alternative vision. In contrast to the conventional male–female
roles presented in the *Goethe* book, with its paradigm of the
young, impressionable, adoring child worshiping at the feet of the
great poet, *Die Günderode*, focusing on the experiences of women,
presents a topic that was anathema to the literature of its time:
the passionate friendship between two women. The hyperbolic and

excessively emotional language of romanticism that informs *Die Günderode* initially inhibits the modern reader's access to the text, making it difficult to assess the significance of the women's relationship, to bracket the specificity of their friendship from the conventionality of romantic literary discourse. The intensity of their interaction, however, soon makes it apparent that their relationship transcends usual romantic norms. While it is doubtful that the women were physically intimate, there are distinctly erotic overtones in many of Bettina's letters. Moreover, both characters, as presented in *Die Günderode,* are to a degree woman-identified,[46] and it is precisely this female identification and their rejection of male values that enable the two women to develop an alternative social vision.

According to Christa Wolf, marginality proved an asset to Bettina von Arnim and Karoline von Günderode. Recasting a potentially negative situation positively, Wolf believes that women, precisely because of their exclusion from the public sphere, are sometimes able to turn their marginal status to advantage and, although still economically and socially dependent, may be able to develop a new, independent, and utopian perspective. This, Wolf maintains, was true of von Arnim and Günderode. It was certainly true to a greater degree of Bettina. Consciously resisting all attempts to mold her, including those of her beloved brother, Clemens, Bettina, a truly self-defining, independent spirit, attained an extraordinary degree of self-awareness. In contrast to Günderode, who, as a published poet, was judged by male literary norms and hence was more vulnerable to patriarchal expectations, Bettina, who did not start publishing until she was fifty, consciously resisted normative canonical restrictions. Iconoclastic in both form and content, *Die Günderode* marks a radical departure from traditional literary structures.

Although by far the majority of letters stem from Bettina, the epistolary text is properly called *Die Günderode,* for Günderode is present throughout the text. *Die Günderode* recreates the relationship between Bettina and her friend. It celebrates the reciprocity of friendship between two temperamentally very different, yet complementary individuals who respected each other's uniqueness and who shared experiences, thoughts and emotions with each other. More than a *confession à deux, Die Günderode* depicts the process of self-definition undertaken by the two women as a process of self-understanding achieved in large part through an understanding of the other. Their relationship, an expression of romantic

Geselligkeit, allowed both to grow as individuals. For Bettina, Günderode was the only person with whom she did not have to dissemble. This was also true, although to a lesser degree, for Günderode. The dialogic structure of von Arnim's epistolary text underscores the mutuality of their relationship. The preponderance of letters by Bettina, reflective of her more extroverted character, her more active role in the friendship, in no way diminishes the sense of the other's presence in the friendship and in no way diminishes the sense of the other's presence in the text. The consistent personal form of address, either by name or through the use of the intimate "Du," creates a conversational form and assures that Günderode is never absent from Bettina's consciousness. Their commonly shared experiences as women and their respect for each other's subjectivity enable these women to circumvent the hierarchical binary oppositions of hegemonic discourse and to articulate a discourse of intersubjectivity.

Their egalitarian stance, not restricted to their personal interaction, also informs the creation of a nonhierarchical social vision. Recent feminist scholarship has noted the utopian ramifications of *Die Günderode.*[47] The community envisioned by Bettina von Arnim and Karoline von Günderode—democratic, antiauthoritarian, nonrepressive, encouraging individual self-actualization—stands in sharp contrast to the society of their time. Yet their utopia should not be understood in the traditional sense of *u-topos*—that is, as a future-oriented, fantastic projection of an unrealizable ideal, a "no place"—but rather in the Blochian sense of a "concrete utopia." For their caring, nonobjectifying relationship is the concretization of their utopia in everyday experience in the present.[48]

Bettina von Arnim's utopian vision emerges out of the early romantic call to romanticize the world. "Romanticization," understood here in Novalis's sense of an intensification (*Potenzierung*) of life, is part of the romantic program of spiritual reintegration. In their attempt to romanticize the world, the romantics strove to break down boundaries perceived to be artificial, such as those between objective and subjective reality, and between art and life. The fact that for the Jena romantics everything, even the most mundane topic, was a potential source of art, may explain the heterogeneity of Bettina's text. More importantly, however, the early romantic program of romanticization evolved into a poetological critique of emerging capitalism.[49]

In criticizing obstacles to "self-actualization," the writings of the early romantics are contiguous with the writings of Christa Wolf, which in part explains her great interest in Bettina von

Arnim. Although writing in very different social contexts, von
Arnim and Wolf create their utopias as projections of that which is
lacking in their respective societies;[50] their preferred model of
human interaction, predicated on the possibility of individual self-
realization through community, is strikingly similar.

At the heart of what Christa Wolf has called von Arnim's and
Günderode's *Weiberphilosophie* (female philosophy) is the notion of
Schwebereligion (a virtually untranslated term coined by Bettina,
perhaps best rendered as "religion held in suspense or abeyance").
One of the chief tenets of this religion is the renunciation of the
traditional concept of education. Education, in Bettina's view,
should not be accretive, should not be the superimposition of
knowledge and values onto the individual.[51] Instead "everyone
should be the object of their own curiosity and should bring themselves to light like a piece of ore or an underground spring. The
whole purpose of education should be to allow the spirit to reveal
itself."[52] For Bettina, traditionally "educated people are the big-
gest dullards under the sun"; for her "true education lies in exercising those powers that lie within us" (173).

Bettina's call for an organic education reflects her distrust of
all systematic thought. In her critique of cultural ideology, she dif-
ferentiates between "being knowing" and "knowledge." The former,
an organic, open concept, she describes as a state of "thriving in
the healthy soil of the spirit, where the spirit flowers," in which
there is no demarcation between imagination and reality. The latter, on the other hand, denotes mastery of a body of information.
Thus for her "a mathematician, historian, lawyer belong to the
petrified world." That type of knowledge is for her "philistinism in
a certain deeper sense" (325). To the more philosophically inclined
Günderode she declares, "I find your Schelling and your Fichte
and your Kant completely impossible fellows" (17).

The structure of *Die Günderode* reflects Bettina's disdain for all
systematic models. Its unsystematic, associative, nonreductionist
form reflects the open-ended process of heightened self-awareness
described in the text and challenges the reader to participate in
this process as well. Bettina counters closed symbolic structures and
dichotomous oppositions with the complementary notions of *Selbst-
denken* and *Selbst-fühlen* (to feel and think [for] oneself), which
are aimed at challenging such artificial oppositional structures as
reason/emotion and nature/spirit and at furthering holism
through both empathetic communion with nature and communication with another person.

The critique of culture presented by Bettina von Arnim's *Die Günderode* and Christa Wolf's *The Quest of Christa T.*, a critique of failed community in incipient Western capitalist and contemporary Marxist-Leninist societies, is articulated by women who are both part of and marginal to their respective cultures. In both texts marginality is perceived as an asset. In von Arnim's text, Karoline von Günderode, the more culturally colonized of the two correspondents, is obviously taken by Bettina's free spirit. She asks to become Bettina's "disciple in insignificance" (70); that is, she seeks to counteract the male-defined notions of the "significant" that she has internalized. In *Christa T.* the narrator assesses her friend's marginality positively and consciously assumes herself a more marginal position. In so doing she, together with Bettina von Arnim, exploits the possibilities open to women whose "history of reading and writing in the interstices of masculine culture"[53] allows them to transform oppositional consciousness into texts that resist canonical aesthetic norms. In their "failure" to create biographies in the traditional sense, these writers undermine the male literary canon. At the same time they create texts that can be read within the context of an alternative, subversive literary tradition.

Chapter Two

"Double Singleness": Gender Role Mergence in the Autobiographical Writings of Charles and Mary Lamb

 *Jane Aaron*

In May 1833 an Edmonton schoolmistress noticed that her neighbours, the Waldens, had acquired two new lodgers; as Mr. Walden, formerly an asylum keeper, let lodgings to the mentally ill, "the reputation of insanity," not surprisingly, attached itself in the schoolmistress's mind to both of the newcomers.[1] In fact, of the two new lodgers, Charles and Mary Lamb, only Mary suffered from attacks of what has subsequently been categorised by their biographers as a manic depressive disorder.[2] Her brother chose to live with her at the Waldens because he believed that the strain of moving to and fro from their own home to an asylum whenever she became ill was increasing the frequency of Mary's attacks, and he could not tolerate the thought of their living permanently apart. As he wrote to a correspondent at that time:

> It is no new thing for me to be left to my sister. When she is not violent her rambling chat is better to me than the sense and sanity of this world. . . . I could be nowhere happier than under the same roof with her.[3]

As well as illustrating an unusual degree of closeness, this description of their sibling relationship also reverses the conventionally overt power relation between the sexes: Charles presents himself as the dependent partner, and he moves according to Mary's needs rather than she according to his. At the same time, given Mary's vulnerable condition, his allegiance to her functioned on a caring, mothering level, as well as on a dependent child-like one. The symbiotic bonding of their two lives appears to have re-

sulted in a relationship in which both played alternating mother/
child roles, and valued qualities connected with either femaleness
or the childlike, rather than with manliness. My intention in
this article is to assess the effect of their sibling tie on the presentation of gender in the Lambs' autobiographical and semi-
autobiographical texts and its influence on the development of
their work.

As with all individual histories, the patterns and processes of
the Lambs' lives developed in response to interacting public and
private pressures; their personal domestic history and the social
and cultural context of their times worked together to establish
the framework of their lives, and to direct their understanding
of it. Culturally, theirs was an age of transition—from the cults of
sensibility and gothic writing characteristic of the second half of
the eighteenth century, with their particular appeal to a new generation of women readers, to a more patriarchal aesthetic in which
the popular styles of the earlier epoch were dismissed as
unmanly.[4] A change from relatively fluid approaches to gender to
an insistence upon opposing "manly" and "womanly" ideals is de-
monstrable in the work of those few amongst the Romantic writers
who both survived their early years of creativity and retained
links with their audience and with changing social practices.
Nineteenth-century admiration for the manly appears to have
originated in part in an aesthetic reaction against the eighteenth-
century school of sensibility, and in part in a political attempt to
control the danger of social unrest through a revival of what was
considered to be an old feudal ideal of benevolent paternalism.
Coleridge, for example, in his didactic *Aids to Reflection in the Formation of a Manly Character* (1825), condemns the lack of manliness in eighteenth-century sentimental writing, and his treatise
On the Constitution of the Church and State (1829) deplores the
"emasculation" of the nation and stresses the need for a revival of
paternalistic powers.[5] Poems characteristic of Wordsworth's later
works, such as his "Ode to Duty" and the "Character of a Happy
Warrior," also function as moral guides to the formation of an orderly, responsible and authoritarian male identity.

Charles Lamb's work, however, stands out in marked contrast
to this prevailing spirit of the age. At no point in any of his writings, the bulk of which belong to the 1820s, does he ever identify
with the voice of authority or leadership. This is not to say that
the ethos of paternalism does not often function as a potent force
in Lamb's writings, but when it does, he associates himself not

with the ordainers of authority but with its recipients, with the governed rather than the governor. His voice at such times is that of the obedient child, the faithful servant, or the admiring disciple, but never that of the father, master or teacher figure. At other times, often in the same piece of writing, a very different note predominates, and Lamb, through his characteristic use of the first person pronoun, identifies himself with those voices that puncture and subvert the paternalistic rhetoric—with the ironist, the jester, or the trickster, with drunkards, liars, felons, and witches. Furthermore, whether playing the part of the gentle servant or the subversive trickster, he often deliberately draws the reader's attention to the prevalence in the roles he adopts of characteristics usually designated as female or childlike. The Elia essay "Old China," for example, begins "I have an almost feminine partiality for old china,"[6] and in the mock-elegiac "Preface, by a Friend of the late Elia" he writes of the Elia persona "the impressions of infancy had burnt into him, and he resented the impertinence of manhood" (ii, 153).

Mary Lamb's writing similarly avoids the least hint of an authoritative, dominating voice. Her tone, normally more measured and controlled than that of her brother, suggests always, even in her writing for children, a concern for the reader as an equal or a friend, and an anxiety with regard to any influence her position as writer may give her. Critics of her children's books have recognised her unusual degree of ability to merge with her characters, and identify with the lives she describes;[7] her letters also reveal the same capacity. In a letter of 1814, for example, she writes to Barbara Betham, a fourteen-year old who had visited the Lambs three years previously:

> You wish for London news . . . I have been endeavouring to recollect who you might have seen here, and what may have happened to them since, and this effort has only brought the image of little Barbara Betham, unconnected with any other person, so strongly before my eyes, that I seem as if I had no other subject to write upon. Now I think I see you with your feet propped upon the fender, your two hands spread out upon your knees—an attitude you always chose when we were in familiar confidential conversation together—telling me long stories of your own home . . . I remember your quiet steady face bent over your book.[8]

Here, Mary's empathic capacity to mirror the remembered life of the child until it lives again in her representation of it exempli-

fies her readiness to merge her interests, and even her very sense
of being, with those of others. Such an ability has recently been
identified as the psychological consequence for women of the conventional allocation by gender of childcare and mothering. It is
argued that because women mother, girls, identifying with their
mothers, develop a sense of self which they see as more continuous
with that of others, and more permeable in its ego boundaries,
than a boy's more detached and separate sense of himself.[9] In the
Lambs' case, however, the brother also to some degree shares in
his sister's unusually pronounced capacity to identify with others.
In a letter of 1824, for example, Charles complains of a compulsive,
unwilled tendency to identify with the afflictions of others, and to
lose his sense of a separate existence in the process.[10] That he
should undergo such experience validates the views of those who
would stress that the development of empathic capacities has
nothing to do with any inherent differential linked to biological
sex but is the consequence of sex-related social role patterning,
and its conditioning effects. From infancy Charles had apparently
been left very much to the care of his sister, ten years his senior;
many of his autobiographical writings record the details of Mary's
caretaking role in their childhood, always with deep affection
and gratitude.[11] Little has been written on the psychological
consequence for the developing subject of sibling nurturance, as
opposed to parental care, but such attempts as have been made
at evolving an analytic understanding of its effects suggest that,
for both the younger and older children involved, and for fe-
males and males alike, it results in interdependent cooperative
behaviour with a relative lack of competitive ego assertion, and
a capacity to change roles, from, for example, a nurtured role to a
nurturing one, in accordance with the changing needs of the
family.[12]

The social conditions of the Lambs' early lives played their
part, in addition to the familial roles, in accentuating Mary's
sensitivity to the needs and existence of others and in creating
Charles's propensity to share in her so-called "feminine" and emphatic characteristics. For both, their inherited position in the
hierarchical ranking of their society must have constituted a factor in their reluctance to conform with the cultural development of
their time and play an authoritative role as writers. The details of
their early family life are readily available in many biographies.
The Inner Temple chambers in which they were reared were the
property of their father's employer, Samuel Salt, a barrister of

the Temple and a Whig member of Parliament. Their father, John Lamb, after a period of early employment as a footman in Bath, established himself as a waiter at the Inner Temple Hall, and Salt's personal servant and assistant. Salt had probably to some degree been an agent in his servant's marriage, for John Lamb's wife Elizabeth was the daughter of a housekeeper to one of his master's friends and colleagues in Westminster, William Plumer. Salt's benevolent influences also secured for Charles and his older brother, another John, their schooling at Christ's Hospital, and assisted them to subsequent employment as trading-house clerks. Mary, after a very elementary dame's school education, contributed to the meagre family income through work as a needlewoman and mantua maker. In September 1796, when she was thirty-one, the stresses of her employment and of the family's financial difficulties after Salt's death, along with the domestic strain of caring for both an invalid mother and a father suffering from senility, were too great for Mary's equilibrium; in a very sudden and violent attack of insanity she took her mother's life, stabbing her to death, in a moment of intense manic rage, with a carving-knife snatched from the supper table.

My concern here, however, is not so much with the factual details of their lives as with the manner in which their experiences are presented and understood in the many autobiographical references to be found throughout their published writings and correspondences. Of particular significance for the development of their concept of gender was the manner in which both struggled to redeem the exploitative and potentially alienating tensions inherent in the power structures of their parents' lives by emphasizing the importance of feudal devotion and love in service roles. The attempts made by Charles, in particular, to transcend the reality of the family's dependency—by stressing the loving emotional tie which connected master and servant in their father's case—is analogous to the common tendency to obscure the imbalance of rights and privileges in conventional male/female relations by emphasizing the value of romantic love. In the Elia essay "The Old Benchers of the Inner Temple," for example, he portrays his father as "Lovel," the perfect servant, who plays a nurturing, motherly role in his relationship with his master. Lovel "took care of everything," and was at once his master's "clerk, his good servant, his dresser, his friend, his 'flapper,' his guide, stop-watch, auditor, treasurer." Salt is described as utterly dependent on the caring capacities of his servant. Elia continues:

I knew this Lovel. He was a man of incorrigible and losing honesty.
A good fellow withal, and 'would strike' (ii, 87).

The reference is to the last act of *King Lear,* to the scene in
which the Duke of Kent attempts to disclose to the dying king the
double role he has played. Through this connection with the figure
of Kent/Caius and the ideal of self-abnegating, voluntary service
he represents, Lamb adds to the portrait of his father a grace and
a dignity which John Lamb may have had in spirit but could not
have had materially, for he, unlike Kent, was never in a position to
serve "for love." The son's portrayal emphasizes, with approbation,
the female aspects of the father's role and presents his life of service as one of voluntary self-sacrifice, akin to that conventionally
attributed to a wife or mother.

Contrary to the commonly accepted figure of the subordinate
at work who becomes a petty tyrant at home, John Lamb does not
appear to have taken advantage of his role as husband, or to have
established in his immediate domestic circle a pattern of marital
or paternal dominance which would compensate for his working
life.[13] In her letters Mary refers very rarely to her parents, but
from Charles's correspondence it would appear that the dominant
figure in the marriage was their mother, Elizabeth, rather than
their father. She emerges from his letters as a mother whose manner towards her two younger children lacked the tender nurturing
care he saw in his father's relation to his master. Had not Mary
mothered her little brother, he might well have suffered from the
same neglect in childhood as his sister had herself. Elizabeth was
extremely attached to her eldest son, John, who had inherited her
handsome, statuesque physique and commanding presence,
whereas Mary and Charles were more like their small-framed father. Charles does not complain of his family's conduct towards
him, but he felt his mother's neglect of Mary strongly. In describing their upbringing to Coleridge he records that his mother could
never accept her daughter's love,

> but met her caresses, her protestations of filial affection, too fre-
> quently with coldness & repulse ... she would always love my
> brother above Mary, who was not worthy of one tenth of that affec-
> tion, which Mary had a right to claim.[14]

In the autobiographical Elia essay "Mackery End in Hertfordshire," he presents Mary, or "Bridget Elia" as she becomes in the

essays, as one who suffered neglect in childhood: her "education in youth was not much attended to" and she "missed all that train of female garniture" with which an affectionate mother might have been expected to adorn her daughter (ii, 76).

Although one would not wish to cast Elizabeth Lamb unequivocally as the villain of the family saga, it is true that there are very few positive images of biological mothers fulfilling nurturing roles in the Lambs' writings. In *Mrs. Leicester's School*, a volume of stories for children they wrote together in 1808, accounts of maternal absence or inadequacy and of emotionally deprived childhoods abound. The framework of the book allows for the presentation of a variety of differing family patterns: a consignment of new pupils arrives at Mrs. Leicester's school for girls, and she suggests that the girls spend their first evening together relating to each other the histories of their past lives. But the tales that follow tell, almost without exception, of isolation and suffering, usually stoically endured by the children. Many of the little girls are orphans; others have lost their mothers at birth; others were abandoned by their parents and left to the mercy of uncaring relations; another is discovered to be a changeling, exchanged by her biological mother. The standard biographies on the Lambs have always stressed the autobiographical nature of many of the tales of *Mrs. Leicester's School*.[15] Both Mary's story "Margaret Green: The Young Mahometan" and Charles's "Maria Howe: The Witch Aunt," for example, are based on the childhood holidays the Lambs spent at Blakesware, the Plumers' country residence, uninhabited except by their grandmother, the housekeeper. In both tales the little girls, grievously neglected by their relations, who have "wholly discontinued talking" to them (iii, 308), find solace and distraction from their loneliness in browsing in the large libraries they discover; however, their entire absorption in tales of Mahomet, or of witches, affects their sense of reality and their mental balance; and both develop nervous illnesses. Their distress is understood and cured not by their immediate family but by visitors, an aunt in one case and a doctor in the other, who remove them from the home environment and introduce them to "lightsome rooms and cheerful faces," affecting a cure through sociable kindness (iii, 323).

The autobiographical similarities suggest that by means of these tales the Lambs were attempting to assuage the sorrows of their own neglected childhoods, particularly Mary's, and to rewrite with happy endings their own histories, which had in fact in

both their cases resulted in mental illness: Charles suffered from
one attack of delusional insanity when he was twenty, spending
six weeks at "a mad house in Hoxton."[16] The little girls are often
provided in the tales with nurturers who give them the loving attention that their biological parents do not offer: what is surprising, however, is the extent to which these substitute mothers are
male. In the first tale to be told, Mary's account of "Elizabeth Vil-
liers," a visiting uncle cares for his niece, curing her of her obses-
sion with her dead mother's grave; in the last tale of the volume,
Charles's "Arabella Hardy," an orphan, travelling alone on a long
sea voyage, is very effectively mothered by one of the ship's crew.
Charles's awareness of the stigma attached to male mothering is
shown by his preoccupation with the way in which the sailor, Atkinson's, behavior is regarded by his mates: they taunt him with
the name of "Betsey" and see him as effeminate. The close of the
tale stresses Atkinson's heroism and self-sacrifice in the child's
eyes as one

> whose womanly care of me got him the name of a woman, who, with
> more than female attention, condescended to play the hand-maid to
> a little unaccompanied orphan, that fortune had cast upon the care
> of a rough sea captain, and his rougher crew. (iii, 335)

Atkinson, like Lovel or Kent, is one who serves for love; he is ready
to take upon himself the role of a servant, and of a female servant
at that, a "hand-maid," to the lowliest of beings, a female orphan.

    Such portrayals exemplify Charles's tendency to idealize self-
sacrificial life patterns, which involve not so much a rebellion
against the injustices of a system as an attempt to redeem the
suffering and humiliation it entails through refusing to adopt
dominant roles, and accepting subordinate ones voluntarily, in the
name of love. But the passivity of this stance involves him at times
in a torturous contradiction which is dangerously close to collud-
ing with the hierarchical structures it in part resists. In one of the
anecdotes included in his portrayal of "Lovel," for example, a tale
intended to exemplify how "L. never forgot rank, where something
better was not concerned," Lovel attacks a gentleman for insulting
a woman, only to apologize for his interference, "bare-headed," to
the same person, the next day (ii, 88). Both actions appear to be
recorded approvingly by Elia. Inheriting an ideology commonly
more impressed upon women and children than upon the male,
usually of the upper classes, who becomes a writer, Charles finds

in positions of childlike humility, obedient service, and passive endurance of suffering the highest moral beauty. The iniquities and injustices of the system in which he was reared are not challenged directly, for his moral and aesthetic sensibility could not validate such protest without experiencing itself as selfish, ungrateful, and ugly. But by means of the abrupt transitions and paradoxes of his work and its overriding use of the ironic voice—stylistic techniques generally associated with the muted protest of the nineteenth-century woman writer—he does at times voice a subversive resistance.

Mary Lamb's work shows this same contradiction: at one and the same time an acute awareness of the underprivileged position of lower-class women in early nineteenth-century society, and a loyalty to English class and familial systems which will not allow her to protest unequivocally. Based on her own experience of sweated, and, in her case, permanently damaging, labor, her essay "On Needle-Work" (1815) concerns itself with the problems of female employment generally, and with the aptitude of women for occupations conventionally monopolized by men. Few other lucrative forms of employment apart from needlework are available to the unmarried woman whose parents' income "does not very much exceed the moderate," not because she lacks the capacity for acquiring new skills or the robustness for furthering them, but because she has never been properly trained or educated. The essay argues that men, were they subject to the same upbringing, could fare no better:

> Even where boys have gone through a laborious education, superinducing habits of steady attention, accompanied with the entire conviction that the business which they learn is to be the source of their future distinction, may it not be affirmed that the persevering industry required to accomplish this desirable end causes many a hard struggle in the minds of young men, even of the most hopeful disposition? What then must be the disadvantages under which a very young woman is placed? (i, 179)

"I believe it is every woman's opinion that the condition of men is far superior to her own," she maintains (i, 177). Yet for all the power of her argument that only conditioning stops women from sharing in the occupations of men, and that as a result of this deprivation they suffer both materially and in terms of thwarted potential, Mary would not have the status quo essentially changed. On the contrary she asks her reader

to contribute all the assistance in her power to those of her own
sex who may need it, in the employments they at present occupy,
rather than to force them into situations now filled wholly by
men. (i, 179)

No arguments sustain this reversal: it is interjected abruptly
and baldly into the protesting body of the text. In composing the
essay Mary underwent "great fatigue;" the strain of it brought
about an attack of her illness.[17] That this should be so is not surprising. To have felt and to be able to communicate vividly the underlying iniquities of a system, as well as its more blatant
injustices, and yet to forbear from formulating such grievances effectively, acquiescing, rather, with the preconceived habits of society—such a self-confounding must have been painful to confront
and to attempt to order. The thoroughly reasonable tone of the essay and its lack of bitterness may in part have furthered the cause
for which it pleads by not antagonizing or alienating its more reactionary readers, but this effect was produced at the expense of a
discrepancy between the ills perceived, and actually experienced,
and the conclusions drawn. Like her brother, Mary had imbibed
from her parents the ethos of loving service with its inherent contradiction or "double bind,"[18] but in Mary's case her very being
became the material on which the resulting conflict was written.
Her "sweet reasonableness" and patient self-restraint were shattered at yearly intervals throughout her life by violent fits of
insanity.

Mary's habits of self-repression were manifest to her acquain-
tances; not only did she write very little, and with difficulty, she
also forbade herself free expression in speech—except during her
periodic illnesses, when she would apparently converse at great
length, with a lively wit, and to vivid descriptive effect.[19] Her
brother also found it difficult to summon the confidence and control necessary to write, and his literary output is slender. Certain
of their biographers imply that his attachment to his sister, and
the care he provided for her, prevented his full maturity as a
writer; others point out that the traumatic outbreak of Mary's illness in 1796 seems to have stabilized her brother's life, and
brought to an end his own mental instability.[20] It is clear from
Charles's letters and actions at this time that the symbiotic bond
between himself and his sister was strengthened rather than
shaken by the manner of their mother's death.[21] Before the passing of the 1799 Act on the criminally insane, persons who commit-

ted such an act could be released if sufficient security was given that they would properly be taken care of as potentially unstable for the rest of their lives. This pledge Charles gave, and the two lived together for the next thirty-eight years, their lives intermittently interrupted by recurring bouts of Mary's illness. Charles identified with her fate to such an extent that he saw the two of them as *"marked"* by madness and matricide, and equally the object of curiosity and scandal.[22] His biographers tend to present him as martyred to his sister and her illness, but he himself stresses throughout his writings his dependency on Mary. He felt a "widow'd thing" (v, 22), with his support gone, when their lives of "a sort of double singleness" (ii, 75) were shattered by her absence. Mary's letters similarly record the free but united nature of their sibling tie. She tells her friends the Stoddarts, for example:

> you both want the habit of telling each other at the moment everything that happens,—where you go—and what you do—that free communication of letters and opinions, just as they arise, as Charles and I do, and which is after all the only groundwork of [any (?)] friendship.[23]

Given Mary's illness, and the shared anxiety involved in awaiting the onset of an attack, one significant feature of their relation was the importance both attached to a healing and sustaining appreciation of the immanent "here and now" of experience. In their day-to-day life when Mary was observed by Charles to be withdrawing into a torpor or extreme silence, he would perform some sudden, whimsical or unexpected act to restore her to an awareness of her surroundings.[24] When Mary was well, part of their popular appeal as hosts was their ability to harmonize a company during their regular social evenings, creating a special festivity out of a habitual gathering. The celebration of everyday experience, particularly of everyday social relations, is a feature of their writings, from the tales of *Mrs. Leicester's School* to the Elia essays. In such essays as "The Convalescent" and the "Popular Fallacies XVI. That a Sulky Temper is a Misfortune," for example, Elia abruptly interrupts and punctures his own hyperbolic and fantastical flights of fancy—a self-aggrandizing flight in the first essay and a paranoid one in the second—and restores himself at the close of each to human proportion. His "preposterous dreams of self-absorption" are interrupted, in the first instance by an editor's request for a late article and in the second by a visit from

cheerful friends, and he returns to his "natural pretensions" as
"your insignificant Essayist," as he tells his readers (ii, 186 and
187). The essays generally close harmoniously in a mood of acceptance and reconciliation, not brought about through any transcen-
dence of human complexity, but through an appreciation of the
trivial or of the transitory—the pleasures of teacups or a game of
cards, of laughing faces in the street or an unexpected welcome.

An appreciation of what is mundane or immanent rather than
transcendent, and of mere "being" as opposed to "doing," has generally been viewed as a female attribute,[25] and it is perhaps no
coincidence that when Elia celebrates these states of joyful immersion in the "here and now" he usually presents himself as being in
Bridget Elia's company at the time. It is she who brings about the
unexpected welcome afforded to them both in the essay "Mackery
End in Hertfordshire," in which Elia presents himself in a childlike role in relation to his "cousin," remembering at the close how
"in the days of weakling infancy I was her tender charge—as I
have been her care in foolish manhood since" (ii, 79). She shares in
his "feminine partiality" for the aesthetic charms of old teacups in
the essay "Old China," though in this essay it is Elia who assumes
the mothering role, comforting Bridget when she mourns for their
lost youth by reminding her of the pleasures still to be gained in
the present moment. And at the close of the essay "Mrs. Battle's
Opinions on Whist," a game of cards becomes a free-floating moment, with no before or after, in which both play together:

> That last game I had with my sweet cousin (I capotted her)—(dare
> I tell thee, how foolish I am?)—I wished it might have lasted for
> ever, though we gained nothing, and lost nothing, though it was a
> mere shade of play: I would be content to go on in that idle folly for
> ever. . . . Bridget and I should be ever playing. (ii, 37)

For the Lambs such moments of peace had, of course, their own
significance; but in these essays, in the children's tales, and in
their letters, their work reaches out to enfold the reader also
in the embrace of such a moment. In the above quotation, for
example, Elia, in his direct approach to the reader, does dare to
disclose his foolish childlikeness, trusting in, and thereby creating,
either a mothering or a childlike response. The reader, too, is
guided towards ways of experiencing relationship which have conventionally been limited either to women or to children, and sys-
tematically undervalued as such. The unusual bond between

Charles and Mary created a shared identity which was essentially either female or childlike in its nature, and their writing constitutes a celebration of female and childlike perspectives, and an avoidance of "the impertinence of manhood." Even though their refusal to confront "manhood" directly with the consequence of its "impertinence" at times deflects the impact of their writing, and depleted their own confidence, their work, at its best, can bring about for the reader sudden shifts of perspective, creating—through an experiential as opposed to theoretical understanding—an awareness of the blinkered and damaging limitations of conventional gender role difference.

Chapter Three

A Woman in the "Man's World":
The Journals of Nadezhda Durova (1783–1866)

Mary Fleming Zirin

On September 17, 1806, Nadezhda Durova disguised herself in Cossack uniform and ran away from her father's house in the Urals to enlist and serve as a man in the Russian light cavalry throughout the Napoleonic wars. Thirty years later, in a brief literary career almost as unprecedented as the military one, Durova published a number of fictional tales that were popular during the last spate of Russian Romanticism. Her most significant work, however, was *The Cavalry Maiden: It Happened in Russia* (St. Petersburg, 1836), a selection of edited excerpts from the journals of her ten years with the army. Except for a few Sternean travelogues and some conventional military memoirs, it was the first full autobiography to appear in Russian during the author's lifetime. Perhaps, to use Domna Stanton's formulation, Durova's wielding of one phallic instrument, the sword, enabled her to overcome a "symbolic order that equates the idea(l) of the author with a phallic pen transmitted from father to son" and commit the daring act of opening her extraordinary life to public scrutiny. "My Childhood Years," the insightful memoir with which Durova prefaced her record of the military years, was just as innovative in its attempt to define the psychological roots of her lifelong rebellion against social norms.[1]

By Durova's own account, she compiled *The Cavalry Maiden* in 1835 from loose sheets of scribbled paper stored in a valise during her years in retirement. While her fresh, unmediated voice and the language and cultural references are consistent with those of a text dating from the 1810s, there is a retrospective element in *The Cavalry Maiden* that sets it apart from raw diaries. The very fact of *selection* gives the journal autobiographical unity: the incidents she chose for inclusion portray—one can even say, betray—

her adaptation of her male persona over the years and her growing disillusionment with peacetime service in the Russian provinces. By contrast, Durova's later published excerpts from the military journals (the leftovers, as it were), *Notes of Aleksandrov-Durova: Addendum to "The Cavalry Maiden,"* (Moscow, 1839), consist of unrelated incidents that give little impression of Durova's inner life.[2] The patterns of adaptation to and estrangement from masculine norms that permeate *The Cavalry Maiden* offer thought-provoking materials for investigation of both conscious and indirect expressions of gender in more conventional memoirs and diaries.

The Cavalry Maiden speaks for all the women who have ever led a life of action outside the accepted female sphere, and particularly for the "Amazons." Women who fought as soldiers are tucked into the corners of myth and history throughout recorded time, but they have left few direct accounts of their lives. Joan of Arc, whose remarkable testimony was recorded at her trial, is the major exception.[3] Unlike the medieval Joan, Durova is a modern woman, a product of Enlightenment values and the romantic ethos of her times, and her terms of reference are mostly comprehensible to us today. In one way, however, Durova's experience may seem as remote from the late twentieth century as Joan's voices. Viktor Afanas'ev describes Durova as putting on the military uniform like a nun's habit, and the description is apt.[4] Like the legendary Amazon of the south Russian steppes, the nun, and the American spinster schoolmarm, she had to sacrifice (or reclaim) her sexuality in order to attain at least honorary masculinity. Joan of Arc took advantage of a tradition of female prophecy to impose her persona on the dauphin and the French armies. The Amazon renounced men's society, and the nun and the schoolmarm were required to maintain the aspect and uniform of chastity.[5] Durova made a further sacrifice. In order to gain the masculine freedoms she sought, she first chose, and then was required by the tsar himself, to mask both her identity and her sex.

Durova later recalled with pride her first months of service as a common soldier:

> Nothing can ever expunge from my memory that first year after I entered upon my military career, that year of happiness, complete freedom, and total independence, which were all the more precious to me because I found a way to attain them by myself, with no outside intercession (chap. 6).

She reached Russia's western borders early in 1807 when a renewal of the Prussian campaign against Napoleon was looming and regiments were recruiting to replace losses in the winter's battles. No commander was apt to challenge the credentials of a boy who frankly admitted running away from home. Durova was accepted as a "cadet"—an unschooled soldier from the nobility—in the Polish Horse regiment and sent to the front in late May.

When her father submitted a petition to Alexander I that autumn asking that his runaway daughter be located and returned home, Durova's unlikely story won her a personal interview with the tsar. Impressed by reports of her "peerless" courage during the campaign and touched by her impassioned plea to continue in the career she felt to be her destiny, Alexander granted her a commission:

> "If you presume," said the emperor, "that permission to wear a uniform and bear arms is your only possible reward, you shall have it!" At these words I began to quiver with joy. The emperor went on, "And you will call yourself by my name—Aleksandrov. I have no doubt that you will make yourself worthy of this honor by the distinction of your conduct and actions. Never forget for a moment that this name must always be above reproach, and I will never forgive you for even the shadow of a spot on it . . ." (chap. 3).

Thus Durova received official sanction for life as an honorary male and a distinct warning that the "privilege" extended beyond public persona to private sexual behavior. Durova grasped the message and lived up to her side of the bargain; reveling in a few months of idyllic leisure in 1813, she wrote (protesting too much?): "Truly, His Majesty fathomed my soul. My thoughts are completely innocent. Nothing occupies them except the beauties of nature and the duties of my post." Until her retirement in 1816, Durova served as an officer apparently too young to grow the mustaches which were the pride and prerogative of the light cavalry. In the same passage of The Cavalry Maiden, a Durova at ease in her masquerade speculated that her colleagues might well know more about her than they admitted:

> . . . there are times when the conspicuous courtesy of their behavior toward me and the decorum of their words serve notice that, although they are not quite convinced that I shall never have mustaches, they at least strongly suspect the possibility. My fellow

officers, however, are very amicably disposed toward me and think
quite well of me. There is no way I can lose their good opinion:
they have been the witnesses and comrades of my life under arms
(chap. 10).

From the privileged vantage point of a masculine status validated
by the tsar (and thus not open to challenge even by those who sus-
pected her real sex), Durova observed and reported on men's mores as, so to speak, an infiltrator into the enemy camp.[6]

It is instructive to compare Durova's journals to military diaries and memoirs published by fellow veterans of the Napoleonic
wars.[7] The male authors tended to be from rich families with
homes in the two Russian capitals; they saw the army as an ad-
vantageous career leading to high rank. Durova was the provincial
child of a retired cavalry captain; she had already advanced beyond her wildest dreams. The men focus their autobiographical
works on military strategy and the excitement of wartime. Durova
covers combat lightly. She is a diffident and amused narrator who
describes her masculine persona as heroic by accident; she speculates on her fearlessness almost as an external phenomenon.
Early childhood years spent on the march with her father's hussar
regiment gave Durova a genuine sense of military vocation. However, while she never avoided the heat of battle and led her men
with fiery courage, her scruples stopped short of actual killing,
which was a job she felt that the infantry carried out much more
efficiently (chap. 12). During the 1812 campaign she lamented
with tongue in cheek the murder of a goose as a lasting stain on
her conscience (chap. 8).[8]

A striking difference between Durova's journals and masculine
memoirs is the fact that most of *The Cavalry Maiden*'s pages are
devoted to peacetime "adventures" which the men find too trivial
to mention. It was those idle days rather than the heat of battle
which brought her opportunities to test her freedom from the constraints of the female role: exploring new localities, reveling in the
glories of nature, and exercising her talent for making friends.
Durova includes in *The Cavalry Maiden* no less than five separate
incidents during which she overcomes frightening situations encountered alone in strange places at night.

These minor victories that Durova chooses as emblematic of
the wider freedom she gained through her disguised life in the
Russian cavalry can be illustrated by passages in chapter 10 about
her participation in the 1813 campaign. She mentions a heroic ac-

tion in passing, citing her captain's gift of "a bottle of first-rate cream for a little clash with the enemy and four prisoners." She devotes brief paragraphs to the two-month siege of Modlin and the regiment's march through Prague and the Bohemian mountains. The bulk of the section, however, is an embedded tale which Durova entitles "A Night in Bohemia." Left behind to watch for stragglers when a foul-up in orders forces her regiment to move on late at night, she finds herself alone in pitch darkness trying to master an unruly steed amid wolves and treacherous ravines. She does not even attempt to share this "adventure" with her fellow officers:

> However much I would have liked to tell my comrades about the events of that stormy night, I refrained from doing so. What use would it be? To them it all seems either too ordinary or altogether improbable. For example, they would not believe in my wolves and tell me they were dogs—and that might well be the truth. And my valiant leap into the river is such an ordinary matter that they would find it comical to hear me relating it as something of a wonder. It never enters their minds, of course, that everything they find ordinary is quite extraordinary to me.

Durova relished the physical freedom and challenge of cavalry life, but the journals also testify that she kept her identification with and connection to her own sex. In Russian the duality (public man, private woman) of Durova's sense of herself is mirrored even in the grammatical choices she makes. There is no way to reproduce in English the effect of Russian inflections. Uninitiated readers can scan entire sections of Durova's text in translation without being aware that they have before them anything but the confessions of a young, independent-minded officer, whereas in the Russian original gender-linked adjectives and past-tense verbs appear in virtually every paragraph to remind the reader of the anomaly of a woman describing herself as a soldier. Throughout the journals Durova uses the feminine grammatical forms that she could never slip into in direct speech without betraying herself, and four of her fictional tales feature a woman officer as frame-narrator. This is particularly interesting since, throughout her long years of retirement, Durova retained what she could of the honorary masculinity that was her warrant of freedom from female restrictions by wearing men's civilian clothing, using men's speech forms for herself, and demanding that others address her as a man. The cynical might assume that she used a woman's voice in order to exploit her fame as the "cavalry maiden." I would propose instead that the feminine first-person forms are an integral part of the text, an assertion of Durova's continued connection to her own sex, just as the demand that she be treated like a man in retirement years expressed her determination to retain what she could of male autonomy.

Durova's rebellion in running away to join the army was born of personal desperation. The domestic arena to which her contemporaries were confined could not satisfy her free spirit; however, it took a complex set of circumstances to drive her out of the female sphere altogether. In "My Childhood Years" she outlined the conflicting influences that led to her final rebellion. During her early childhood with the regiment, her father's orderly served as her nanny, and he taught her to love horses, swords, pistols, and the blare of military music. After her father retired to a civil post in the remote Ural town of Sarapul, Durova was returned to the strict custody of a mother who was determined to force her active, tomboyish daughter to accept a restricted female life that she herself deplored. In Durova's adolescence, her mother despaired of trying to change her "hussar ways" and sent her to live with maternal relatives in the Ukraine for a few years. There Durova learned to appreciate the positive side of female life and "the polite and obliging attentions" of men. Perhaps, she speculated:

> I would at last have forgotten all my hussar ways and become an ordinary girl like the rest if my mother had not kept depicting woman's lot in such a dismal way. . . . resolved, even at the cost of my life, to part company from the sex I thought to be under God's curse. Papa, too, often said, "If I had a son instead of Nadezhda, I shouldn't have to worry about my old age; he would be my staff in the evening of my days." I would be ready to weep at these words from the father I loved so extravagantly. These two contradictory emotions—love for my father and aversion to my own sex—troubled my young soul with equal force. With a resolve and constancy rare for one of my age I set about working out plans to escape the sphere prescribed by nature and custom to the female sex.

Durova had another unpleasant experience of female life, the details of which will probably remain only a matter for conjecture. She always insisted that every word in her journals was true, but there is one important truth that she omitted. In "My Childhood

Years" Durova says that she joined the army when she was sixteen. Actually, she was twenty-three years old, had been married
at eighteen, and had a young son. She left her husband and returned to what must have been a tense situation in her parents'
home before finally running away to the cavalry. She does not
mention her failed marriage in the memoir (or elsewhere). Perhaps the censorship of Nicholas I's Victorian reign found her status as runaway wife and mother a bad example for her female
contemporaries, or perhaps Durova herself omitted those seven
years in the conviction that the Russian public would more readily
accept a sixteen-year-old virgin as Alexander's *chevalier pur et
sans reproche*.[9]

Despite this failure of candor, Durova's experiences of repressed girlhood and broken marriage underlie her descriptions of
and references to women in *The Cavalry Maiden*. The journals are
written in the canonical form of anecdotes recorded for her family,
but it is clear that she sees her own sex as the audience best prepared to understand her experience:

> You, young women of my own age, only you can comprehend my
> rapture, only you can value my happiness! You, who must account
> for every step, who cannot go fifteen feet without supervision and
> protection, who from the cradle to the grave are eternally depen-
> dent and eternally guarded, God knows from whom and from
> what—I repeat, only you can comprehend the joyous sensations
> that fill my heart at the sight of vast forests, immense fields,
> mountains, valleys, and streams and at the thought that I can
> roam them all with nobody to answer to and no fear of anyone's
> prohibition. I jump for joy as I realize that I will never again in my
> entire life hear the words: *You girl, sit still! It's not proper for you to
> go wandering about alone.*

Durova records passing glimpses of women of a wide variety of
class and nationality that male memoirists never seem to notice:
officers' wives, children, and lovers; landowners; the wife of a Uni-
ate priest who is suspiciously tender to the young "Aleksandrov";
women who keep post-stations and wayside taverns; Polish, Ukrainian, Lithuanian, Russian, German, and Jewish women; a French
orphan stranded by Napoleon's headlong retreat—all of these appear in Durova's pages. She is tolerant of the convictions and way
of life of more conventional women to an extent that occasionally
drifts over into support for the patriarchal mores of her time.

Durova was apparently convinced that a sensibly arranged marriage was as viable as a self-willed romantic match, but the tragic "Tatar's Tale," which Durova embedded in *The Cavalry Maiden,* treats doomed runaway lovers with intense compassion.

There are times when Durova seems virtually androgynous in her psychological sense of female identity combined with a fully internalized accommodation to the masculine persona. She forgets the degree to which "clothes make the man" and interacts with others, male and female, as an integrated person. Occasionally, however, her innate femaleness makes her heedless of the proper distance to be observed between gentlemen and ladies; carefree reversion to youthful norms of contact—touching and hugging other women—got her into serious trouble at least once. She became especially supportive of parental rights when the hopeless infatuation of her colonel's daughter for the merry, enigmatic "Aleksandrov" forced Durova to transfer from the hussars to the uhlans in 1811. Durova's attempts to persuade her unwelcome lover to accept the colonel's preferred candidate for her hand are understandable (although hardly commendable): to change regiments meant starting over again as a stranger under scrutiny, open to curiosity and discovery, until she could prove herself as a soldier and a comrade, not an easy situation even for a person of integrated gender.[10]

In the early pages of *The Cavalry Maiden,* Durova portrays herself as a fumbling, comic character, the butt of her own anecdotes. Later, there is a partial reversal. As she becomes more confident, both in her inner self and her outer persona, she tends increasingly to see her fellow officers as equally comic and to turn her wit on them. The strategy of combining self-criticism with increasingly barbed humor directed against the foibles of her male comrades may have been a manifestation of Durova's sense of vulnerability, a way of deflecting the criticism to which she felt she might be subjected "when my sex is revealed." It seems to me, however, that Durova may also have had her female audience in mind when she portrays herself as out of place, slightly ridiculous, and yet functioning on a level acceptable to equally bumbling colleagues within one of the bastions of masculinity. The implicit message is that other women, too, could function ably in roles outside the restricted sphere to which "nature and custom" confined them. Her last known work, an unpublished essay dating from 1858, confirms this feminist reading. Commenting on the need for women to participate in the impending reforms of Alexander II's reign, the 75-year-old Durova wrote: "Now more than ever Russian society needs active, hard-working women who sympathize judiciously with the great events taking place around them and are capable of adding their mite to the structure of social welfare and order which is being erected by the common effort."[11]

Durova never admitted regretting the draconian bargain she struck with Alexander I, and there is little direct evidence from which to assess the longterm psychological cost. Stuck in muddy provincial posts, fretting under the mean-spirited discipline of the post-Napoleonic Russian army, urged by her father to return home, Durova retired in 1816. In the late 1830s she emerged from obscurity long enough to publish her autobiographical and fictional works. In 1840 she left St. Petersburg for good. The long years she spent in retirement in the remote town of Elabuga are documented only in the early 1860s. Except for the independence guaranteed by her veteran's pension and the eccentricity of her dress and speech, her life differed little from that of many other elderly spinsters. She could be depended on to intercede with the local mayor for anyone in trouble or offer help from her own slim purse; she lavished her affection on stray dogs. One visitor described Durova at 78 as "still brisk, she has not lost the gleam of her intelligent blue eyes, nor her playful thoughts. . . . They say that it was only ten years ago that she gave up dancing, where she, of course, always played the masculine role to which she had become accustomed."[12]

Durova exchanged her personal and sexual identity for the masculine freedoms of the cavalry because she saw no other way to lead an active, useful life. The patterns of *The Cavalry Maiden*—interest in and, by and large, sympathy with her own sex; a distanced, amused attitude toward her male colleagues; pride in her ability to function as an equal in the "man's world"— reveal a complex sense of self that transcends traditional gender distinctions.

Chapter Four

Biography as Autobiography:
Adèle Hugo, Witness of Her Husband's Life

 *Marilyn Yalom*

In an attempt to create a bibliography of French women's autobiographies published since the Revolution, I stumbled into the murky area of biography-cum-autobiography.[1] While it was relatively easy to identify and categorize the numerous women who wrote their lives because they had been exceptional women of letters, historical memorialists, travelers, actresses, singers, and courtesans—or, conversely, religious figures—what was I to do with a group of women who assumed authorial worth vicariously and wrote from the ostensible position of a biographer? This problematic group included such choice entries as the *Mémoires de Charlotte Robespierre sur ses deux frères, Dix Ans chez Alfred de Musset,* and *Victor Hugo raconté par un témoin de sa vie,* this last published anonymously in 1863 by Hugo's wife Adèle.[2] The authors had in common only their relationship to a great man, assessing themselves, just as society had assessed them, as "relative creatures," to use the English translation of the title of Françoise Basch's book on Victorian women.[3] This contingent role for women should not surprise us; many women in the past were seen as appendages to their fathers, brothers, husbands, lovers, sons and employers. Even notable women such as George Sand, Daniel Stern, and Simone de Beauvoir, as Nancy K. Miller observes, were "known for (or even through) their liaisons with famous men."[4]

Could any of these works, composed around the figure of a significant other, be considered as autobiography according to its conventional definition: the story that a real person writes about his or her own life? To what extent did these women record their own life histories along with those of the men who figured so prominently in the books' titles? What subversive means might a female

author have devised to make her presence felt in a work conse-
crated to a male protagonist?

The case of Adèle Hugo provided an obstinately ambiguous example. Adèle has come down through literary history as the least
interesting of wives, "a pious, prudish middle-class woman" ("une
petite bourgeoise prude et dévote")[5] according to one twentieth-
century critic who was echoing earlier assessments ("the most ordinary woman in the world" in Adèle's own words).[6] Like many of
my contemporaries bred on this version of the mouse-spouse, always compared unfavorably to Hugo's colorful mistress, Juliette
Drouet, I did not expect to find Adèle overtly present in her account of her husband's life.

It is true that Adèle Hugo is the most circumspect of biographers and that she depended largely on those incidents recounted
by Hugo himself at mealtime during their long political exile on
the islands of Jersey and then Guernsey, where they had settled in
1851 for the duration of the Second Empire. It is true too that she
was subjected not only to Hugo's control, but to the supervision
and revision of several professional editors, most notably Auguste
Vacquerie who was, according to Hugo's most recent biographer
Alain Decaux, "pre-occupied more than Hugo himself with the image of the poet that had to be transmitted to posterity."[7] There is
little that could be called self-promotion in the text, subscribing,
as Madame Hugo did, to a self-effacing mode of decorum for
women, especially married women. There are certainly no indis-
creet revelations, no mention of those conjugal infidelities that
have intrigued subsequent biographers (hers with the critic
Sainte-Beuve, his with any number of women, including his "second wife" Juliette Drouet, who accompanied them to Guernsey).
But there is more of Adèle in these memoirs than one had previously believed. Now that they have been reissued in their unexpur-
gated form on the occasion of the 1985 centenary of Victor Hugo's
death, we discover a text twice the size of the 1863 version and one
in which Adèle figures more conspicuously. Passages focusing on
the author, rather than on her husband, which had been elimi-
nated or greatly truncated in the first published edition, give us a
feel for her personality and for the female sphere. Moreover, the
new edition has restored to Adèle the first-person voice of the
manuscripts—a voice that was consistently transposed by her editors into the third person for the 1863 publication. Only now is it
possible to understand why Adèle thought of her work as memoirs,
as is evident from two of her letters, preserved in the Victor Hugo

Library in Paris, wherein the words "mes mémoires" are used in reference to the imminent publication of her book (letters of April 13, 1863, to her aunt Madame Asseline, and of April 28, 1863, to Victor Hugo). Clearly this incident of censoring and altering a female voice in the service of the masculine literary canon provokes feminist questions that are not unrelated to our central formal question of whether Adèle's biography of Victor is simultaneously an autobiography.

To begin with, what was Adèle's situation when she set out to write her husband's life? We must remember that it was not uncommon for a biographer in the past to know his or her subject: for example, Boswell's *Life of Johnson,* Godwin's memoirs of Mary Wollstonecraft, and Forster's *Life of Charles Dickens* were all written by individuals closely connected to their subjects. The notion of an "objective" biographer detached from the biographical other is a comparatively recent nineteenth-century phenomenon, corresponding to a scientific model that has already begun to fall out of favor in the twentieth century as we better appreciate the biases of biographical choices. In France, the memorialist tradition had permitted both men and women to bear witness to extraordinary lives and times; for women, this was never truer than in the wake of the French Revolution.[8] Still, despite a history of female-authored texts stretching back to the Middle Ages, prejudices against the woman writer had always existed and they were never more evident, nor more virulent, than in the nineteenth century when the number of women publishing was greater than ever before. Others have documented the varied disadvantages and insults to which nineteenth-century women authors were subject: Daumier's maliciously funny series of caricatures titled *Les Bas Bleus* (*Bluestockings*); the necessity for women writers to use male pseudonyms so as to be taken seriously; George Sand, admonished by an older male writer to go home and make babies instead of books. As late as 1878 Barbey d'Aurevilly was able to publish in yet another book titled *Les Bas Bleus*—and this under the auspices of a Catholic press—the most overtly vicious attacks on women writers to date: "Women who write," he declares, "are no longer women. They are men—at least by pretension—and failed men at that ('manqués'). They are Bluestockings. . . . Bluestockings have, more or less, given up their sex."[9] Little wonder that Adèle Hugo, in one of her rare polemical moments, seeks to disassociate herself from the bluestocking label as she cautiously defends her right as a woman to author texts.

One says that the woman who writes is a *bluestocking,* a formula which in itself has no meaning but which suggests an amphibious being, unclassified in society, neither man nor woman, not enough of a man to have his intellectual faculties, not enough of a woman to have her charm and grace: well then, a ridiculous being.

What is shocking is not that the woman who has a thought in her head is able to reproduce it. The woman painter, the woman sculptor, and the woman musician have thoughts and reproduce them without appearing ridiculous. What is shocking in the woman who writes is only the form of reproduction—the fact that instead of expressing ideas through the medium of musical notes, drawings, or colors, she expresses them in writing.

You may object that the woman who writes puts herself forward more obviously than those who paint, sculpt, or compose music, and that woman's chief attraction deriving from her sex is that she forgets herself, that she veils herself. This has a very true aspect: woman is, in general, made for the shadowy light and not for the bright light of day; she is made for self-effacement rather than for publicizing herself.

And that is exactly why I cannot understand the acerbic mockery of the woman who writes. What does this woman need? A little time for meditation, a peaceful corner in her home, a sheet of paper, a pen. Nothing prevents her, if she so desires, to have at her side, as I have, her basket for mending stockings, her embroidery, her needlework. . . .

But you will say that the woman who writes also writes so that her thoughts will be published, and consequently her name delivered up to publicity. To that there is an uncontestable response: talent itself is very rare, as rare among women as among men, and women like men only find editors, newspapers, and magazines if they have talent. . . . One must admit that the woman who endows society with a work of true merit will compensate for the fact that this work will have made her lose her power of feminine seduction.[10]

What are we to make of this tortuous defense of the woman writer, inserted into the biography of the male writer *par excellence*? Although the author tries to remain hidden among the throngs of her sister artists, ambivalently sharing their professional malaise in a society that dictated self-effacement for any woman who wanted to maintain a claim to a "feminine nature," occasionally Adèle sticks her head out of the masses and sketches her own self-portrait—oh, a very modest self-portrait to be sure, one that is thoroughly in keeping with received ideas about woman's domestic essence.

Note how the language shifts from the impersonal "on dit" and "on objectera" (translated as "one says" and "you may object") to the first person, and how Adèle subtly wedges her own image into the text with three banal, easily overlooked words—"ainsi que moi" ("as I have"). We glimpse a domestic Adèle seated in a peaceful corner of the house, pen and paper in hand, her sewing basket at her side—the stocking-mender covering for the bluestocking. Are we so very far away from Jane Austen, a half century earlier, hiding her manuscripts "with a large piece of muslin work . . . whenever genteel people came in"?[11]

This is the situation of Adèle as a woman daring to write her memoirs as witness to her husband's life. Let us note that Adèle was not unfamiliar with authorship at this time. She had already published three articles under the pseudonym of Cécile L. in 1849 and 1850 in the journal founded by her husband, L'Événement. These obituary pieces on the Hugos' close friend, the writer Charles Nodier, on the actress Marie Dorval, and on the working class writer Alphonse Petit reveal not only the progressive ideas that one might attribute to her husband's influence, but also—especially in the piece on Marie Dorval—a feminine sensibility that is undoubtedly her own.

By "feminine sensibility" I mean a heightened awareness of those aspects of human existence that traditionally devolve upon women, specifically the cluster of concerns surrounding maternity and children. Adèle—who had borne five children, losing one at birth and her beloved Léopoldine at nineteen, and who was to see her last-born, her namesake Adèle, go mad as a young woman—was no stranger to maternal solicitude and grief. Her obituary for Marie Dorval bypasses the public life of the great comédienne and zeroes in on a maternal loss similar to her own—that of Dorval's intense attachment to her four-year-old grandchild and her inconsolable grief at his death. Others may eulogize Mme Dorval in her professional role as one of the most celebrated actresses of her age; Adèle gives us the Dorval she can best understand—a good and simple woman, "made for family life, humble, discrete, domestic, a mother and a grandmother."[12]

This same feminine sensibility that privileges the domestic sphere and the nurturing of children asserts itself frequently in Adèle's biography of Victor. For example, when Adele narrates the story of Victor as an eight-year-old entering boarding school for

the first time, she turns the event into something peculiar to her
own imagination; the story is told from the perspective of the
mother as well as the son. First, true to the facts, Victor and his
brother are taken by their mother to the Collège des Nobles in
Madrid, where the family had joined Victor's father Léopold, a Napoleonic officer. There is a two-paragraph description of the children in their new setting, a huge scantily populated abbey, that
ends with a pathetic scene of abandonment. "The children's hearts
were so filled with sorrow that they were almost stupefied. They
broke into tears when their mother left them in that vast and
solitary prison."

Then Adèle allows herself a two-*page* imaginary recapitula-
tion of the scene, opening out to encompass all mothers and children who are separated by what she considers an inhuman
educational system designed to perpetuate questionable male
values.

> Many boys pass through such sorrows and consequently their
> mothers as well. We take such good care of them, our children—we
> wash them, comb them, dress them ourselves, help them with their
> appearance. I remember my little François-Victor telling me, when
> I combed his hair: 'Make my part straight.' We tuck them into their
> beds, we give them hot water bottles in winter. If during the night
> they have those inexplicable fears, they come to cuddle up next to
> us. We try to create for them as much of paradise as is possible.
>
> At a certain moment, it is decided that they should go to
> boarding school. We know it is inevitable; we have been preparing
> for it for a long time; they say it is in the child's best interest. The
> child doesn't take it too badly. Boarding school is a step towards
> becoming a man. . . .
>
> They leave for school rather cheerfully. They see a large cere-
> monial *porte cochère*. This door is so heavily locked that it does not
> seem to be made for being opened. . . . In a second the child realizes
> that in this big world he will be isolated—in all of these hearts, not
> one will be open to him. He clings to his mother. . . . The mother
> recommends her child [to the headmaster] without thinking about
> what she is saying. She does everything she can for her child, who
> opens his mouth wide and cries so hard. She tells him she will
> come back tomorrow.
>
> The next day she goes to see him. The child has felt her pres-
> ence, he is in her arms in a minute. He cries as he had the day
> before. He tells her: 'If you knew how disgusting it is in the dormi-

tories. I can't eat, it's so bad, it's so cold, things stick to the plates.' And then, a story of how mean the teachers are, how spiteful the other children. . . . Twenty-four hours have killed off eight years of happiness. You certainly feel like restoring him to his former happiness, but you tell yourself: 'Let's wait a bit, it will pass. It's for his own good. They've told me this so often that it must be true.' Only, it is amazing that so much evil is necessary to produce something good.[13]

Whose story is this, we ask—Victor's as a boy or Adèle's as a mother? By giving voice to what she and her two sons (Charles and François-Victor) had felt under similar circumstances, Adèle slips into the form of Victor's mother and artfully takes her place, substituting her own maternal sentiments for those of the senior Mme Hugo (who might not have had such tender feelings at all). As in the earlier example of Adèle as woman writer, the strategy entails merging with the collective identity of other women so as to simultaneously conceal and reveal her own identity.

The strategy of inscribing one's history obliquely—telling one's story "slant" in the words of Emily Dickinson—may indeed be characteristic of women writers, both as biographers and auto-biographers. Sometimes, however, even as biographers they are able to tell their personal stories more directly, at least from the time at which the biographer—wife, sister, daughter, or friend— has memories of the great man. Oddly enough, in Adèle's case, she most freely records her own history in the premarital years, in those sections dealing with Hugo's parents, childhood, and adolescence. One wonders if she writes more personally and more expansively about the early years because they represent for her a more joyful period, unmarred by the trauma and tragedies that, some have argued, began with the wedding night.[14] We should remember that Adèle had an unusual claim as Hugo's biographer in that their respective parents had known each other since before their marriages; Léopold Hugo and Pierre Foucher (Adèle's father) had even been witnesses at each other's weddings.

Adèle justifies writing about her family because, as she puts it, " . . . his family and mine were always linked together." The extent to which she describes her family life does, however, seem exaggerated in a memoir centered around her husband. Like George Sand, whose autobiography in serial form Adèle read between the autumn of 1854 and the summer of 1855 when she was working on her own manuscript, the author begins her book with a pre-history along paternal lines. The first chapter begins with the sentence: "General Hugo, Victor's father, was born in Nancy in 1774," and, like Sand, who included voluminous letters from her father to her grandmother, Adèle excerpts long passages from her father-in-law's own memoirs. This fixation on the paternal lineage, with scant attention to the maternal heritage, was common in the past, as any perusal of nineteenth-century dictionaries of biography makes manifest. What is more surprising is the fact that Adèle gives equal coverage to her own father, the court clerk Foucher, whose peaceful secular life contrasts markedly with the general's agitated military career. It is as if Adèle wished to establish a "masculine" and a "feminine" dichotomy in the two paternal legacies that were to be united in her future marriage to Hugo.

In these early chapters, where Adèle has not yet established the boundaries of her biographical territory, it is not clear to her (or to the reader) where Hugo's story ends and hers begins; indeed, it seems for a moment that it will be "their" story, the story of two young people paired before birth. She writes: "I do not know anything more about those two marriages from which were to issue two children destined for one another, my husband and myself."[15]

This vision of a dual destiny often determines the choice of content—the Hugo children play with the Foucher children, Mme Hugo depends increasingly on the Fouchers for domestic intimacy as her husband's military career carries him to distant wars, the Fouchers offer a stable two-parent family to Victor and his brothers, who become accustomed early in life to the distance between their parents that is to end in legal separation.

Adèle depicts herself as a cheerful child, domestic enough to have enjoyed embroidering and marking linens, spirited enough to have spit upon the fur jackets of two older girls whom she envied. She was very close to her mother, who combed her hair until she married, and she adored her father. One remarkable description of a visit to the Hugos at the Feuillantines can stand unashamedly beside Hugo's more celebrated poetic evocations of this former convent, turned residence, where he spent his most happily remembered childhood years.

> When I went to the Feuillantines, it was in search of joy. I went there, running and jumping all the way. . . .
>
> The front of the garden was decorated with beds filled with flowers. At the back end there were big, bushy trees. Attached to those trees was a swing, for me the source of vivid emotions.

My husband—the little boy that he was—was very proud of being able to go up very high. He stood up on the swing, stood as straight and as taut as the rope he had in his hands, then he gave himself vigorous jolts until his body got lost in the green plumage of the trees, which the swing caused to ondulate from top to bottom. It seemed to me that little Victor was going to break everything— trees, rope, swing, and himself. I walked far away so as not to see.

Everyone took a turn on the swing. I got on when my turn arrived. I preferred to swing alone rather than to be pushed because the boys, who take pleasure in force, made me go up too high. However, sometimes I let them do it, after I had stipulated my conditions. But I wouldn't let little Victor take the rope because he never gave in to my prayers. No matter what I said, he pushed the rope with all his might—whereas the others, after long petitions, yielded to them.[16]

The editors of the 1985 edition of *Victor Hugo raconté par Adèle Hugo* suggest that "the destiny of this couple was already sealed next to this swing."[17] Certainly this passage, with its contrast between the phallic aspirations of the young Hugo and Adèle's desire to follow her own rhythms rather than his, can be seen as a paradigm of their future relationship, a symbolic microcosm within the macrocosm of their entire lives. This is not the place to speculate upon their psychological and sexual incompatibilities or, equally pertinent, the rigid division of gendered spheres that led to unhappiness and misunderstanding in the Hugo *ménage*. But a careful, sympathetic reading of the text does lead to the conclusion that Adèle was hardly the colorless person she has been made out to be. She was, by her own accounts, a happy and beloved child, even "spoiled and strong-willed."[18] By the age of ten she was considered pretty, and by sixteen she was receiving love letters and poems from the man who was to become the greatest French writer of the century. When Adèle's parents discovered the letters, they went immediately to see Mme Hugo who, despite her careful surveillance of every aspect of her children's lives, had noticed nothing. She was, it appears, miffed at the idea of such a union, considering her son too young and the prospective bride perhaps not good enough, which put an end to the parental friendship. Yet Adèle and Victor did marry when she was nineteen and he twenty, literally over the dead body of Mme Hugo.

Adèle's written story does not end here, but it peters out as her husband's literary importance increases. Aside from one lighthearted interlude during the first years of their marriage when they traveled with the Nodiers to Switzerland, one senses the oppressive weight of Hugo's growing glory. As he ascends in the literary pantheon, she adopts the stance of the official biographer: at first, in the early chapters, she simply calls him "Victor," midway in the book she begins to refer to him as "Victor Hugo" and, toward the end, increasingly as "Monsieur Victor Hugo."[19] The last third of the biography is devoted almost exclusively to Hugo the writer, Hugo the Great, the public figure and national institution. He has expanded to Olympian proportions and she is virtually nonexistent.

How is it then that this work can be seen as Adèle's autobiography? Obliquely, directly, and even silently. Obliquely, when she inserts her own person into the collective body of "women" and when she gives expression to a recognizable feminine sensibility. Directly, when she speaks in a straightforward manner of her own experiences as a child and adolescent and even occasionally as a young wife. Silently, as she becomes incorporated into the Hugo industry and merges into the making of the Hugo myth.

Silence is by now an all-too-familiar subject of feminist inquiry, especially as it affects female creators.[20] Adèle's memoirs only hint at the patriarchal silencing that took place in her life; other sources are more explicit. For example, Nefftzer, the editor of the journal *Le Temps,* described to the Goncourt brothers a dinner during which "Mme Hugo began to talk a little too much." He added: "I'll never forget the indescribable look Hugo gave her ("par leqeul Hugo l'a foudroyée") and reduced her to silence."[21] It comes as no surprise to us that Adèle's book suggests a progressive erosion of her sense of self in her role as the spouse of the colossus Hugo had become. Whereas she writes directly and unselfconsciously of herself in her youth, leaving for posterity the picture of the girl swinging at her own pace, she gradually fades from the record in later life, as one hidden in the shadow of a towering edifice.

Adèle Foucher Hugo's biography of Victor Hugo is clearly, then, an example of female-authored life-writing containing both the story of another and the story of oneself. The other's story provides an excuse, as it were, for the woman witness to enter into history as a writing subject. This form of borrowed glory may be less prestigious than celebrity in one's own right, but it was undoubtedly better than no glory at all. And those women living in the shadow of great men—Adèle Hugo, Anne Thackeray Ritchie (see the following chapter), Charlotte Robespierre, the widows of certain Revolutionary officers—were not afraid of assuming the autobiographical "I," though they often did so in the guise of biographers and with sufficient disclaimers to justify putting themselves forward as active players in their scripts.

Perhaps, too, it is characteristic of women to write their stories through the stories of others, as the late Joan Lidoff maintained in her work on women's autobiographies.[22] In light of the psychological theories of Nancy Chodorow and Carol Gilligan, it is not unreasonable to assume that women's sense of self—for better or for worse—is intimately entwined with their relationships to others, and it is not surprising that their autobiographical texts, reflecting more fluid ego boundaries than found in men, are more relational in character.[23] In our own time, some of the most innovative works—those of Maxine Hong Kingston, Kim Chernin, and Nathalie Sarraute, for example—interweave the stories of mothers, grandmothers, aunts, sisters, daughters, caretakers, female friends, and even mythical women within the narrator/protagonist's life history. Does this indicate that women, newly conscious of their female connections, are beginning to validate themselves more overtly through members of their own sex rather than through the male figures who have been traditionally foregrounded throughout history?

Carolyn Heilbrun has argued that a new period in the writing of women's autobiographies and biographies has begun, that in the past two decades women have started to inscribe their lives with greater honesty.[24] In allowing for and even lauding this development, we should not, however, overlook the courage of those women in the past who, like Adèle Hugo, used whatever means were available to them, masquerading as biographers when necessary, so as to leave behind a textual manifestation of their will to be heard and remembered.

Chapter Five

Biography as Reflected Autobiography: The Self-Creation of Anne Thackeray Ritchie

 *Carol Hanbery MacKay*

"I love my recollections, and I now understand why everybody writes them. One begins to dance again, and lark, and frisk, and thrill, and do all the things one can hardly believe one ever did." So observes Anne Thackeray Ritchie (1837–1919), daughter of Victorian novelist William Makepiece Thackeray, upon publication of *Chapters from Some Memoirs* in 1894.[1] These essays, originally published over a five-year period in *Macmillan's Magazine,* were not undertaken, however, as an overtly autobiographical endeavor. They served Ritchie as a gradual approach to writing her distinguished father's biography. Yet we can also read this text, as well as her other "records" and biographical introductions, including those to the works of many women authors, as autobiographical reflections on the experiences that shaped her life and determined her vocation.

Behind these various auto/biographical activities lies an ambivalence about disclosing any private self or purporting to sum up a life. Ritchie shares this ambivalence with many other women autobiographers whose fragmented self-portraits mirror not only the complexities of their interwoven relationships but their unwillingness or inability to assert an independent ego as well.[2] Self-effacing, yet not denying her personal voice or intimate connections, Ritchie does not write in the ego-centered tradition of autobiography that has been especially associated with male authors; instead, by evoking herself through her subject, she creates "reflected autobiography." The result for Anne Thackeray Ritchie, in terms of both biography and autobiography, is a rich literary form created in response to a characteristically Victorian ethical dilemma. Apart from the specific proscription against writing his biography uttered by Thackeray, Ritchie had her own reserve to contend with, but she also held in common with other women writers what George Eliot called that "precious specialty"—which leads them to quiet self-discovery.[3]

Ritchie left us many clues to her ambivalence about biography and autobiography—in her piecemeal approach (she wrote "chapters" and "introductions," not complete studies), in the original ascription of her memoirs as "unwritten," even in the subcategories of "records" and "memoirs." In fact, memoirs seemed the appropriate mode for recounting the writer's secondary place in relation to the public figure whose life he or she chose to chronicle. In this case, the subject of the memoir was clearly intended to be someone other than the writer. This designation of memoir has caused Avron Fleischman to say of the form: "If there are to be axiological distinctions between *classes* of autobiography, we may ascribe higher value to those works where *mise en abyme* occurs, for its absence in another breed of writings designed to obscure their own artificiality has led to their relegation to the class of memoirs."[4] By using *mise en abyme* (essentially, trapped in a linguistic labyrinth or abyss) in this context, Fleischman is judging texts on the basis of their degree of self-referentiality. As we shall see, however, Ritchie's imagery contains creations within creations, mirror-image reverberations that raise her memoirs to a higher status within Fleischman's evaluative schema.

Ritchie has evolved a form which at once establishes and denies a center. It is, in other words, a unique kind of *mise en abyme.* Her images of creativity draw on two resources—one a reflection of her own life, the other a reflection of her father's. These two reference points function like a pair of mirrors, plunging us into the abyss of the creative realm. The negative side of this effect is a sense of loss or confusion; we may seek but not find a single center to the text. On the other hand, as I think Ritchie confirms in her generally optimistic tone, there is a positive side: the reader feels surrounded by the richness of repeatedly renewed creativity.

For our purposes, the text's center can be found in Ritchie herself as autobiographer within the act of writing biography. Fleischman's designation of memoirs as basically of less worth because they lack *mise en abyme* lends itself to a useful critique. On the one hand, his valorizing of self-reflexive texts over apparently objective subject models seems unfortunate; he fails to allow for the full spectrum of biographical and autobiographical activities. Because many women have approached writing for publication through the arena of writing memoirs about others, such thinking serves to denigrate or marginalize their efforts. At the same time, Fleischman's statement raises for our consideration the ways in which we can read Ritchie's extended "memoirs," namely her biographical endeavors, as a rich nexus of autobiographical writing.

A novelist in her own right, Ritchie never saw her life as responding to a purely self-conscious autobiographical impulse, and Thackeray's proscription against ever having his biography written constrained her desire to set the record straight about him.[5] The result in her case was a brand of refracted autobiography that emerged in memoirs overtly about the lives of others—most notably in the biographical introductions to her father's canon (thirteen in 1898–99 and eighteen in 1910–11).[6] In this arena, Lady Ritchie developed her own blend of autobiographical biography, weaving fact and imagination to establish a meeting-ground in which images of fertility conjoin her as a creative writer with her father. Gardens and flowering often inform these images, but Ritchie also uses any focal point of creativity, such as memorable locations and works of art, as the catalyst for an epiphany. This form of autobiography is thus much more than factual information arranged in chronological order.

Ritchie demonstrates how ambivalence may play into creativity. Her unwillingness to adopt the traditional tools of biography collided with her desire to come to terms with her father's lifestory. As a result, she produced a series of memoirs infused by metaphors that highlight the creative process. For many critics of autobiography, such metaphors constitute a "personal myth," particularly as it develops through a sequential narrative.[7] Ritchie's narrative—either her own or her father's story—is hardly sequential, but it can be so reconstructed by the reader. Furthermore, treating metaphor as a conjunction of the conscious and unconscious allows us to recognize the layers within layers operating in Ritchie's text: what better ruling principle for Ritchie's study of creativity than images of fertility, which will force reader and writer alike to admit the role of the unconscious in the creative process?

Thirty years after Thackeray's death, Ritchie attempted a series of autobiographical essays that have as their stated impetus her father's shaping role in her life. Entitled *Chapters from Some Memoirs,* this collection assumes from its opening words her readership's familiarity with Thackeray and his literary circle: "My father lived in good company, so that even as children we must have seen a good many poets and remarkable people, though we were not always conscious of our privileges."[8] Ritchie postpones the "I" voice for several sentences, speaking instead the "we" that invokes her sister Minny—Leslie Stephen's first wife, dead almost twenty years. (A distinguished man of letters, Stephen was also Virginia Woolf's father.) Yet before her first chapter has concluded, Ritchie develops her view of childhood's illusions and the mind's repeated interplay between the past and the present. When her then favorite poet Jasmin fails to live up to her expectations, she acknowledges:

> I can't help laughing even now as I conjure up the absurd little dream of the past and the bitterness of that childish disappointment. How little do we mortals recognize our good fortune that comes to us now and again in certain humorous disguise.[9]

This last sentence reads like a typical Thackerayan generalization—except that the balance is tipped more toward the present than we usually find in Thackeray's brand of nostalgia. Already Ritchie has begun shaping her own double vision, playing variations on her father's theme of time passing.

Chapters from Some Memoirs presents a succession of Thackeray's famous friends parading by an enchanted observer on whom little was missed. Edward FitzGerald, Count d'Orsay, Alfred Tennyson, the Carlyles, Dickens, the Brownings, Fanny Kemble, Adelaide Sartoris, Charlotte Brontë—these and other luminaries were to little Anny part of her daily existence. The self-portrait that emerges here is one of a budding writer, caught up by all the excitement that life has to offer to her pen. The illustrious figures who people Ritchie's pages soon begin to take a back seat to the voice that memorializes them.

In her previous collection of essays *Records of Tennyson, Ruskin and Robert and Elizabeth Browning* (1892), Thackeray's role as man of letters had also served as entré to her subjects, but it was Ritchie who cultivated those subjects through years of independent friendship and observation. These memoirs record her skill at evoking character through place—a place that usually draws on the record-keeper's memory and hence makes an autobiographical statement. Ritchie also uses her personal insights to create intimate portraits that at the same time do not invade privacy. In contrast to the youthful exuberance that characterizes the author of *Chapters from Some Memoirs,* the self-portrait that emerges from these records is measured and reflective. Granting the value of Ritchie's biographical approach in "its essentially personal quality," Winifred Gérin is quick to add: "but it is not that she seeks to put herself in the picture, rather that without her presence the picture would not exist."[10]

These two semi-autobiographical, semi-biographical works preceding Ritchie's biographical introductions to her father's canon show her experimenting with the techniques that serve her unique blend of autobiographical biography. On the one hand, Ritchie seems indifferent to gradations, measurements, dates, and the like, in fact calling the process "incompetent, woolgathering."[11] Yet the pose is a conscious one that allows her "impressions" to unfold in detail. Ritchie's use of place is key in this respect, for a location is at once factual, imagistic, and full of subjective meaning. In the case of Tennyson's birthplace imaginatively evoked, for example, she can use it to tell the poet's story while symbolically creating her relationship to him anew as a fellow writer.[12]

At the heart of Ritchie's biographical introductions to her father's works lay her relationship with him, and to the extent that we recognize that center, we can read her autobiography in these introductions. Furthermore, since Ritchie emphasizes Thackeray as writer, it is equally the daughter as protegée who becomes manifest in these pages. As she cites Thackeray's letters about the vicissitudes of the writing process, recalls her own involvement in taking down his dictation, or reports a scrap of his conversation about the original for a place or character, Ritchie reveals her growing awareness of what constitutes a writer's work. Ritchie's juxtaposition at the end of the *Esmond* introduction of two of Thackeray's letters to his children is a telling one: to Minny he writes in his neat, upright hand, while to Anny he writes in the hurried, slanted one—all the better to communicate rapidly his mental process to the daughter, who was his co-worker and confidante.[13]

Ritchie approached her father's life story piecemeal—working from different angles and apparently taking in small units of time—all in an effort to avoid going against his wishes. Yet in every case, she stakes out more territory, including more "self" territory, than first meets the eye. In 1889, one of her earliest partial biographies of Thackeray appeared in *St. Nicholas*, a magazine for children. Entitled "The Boyhood of Thackeray," this article uses a series of paintings and portraits, including some of Thackeray's own drawings, to address its readers as future writers. By focusing on a spectrum of aesthetic objects, Ritchie structures her presentation through imagery, the passage of time, and personal memory. In fact, she and her own children are present in the article from the outset. By conflating time—the period of the paintings, her memories of seeing them, her children now viewing them, the historical time of the artists, impressions of Thackeray's boyhood—Ritchie dramatizes the uses of shared creative sources.

If Ritchie still remains uncomfortable about making the private public, as her use of passive constructions to describe the reproduction of the pictures and letters demonstrates, the result is also remarkable for its unique amplification of a fairy-tale mode:

> And so it happened that one summer's day this year a little cart drew up at our garden gate, a photographer and a camera were landed on the doorstep, the camera was set up in a corner of the garden, the sun came out from behind a cloud, and in an hour or two the letters were copied, the pictures and the bust were reproduced, the picture went back to its nail, and letters to their drawers, and the cart rumbled off with the negatives, of which the proofs have now reached me from America.[14]

The scene depicts a concentric series of containers, like a Chinese box: the camera forms within itself photographs, themselves inscribing representations of self-contained faces. And as light triggers the process, it is almost as if the reproductions reappear magically, without the practical aid of human intermediaries. In effect, this superfetation is yet another example of Ritchie's application of the principle of *mise en abyme*.

Despite Ritchie's ambivalence, she eventually plunged into the precarious balancing act of her biographical task, and her opening choice is telling. She begins with the "I" voice she denied herself in the first words of her own memoirs:

> I cannot help thinking that, although "Vanity Fair" was written in 1845 and the following years, it was really begun in 1817, when a little boy, but lately come from India, found himself shut in behind those filigree iron gates at Chiswick, of which he writes when he describes Miss Pinkerton's establishment.[15]

Bringing herself to the fore and concentrating on the genesis of *Vanity Fair*, Ritchie uses the personal voice and calls attention to origins, both characteristics of autobiographical endeavors—now all in the name of biography. The facts are present in the dates and places, but the imaginative act is more important, for it shows the novelist-daughter looking at her novelist-father through the eyes of his fiction and recognizing the shaping role of childhood experiences. For Thackeray, the child lives unanalyzed in numerous fictional re-creations, but for Ritchie that life stands both inviolate and subject to empathetic interpretation. Writing this piecemeal biography constituted her primary literary undertaking as well as a major phase of her own autobiography.

Although Ritchie indicates that she has "reconstructed much of what happened from the scraps and letters" of the past, we see a much more intricate layering effect when she rhapsodizes about the fecund imagination of childhood—"these dawning hours, when the whole world is illuminated and enchanting, when animals can speak—nay, when all nature speaks and inanimate things are alive, and when we are as gods, and unconscious of evil, and create existence for ourselves as we breathe."[16] She is here recognizing the creativity inherent in childhood source points—those key moments forming images of genesis that live in memory to feed the imagination—in large part because she has been analyzing Thackeray's own use of childhood memories in the writing of his fiction.[17] At such moments, we recognize a conjoinment of forms—of her father's biography, of their shared life-story, of her own autobiography.

Ritchie plays back and forth between the pages of Thackeray's fiction and the facts of his life. Much of what she reveals, however, are the memories of their *shared* experience. By using Thackeray's fictional labels for the places and events of his actual life (Thackeray's stepfather removes the family to "Pendennisland," for instance), Ritchie not only reveals how much her father's creations permeated her childhood but how her own approach to biography and autobiography has become increasingly playful and innovative.

The child's perspective is readily available to Ritchie through her own memories of childhood, her father's published fiction, and his private letters to his mother and children. Both father and daughter delight in the power of place to unleash personal associations from the past that live again in the present: he in pointing out the source points of his fictional re-creations, she in recalling those moments. In one sense, these are the family secrets that she makes public; in another, this is the process of demythologizing that gradually helps illuminate the creative artist at work.

Ritchie recasts the autobiographer's inherent double perspective as both subject and object into her own dramatic mode, which

allows the past and present to coexist. In a 1891 article that introduced the reading public to her father's unpublished illustrated
tale of "The Heroic Adventures of M. Boudin," Ritchie encapsulates
past moments as a telling comment on the present. After recreating a pleasant evening with her father and sister at a friend's
home, she adds that "the thought of it all faded quietly away; for
in those days, five-and-twenty years ago, tranquility had less
charm and importance than it does now."[18] The past gets its nostalgic due, but more significant is the reflection on the writer's
engagement with the present.

In each of the biographical introductions, Ritchie examines
Thackeray's stated inspirations and seeks out the implied ones. In
her introduction to *Vanity Fair,* for example, she reproduces one of
his youthful sketches of a German actor, accompanied by Thackeray's comment, "I have done nothing but practice drawing his face
since I saw it."[19] Here we see Ritchie's sensitivity to a focal point, a
spot in time, repeatedly examined by the young artist-writer, that
his daughter now reexamines within her own creative endeavor as
she speculates about the connection between the drawing and the
novel. She caps this discussion with the image of her father pointing out the windows of his old room in Germany, the afternoon sun
"shining full."

A writer herself, Ritchie knows the difficulties attendant on
beginnings and endings. Over and over again, she isolates those
moments as recorded in Thackeray's letters, empathetically commenting on them and then setting them in an ongoing recursive
context that denies their isolation from one another. Ritchie epito-
mizes this affirming endeavor in the introduction to *Esmond,*
where she recreates the garden outside Thackeray's writing studio:

> The vine shades the two windows, which looked out upon the bit of
> garden and the medlar tree, and the Spanish jasmines of which the
> yellow flowers scented our old brick walls. I can remember the tor-
> toise belonging to the boys next door crawling along the top of the
> wall where they had set it, and making its way between the jas-
> mine sprigs. Jasmines won't grow now any more, as they did then,
> in the gardens of Kensington, nor will medlars and vine trees take
> root as ours did, and spread their green branches; only herbs and
> bulbs, such as lilies and Solomon's seals, seem to flourish still,
> though one has a faint hope that all the things people put in will
> come up all right some centuries hence, when London is resting
> and at peace and has turned into the grass-grown ruin one so often
> hears described.[20]

In the midst of decay, Ritchie conveys a sense of the ultimate triumph of fertility. Throughout this passage—introduced with the question, "May the writer be allowed to quote a chapter from some unwritten Memoirs in which she had described the study?"—we are aware of the presenter within the presentation.

With each of her eighteen introductions, Ritchie begins anew her attempt to understand her father's life. As she works with Thackeray's various fictions, she acknowledges his own reworkings of his life-story, in effect his recurvate attempts to understand his life anew. But perhaps most importantly, Ritchie's attention to Thackeray's sources of inspiration and to her own emblematic images point to the regenerative nature of creativity. This line of interpretation becomes all the more poignant when we recall that Thackeray repeatedly felt that he was played out, particularly in comparison with his prolific contemporary, Charles Dickens: "I can't but see [The Newcomes] is a repetition of past performances, and think that vein is pretty nigh worked out in me," he writes to his mother, adding, "One of Dickens' immense superiorities over me is the great fecundity of his imagination."[21] But Ritchie reasserts renewal in the face of exhaustion. Even as he writes about completing his novels, Thackeray reveals his resistance to pat conclusions. And when he writes to his mother condemning the "bookolatry" of worshiping established authors (Shakespeare and King Lear constitute his specific provocation),[22] he reaffirms the origins of creativity in the destruction of that which is old and effectively dead. Finally, at the end of her last introduction, Ritchie once more brings herself to the fore, evoking the cross-generational network that helped her give birth to this endeavor.[23]

Each generation, each individual, has something new to contribute and sees life differently. Ritchie seizes upon this idea and combines it with Thackeray's own trademarks—eyes, spectacles, framed views and pictures. In her introduction to Esmond, for example, she recalls Thackeray's "second sight" to explain his descriptions of places he can hardly believe he has not seen,[24] while her own memories of their early years on Young Street coalesce in the happy image of "fruitful years, bringing their sheaves with them and gathering in their full harvests."[25] This attention to viewpoint and image-making confirms Ritchie in her own and in her father's creative energies. Each performs this task with regard to self and other, visually and verbally.[26]

Self-images thus permeate Ritchie's text. Thackeray produced his own self-portraits in both his drawings and his fiction, and

Ritchie duly records this dual activity. But each time she reports on another fictional self-accounting for her father, she must come to terms with another aspect of herself in her relationship to him. Ritchie can be child and confidante, apprentice and co-worker, idolator and critic—moving confidently among these roles, in historical and present time, recognizing a bit of herself in all of them.[27]

This element of self-recognition points to Ritchie's ability to objectify herself and even poke fun at her activity as a would-be biographer. Writing her father's biography encourages her to recall a range of memories, ones that mark significant stages of her personal growth and development. In particular, she remembers and describes Archdeacon Allen, who served as the prototype for Dobbin in *Vanity Fair*. Allen is also the first person Ritchie can recollect as existing outside her family circle, and she pauses at this awareness, taking stock of herself as she might have been viewed by the outsider.[28] This perspective, encouraged by Thackeray's own portraits of his daughter, fosters a healthy brand of self-mockery, which emerges in the biographical introductions in Ritchie's interplay between her impressionistic and dry-as-dust selves. She pokes fun at herself in her own footnotes in the introduction to *Vanity Fair* by pointedly citing a German correspondent's pedantic questioning of the spelling of a name in one of Thackeray's letters.[29] This byplay shows her fussing over inconsequential matters and engaging in flights of fancy that recall, albeit in a more gentle cast, Thackeray's ironic outlook.

Facts can thus be derived from the embedded text of Ritchie's various narratives; however, more important to both the biographical and autobiographical undertaking are the imaginative acts that crystallize Thackeray's and her own different selves. This is how Ritchie uses images of creativity as a means of discovering her own parallel points with Thackeray's creativity and uniting the two of them beyond this time-bound world. For William C. Spengemann, the evolution of poetic autobiography reflects the radical upheavals of the nineteenth century; here we see the autobiographer choosing "enactment" over mere "recollection" in an effort to dramatize self-creation.[30] Multiple viewpoints conjoin in her narratives to underscore further the layers of creativity in both her and her father's work. Even the narrative form confirms Ritchie's choice of imagery: moving round and round in time, the overall narrative reveals its reduplicative story and makes its point through incremental repetition.

Reviewing Aimée Dostoyevsky's account of her father Fyodor, Virginia Woolf asks, "And what is a daughter's purpose in writing a study of her father?"[31] Writing the biographical introduction to Thackeray's works freed Ritchie from the ghost of being her father's protector (a quarter of a century earlier she was still saying, "It is so painful to me to discuss him in any way that I avoid doing so when I can"),[32] and finally measuring Thackeray through her piecemeal portraits of him let her see herself in her various relationships to him.

Each of Ritchie's introductions has a theme, which unites the several layers of creativity that all the works have in common—individual memory, shared memory of father and daughter, the created artifact itself, the wellsprings in life of that creativity.[33] *Vanity Fair*, for instance, is very much about early impressions, and her introduction to it establishes both Thackeray's and Ritchie's awareness of the influence of these impressions on life and art. *Pendennis*, on the other hand, is a novel about ordering one's life, and Ritchie's introduction draws attention to Thackeray's attempts to order life and art in ways that parallel not only Pen's but her own. As for *Esmond*, it tells the story of a protagonist trying to impose order on a repressed life, and Ritchie responds to Thackeray's own repression and reversals by apparently forgetting much about the novel's composition, dictated in large part to her, focusing instead on her own memories of its reception. Pulling back and then putting herself forward, Ritchie uses her absence or presence to shape her art.

Ritchie's art, like Thackeray's, is more circular than linear. The harmonic of Ritchie's introduction to *The Newcomes* confirms the power of incremental repetition, as she rounds out her observations and then circles back in time. In this respect, she intuitively responds to the creative tension between the linear and circular elements in Thackeray's narrative art: he may end *The Newcomes* by drawing a line between its fiction and the "Fable-land" of our imagination, but that fable-land also returns us to the initial "farrago of old fables" that opens his text, inviting us to reread it and reconceive it anew. In contrast, *Philip* is much more about endings than Thackeray himself could have known. His last completed novel, it conveys a curious finality that Ritchie captures by citing his letter about drawing out the moment of finishing it and then trying to stop time.[34] Moreover, Ritchie also reacts to the paradoxical interrelation of beginnings and endings as she returns in her memory to an outing the next day, when "the gardens were

in their prime," conveying "one glow of beautiful, bright colour"—a
fecund memory played off against her present-time experience of
reading about the funeral of the duke who had served as her host
on the day of the outing.

"Being my father's daughter facts still exist for me," Ritchie
writes to Lewis Benjamin [35]—and they do appear as names, dates,
and places—but the imaginative act is more important, especially
as it shows the novelist-daughter examining her novelist-father
through his fiction and recognizing the shaping role of their mu-
tual or parallel experience. Thus, by using Thackeray's fictional
terms to describe factual places and individuals, Ritchie encourages fiction to permeate fact. Even when she discusses ancestry, a
traditional facet of biography, it fits into an aesthetic, speculative
vein, again as if to suggest that the facts do not matter as much as
the feeling.[36]

This, then, is the hidden order of Anne Thackeray Ritchie's
art as Thackeray's biographer and, to a considerable degree, her
own autobiographer: her apparently structureless narratives are
actually governed by imagery and empathy, the tools of a fellow
creative artist.

We would do well, nonetheless, to look beyond Ritchie's memoirs
and her introductions to Thackeray's works to her other biographical
commissions, in order to see how she tells her own story within the
full corpus of her life-writing. *The Cornhill Magazine,* for example,
marks another conjunction of Ritchie's biographical and autobiographical interests. She sees it through both the eyes of childhood,
when George Smith founded the journal and asked Thackeray to be
its first editor, and the eyes of the adult, when she was one of its main
contributors. As its jubilee and Thackeray's centenary approached,
Ritchie was asked to write several recollective pieces for the journal, articles that basically called forth mini-biographies because
they featured the illustrious contributors she had known over the
years. To compare her 1896 article on "The First Number of 'The
Cornhill' " with its reincarnation in the 1898 and 1911 biographical
introductions to *Philip,* however, is to see how much she kept her
own accomplishments in the background when she told her father's
story. In the article, on the other hand, Ritchie acknowledges with
pride the "raptures" of seeing the "printed paragraphs" of her first
novel, *The Story of Elizabeth* (1862), and "hopes she may be for-
given" for quoting Robert Louis Stevenson's poem to her, in which
he woos her in verse to future biographical endeavors: "The sires of
your departed sires,/The mothers of our mothers, show."[37]

Writing about other women authors, both her contemporaries and historical figures, seemed to encourage Ritchie to keep herself at the forefront, almost as if she were providing proof that they lived anew in her. Thus Ritchie's introduction to Elizabeth Gaskell's *Cranford* begins on the personal note of recalling how she felt when she saw Thackeray reading a certain installment of it—"I had a foolish childish wish for my father's sympathy, and a feeling that even yet he might avert the catastrophe"—and ends with a memory of visiting the real-life counterpart of the village of Cranford and sensing the presence of Gaskell's characters: "As I sate there drinking my tea I thought I could almost hear Mrs. Gibson herself conversing. 'Spring! Primavera, as the Italians call it,' the lady was saying."[38] In fact, Ritchie's introductions to Maria Edgeworth's *Our Village* also include visits to their authors' homes and the scenes of their fiction. We see here Ritchie's attempt to steep herself in the atmosphere of her subject matter, to come to know these writers even after their deaths. In autobiographical terms, Ritchie once again cultivates empathetic identification as a primary artistic technique.

Of all Ritchie's biographical endeavors, her life of Mme de Sévigné offers perhaps the most concealed autobiographical message; yet once we uncover the author in her subject, this biography can be considered one of her most self-revelatory works.[39] Published in 1881, *Madame de Sévigné* shows Ritchie's ability to be both honest about her subject's shortcomings and willing to celebrate their shared talent as empathetic creators:

> There is something almost of a great composer's art in the endless variations and modulations of this lady's fancy. She laments, she rejoices, she alters her note, her key; she modulates from tears to laughter, from laughter to wit. She looks round for sympathy, tells the stories of the people all about her, repeats their words, describes their hopes, their preoccupations. Then she remembers her own once more, and repeats again and again, in new words from fresh aspects, the fancies and feelings which fill her heart.[40]

Here we witness the rhetoric of creativity: continual teeming, multiple aspects, duplication, spheres of discourse, the magical and cyclic nature of existence—these are the qualities that Ritchie underscores.

Ritchie's portrait of Mme de Sévigné is in many respects a covert self-portrait. In *Madame de Sévigné* she openly acknowledges the letter-writer's voice and the biographical value of letting the subject tell her own tale: "It has seemed the best and simplest plan to endeavor in this little book to tell her story in her own words, so far as may be possible."[41] A prolific letter-writer herself, Ritchie recognized the importance of these documents for self-writing in both Mme de Sévigné and Thackeray, and hence she gave over considerable space in her biographical studies to reproducing her subjects' correspondence. Ritchie understood only too well that letters are close kin to autobiography.

Those who have turned the tables on Ritchie and tried to capture her life-story have quickly realized that she is her own best biographer, and they have freely reproduced her words in their biographical accounts. Chief among these recorders was Virginia Woolf, who first rose to the occasion within a week of her Aunt Anny's death in 1919. In her obituary notice for *The Times Literary Supplement,* Woolf provides a series of quotations from Ritchie's memoirs—portraits of Charlotte Brontë, Trelawny, George Sand—all of which lead Woolf to conclude, "We feel that we have been in the same room with the people she describes."[42] Five years later, when Ritchie's daughter Hester published a volume of her mother's correspondence, Woolf was still singing her aunt's praises through Ritchie's own words. Woolf's review essay, evocatively entitled "The Enchanted Organ," strings together a succession of Ritchie's most quotable phrases, evoking a unique person "at once so queer and so sweet, so merry and so plaintive, so dignified and so fantastical."[43]

Both of Hester's tributes to her mother decidedly let Ritchie speak in her own voice. The collection of Ritchie's letters is, of course, an obvious case in point, but Hester also adds to the correspondence quotations from Ritchie's various journals and diaries, including selections from her manuscript book, "Notes of Happy Things."[44] Hester's second contribution to her mother's memory, appearing some twenty-five years later, is entitled *Thackeray's Daughter,* with the telling subtitle, *Some Recollections of Anne Thackeray Ritchie.* An anonymous reviewer acknowledges its appropriate form—"Anny Thackeray's gay haphazard personality, which would have been buried forever under the incongruous weight of a formal biography, emerges clear and sparkling from these seemingly casual pages"—adding that "if anything further is to be published about her, let Anny speak for herself, in the words of her own letters and reminiscences."[45]

In large part, that is exactly what Winifred Gérin did when she prepared her full-length biography of Ritchie. Sometimes Gérin seems annoyingly remiss in her unwillingness to analyze and criticize Ritchie's work more thoroughly, but at least she has provided us with extensive excerpts—including many from previously unpublished material—upon which we can base more critical study. Once again, Ritchie emerges from the pages of a biography almost as if she were writing the text of her autobiography. Gérin may conclude that Ritchie was "a natural biographer,"[46] but by now we would have to add that autobiography also came naturally to her and infused itself in all her writing. As a result, it is particularly frustrating to read accounts of Ritchie's life that do not let her speak for herself. A case in point is the entry in the *Dictionary of National Biography,* first edited by her brother-in-law, Leslie Stephen. Not only are Anne's own words missing from this brief account, but she does not even merit an entry of her own: her life appears as an appendage to the one on her husband, Richmond, a civil servant in the India Office.[47]

Reading a range of Anne Thackeray Ritchie's works, and in particular her biographical introductions, produces the impression that she developed a sure sense of when to be factual and when to let her imagination roam more freely. In fact, her manipulation of images of creativity amounts to an impressive control of viewpoint. We emerge from reading the biographical introductions with a strong sense of knowing Ritchie. Although we may not learn very much about the facts that constituted her life, we recognize in her attention to source points the growth of a creative writer coming to terms not only with her biographer's task but with herself.

Chapter Six

The Feminization of John Stuart Mill

 *Susan Groag Bell*

The *Autobiography* of John Stuart Mill, the most famous male feminist of the nineteenth century, is inspired by a presence that has infuriated many critics—that of his wife Harriet. In Mill's words, she was "the most admirable person I had ever known" (p. 114). He insisted that his published writings were "not the work of one mind, but of the fusion of two" (p. 114), "as much her work as mine" (p. 145).[1] He attributed to Harriet "the most valuable ideas and features in these [our] joint productions—those which have been most fruitful of important results and have contributed most to the success and reputation of the works themselves." And, downplaying his own contribution, he added that his own part in them was "no greater than in any of the thoughts which I found in previous writers and made my own only by incorporating them with my own system of thought" (pp. 145–6).

Why are these statements so unpalatable to Mill scholars? Stillinger, for example, who edited various drafts of the autobiography, states that Mill's "encomiums [on Harriet] are a blemish on the work . . . we should object to such extravagances in fiction, and similarly must object to them in autobiography" (p. xvii). An examination of the circumstances in which the autobiography was composed illuminates this question and, additionally, offers a basis for analyzing Mill's pivotal stance in nineteenth-century views on women and gender.

In the first page of the *Autobiography,* Mill presented his intention to describe the story of his "intellectual and moral development;" and further, to acknowledge his debt to others, particularly to "the one to whom most of all is due" [i.e., his wife, Harriet] (p. 3). In fact, one may say that Mill offered a collective self to the world, a self joining Harriet's practical concerns and her emphasis on human connectedness to his own theoretical bent.

81

In an important passage, totally lacking the sentimentality of which he is so often accused, he explained the exact nature of Harriet's contribution to his thought:

> I have often received praise, which in my own right I only partially deserve, for the greater practicality which is supposed to be found in my writings, compared with those of most thinkers who have been equally addicted to large generalizations. The writings in which this quality has been observed, were not the work of one mind, but of the fusion of two, one of them as preeminently practical in its judgments and perceptions of things present, as it was high and bold in its anticipations for a remote futurity. (p. 114)

It is this concern for his debt, this intellectual debt to his wife, that deeply troubles many of his critics. One of these, H. O. Pappe, has devoted an entire book to an attempt to disprove Harriet's intellectual influence on Mill.[2]

Mill describes his mental development with shining modesty and integrity—beginning with his earliest education, when he was obliged to learn classical Greek at the age of three. However, as readers, we are also aware of the clear psychological implications of his story. Prior to Mill's involvement with Harriet, his life had been dominated by his father James Mill, portrayed by his son as a stern, driving, unloving and unforgiving man. Since the dominating presence of Mill's father has been dealt with at length by others, I do not propose to discuss this further.[3] But what of John Stuart Mill's mother? Was she indeed as absent from his psyche as the final version of the *Autobiography* would lead us to believe?

Most commentators find it easy to dismiss Mill's mother since she appears to be totally absent from the published version of the *Autobiography*. A good example of this point of view, and one of the most recent, is offered by A. O. J. Cockshut: "He [Mill] does not appear to see that he was unusual in having no discernible feeling at all about his mother. If he had disliked her, we could understand it. But not to notice her! . . . . Something which Mill never mentions, and (as far as we know) never considered, becomes one of the most fascinating issues in the judgment of his work."[4] Had Cockshut taken into consideration the first draft of the manuscript, he would not have written such a sentence. Ever since 1961, when Stillinger published his edition of the early draft of Mill's *Autobiography*, we have known that at the time of composing this first draft, Mill not only thought about his mother, but actually wrote down some of his negative feelings about her.

The most telling of his observations about his mother (in the first draft) lies in the following remarks: "In an atmosphere of tenderness and affection he [my father] would have been tender and affectionate; but his ill assorted marriage . . . disabled him from making such an atmosphere."[5] And again, "a really warm-hearted mother would in the first place have made my father a totally different being, and in the second, would have made the children grow up loving and being loved. . . . I thus grew up in the absence of love and in the presence of fear."[6] Strong words—an unflinching indictment only few sons would dare to voice. And from the exchange of letters between Mill and Harriet Taylor, published in 1951, we have long known how instrumental Harriet was in editing and censoring Mill's work.[7] These letters clearly show that in order not to aggravate his mother's hurt feelings, Harriet persuaded him to erase everything he had written about her. Harriet's editing, in fact, went so far that in her distress and haste to prevent Mill's negative remarks about his mother from being published, she sometimes led him to expunge certain sections that would have shown his mother's concern for his upbringing and manners. For example, in the passage of the *Autobiography* where Mill describes how as a young boy he had been disputatious and impertinent towards adults, Harriet erased the following sentence: "My mother did tax me with it, but for her remonstrances I never had the slightest regard" (p. 21n). In other passages in the original drafts which Harriet insisted he remove, Mill had bitterly expressed his disappointment with his lack of practical knowledge of day-to-day life and his dependence on others for practical matters. "I had also the great misfortune of having, in domestic matters everything done for me," he had written, and he continued, "it would never have occurred to my mother who without misgivings of any sort worked from morning till night for her children" (p. 24).

What were the psychological pressures, conscious and unconscious, that brought Mill to write negatively about his mother and then to allow Harriet to erase all mention of her?

The autobiography was written at the beginning of Mill's and Harriet's marriage. At this time Mill was deeply angry because he felt his mother had slighted Harriet by not paying her sufficient respect. Apparently the elder Mrs. Mill and her daughters had not called upon their new daughter- and sister-in-law. Thus, in middle age, after living amiably with his mother and sisters until he was forty-five, Mill became estranged from them, and especially from his mother.

According to Bruce Mazlish, Mill defeated his father in a symbolic Oedipal drama when he married Harriet Taylor. With their marriage, Mazlish claims, Harriet replaced Mill's mother and, because of her intellectual capacities, also his father.[8] Mazlish discusses Mill's guilt feelings, when against his father's, as well as society's, standard of morality he conducted his (albeit platonic) love affair with Harriet for twenty years while her husband John Taylor was still alive. At the same time he had been "devotedly attached to his mother" as a young man, according to family friends.[9] One does not have to be a psychohistorian to understand that Mill would subsequently feel guilty toward his widowed mother when, after long years as a loyal bachelor son living in the maternal household, he left her for Harriet. The *Autobiography* emphasizes his craving to be within the orbit of a loving and demonstrative nature. Thus, however foolish or unnecessary the quarrel between Mill and his mother might have been, the break with her left him feeling guilty and unable to deal with her adequately or fairly while he was composing the autobiography.

Mill stated that his aim was to show his mental development, but he and Harriet had another concern: to assure a skeptical world that their twenty-year friendship before their marriage had been purely platonic. Since Harriet and Mill had clearly been in love, spending many days and weeks together in her small house or travelling in various parts of the Continent, with her husband's knowledge and acquiescence, a public statement was in order. Their exchange of letters in January and February of 1854 includes many suggestions as to how this should be done in the *Autobiography*. "Something must be said," Mill wrote, to "stop the mouths of enemies hereafter", and "to make head against the representation of enemies when we shall not be alive." Harriet wanted to provide an "edifying picture for those poor wretches who cannot conceive friendship but in sex."[10] In the original draft of the autobiography Mill finally wrote:

> ... our relation at that time was one of strong affection and confidential intimacy only. For though we did not consider the ordinances of society binding on a subject so entirely personal, we did feel bound that our conduct should be such as in no degree to bring discredit on her husband nor therefore on herself; and we disdained, as every person not a slave of his animal appetites must do, the abject notion that the strongest and tenderest friendship cannot exist between a man and a woman without a sensual relation.[11]

But even the phrase "animal appetites" was later removed as it seemed to be too suggestive. No reading of the short paragraph in the final publication would let the reader suspect the agitated correspondence that had passed between these "married friends," nor their struggle over sexuality.

Setting aside the immediate personal context in which Mill composed the *Autobiography,* let us now consider the broad spectrum of ideas at the time of its composition during 1853–1854. Mill's birth and youthful development coincided with the shaping of industrial capitalism and middle-class ideology painstakingly analyzed in Davidoff and Hall's *Family Fortunes.* Davidoff and Hall suggest that this period was one of co-operation between articulate men and women, particularly in marriages concerned with building the "material, social and religious base of their identity."[12] To that extent, John Stuart and Harriet Taylor Mill fit in with the prevailing models. While their intellectual partnership soared far above that of almost all their contemporaries, and their sexual partnership was possibly equally lofty, the rest of their relationship appears to have followed the conventional pattern of masculinity and femininity of their time. In other words Mill, as the published writer and *acknowledged* "thinker," was the "doer" of the partnership, while Harriet provided the emotional stimulus and practical contribution that Mill had missed in his earlier life and deemed essential for its stability.

This pattern of a gendered partnership was based on two well developed streams in nineteenth-century Western thought that fed into Mill's *Autobiography* and provide the context of the prevailing debate on gender. One of these streams is the scientific discussion on evolution, and the other the discourse of Romanticism. Both of them, to put it crudely, allocated intellect to men, and emotional primacy to women.

By the 1860s, soon after Harriet Taylor Mill's death, a proliferation of scholarly publications by historians, anthropologists, biologists and zoologists attempted to order in a scientific manner the romantic equation of: male = intellect, female = emotion. Thus, for example, in 1861 Johann-Jakob Bachofen in his *Mutterrecht* and Sir Henry Maine in *Ancient Law* published their (by now well known) anthropological and legal histories of male-female dichotomies in which women clearly represented the nonintellectual side of humanity.[13] The French craniologist, professor of clinical physiology Paul Broca, wrote in 1861 that the "relatively small size of the female brain depends in part upon her physical inferiority and in part upon her intellectual inferiority."[14] Similarly sexist and equally racist, the 1864 English translation of the famous German Professor of Zoology, Karl Christoph Vogt, stated that "the grown up Negro partakes, as regards the intellectual faculties, of the nature of the child, the female, and the senile white [male]."[15]

I suggest that Mill's emphasis on his wife's intellectual capacity in the *Autobiography*, which such critics as Stillinger and H. O. Pappe found so exaggerated and unsettling even in the 1960s, sprang from an effort to counter this denigration of women's intellect, something Mill did quite consciously and logically in his other published works.[16] For example, he described in the *Autobiography* how Harriet translated his abstract ideas into concrete human terms:

> ... in all that concerned the application of philosophy to the exigencies of human society and progress, I was her pupil, alike in boldness of speculation and cautiousness of practical judgment. . . . Her mind invested all ideas in a concrete shape and formed to itself a conception of how they would actually work and her knowledge of the existing feelings and conduct of mankind was so seldom at fault that the weak point in any unworkable suggestion seldom escaped her. (p. 149)

Thus Mill tried to answer the evolutionists' "scientific" approach to the problems of gender by pointing not only to Harriet's clear judgment, her loftiness of thought, but also to her common sense.

While Mill attempted to refute the contemporary scientific diminishment of women, we must not forget that he lived in the heyday of Romanticism. Romantics, from Wordsworth in the 1790s to Ruskin in the 1860s, turned to nature as a catalyst for their emotions, generally linking women with nature as the twin founts of beauty and rapture. This Romantic sensibility is present in Mill's *Autobiography*, not only in the sections dealing with Harriet but in those that trace his intellectual development from its origins in the eighteenth-century rationalism of the Benthamite school.

Romanticism affected Mill's style in the *Autobiography*, particularly in his descriptions of Harriet. He was profoundly influenced by Wordsworth, who is presented in the *Autobiography* as Mill's psychic savior when Mill found himself in a deep depression at the age of twenty-two (pp. 88–90). Wordsworth's poems extolling na-

ture and the primacy of the senses[17] spoke directly to the emotionally starved "reasoning machine" Mill claimed he had become
(p. 66). In the *Autobiography,* Mill further tells us how continental
influences—French and German nineteenth-century reaction
against eighteenth-century rationalism—were "streaming in
upon" him (p. 97). He was nothing if not well read, having mastered French, at fourteen when he lived for a year in the south of
France (pp. 36–39), and German at the age of nineteen (p. 72).
Both Rousseau[18] and Goethe,[19] whose work he knew well, expected women to be tender, loving and morally inspiring, and
above all "eternally feminine" helpmeets to men. The French pos-
itivist, Auguste Comte, with whom Mill conducted a philosophical
correspondence for five years, claimed that "the new doctrine
[Comte's vision of a secular religion of humanity] will institute the
worship of Woman . . . . Man will kneel to Woman and Woman
alone."[20]

How does Mill's description of Harriet compare with this Romantic vision? Mill's extravagances on Harriet's behalf are of a
piece with other romantic descriptions of womanhood. But in the
Autobiography he emphasized—in keeping with his intention to focus on his own mental development—both his belief in women's
intellectual equality with men and his androgynous theory of gender. He therefore concentrated on Harriet's intellectual perfor-
mance and how it meshed with his own. Like other Romantics, he
subscribed to the view that women's influence on men and children was important, but his style was quite distinct from the language of other Victorian Romantics.

On the whole, critics do not find it difficult to accept Victorian
hyperbole on "woman." This is shrugged off as the "Victorian
style," in keeping with Victorian religiosity and Romanticism. But
Mill, the rationalist, the interpreter of utilitarianism, the author
of works on political economy, must not be allowed to fall into the
Romantic trap. Perhaps critics find Mill's encomiums to Harriet
unacceptable because they extol her intellectual rather than her
emotional contributions to his life. Mill's assertion that Harriet
offered "a boundless generosity, and a lovingness ever ready to
pour itself forth upon any or all human beings who were capable of
giving the smallest feeling in return" (p. 113) is never commented
upon or questioned by these same critics because such qualities
were in keeping with the conventional view of "woman's nature."

Mill is indeed almost unique in the history of Western thought
for publicly acknowledging the cooperation of a woman in his

highly acclaimed philosophical publications. (We can hardly count all those prefaces "thanking the wife.") The only other that comes to mind is William Thompson, a member of the Benthamite circle, whose work was certainly known to Mill and who, when Mill was nineteen, had published a long feminist essay, which he openly attributed to his friend Anna Wheeler.[21] Even so, there is an important difference. The Thompson/Wheeler essay dealt exclusively with improving the status of women, whereas Mill attributed Harriet's joint authorship to a broader spectrum of his works—those which are acknowledged as a significant contribution to the canon of economic, political and social thought. Particularly controversial is his attribution to Harriet of much of the basic thought in his popular masterpiece *On Liberty,* of which he wrote:

> The "Liberty", was more directly and literally our joint production than anything else which bears my name, for there was not a sentence of it that was not several times gone through by us together, turned over in many ways, and carefully weeded of any faults, either in thought or expression, that we detected in it. . . . The whole mode of thinking of which the book was the expression, was emphatically hers. But I also was so thoroughly imbued with it that the same thoughts naturally occurred to us both. That I was thus penetrated with it, however, I owe in a great degree to her . . . . she benefitted me as much by keeping me right when I was right, as by leading me to new truths and ridding me of errors.(p. 148)

It is instructive to compare Mill's praise of Harriet with other mid-century Romantics. For example, Coventry Patmore's panegyric on his wife in the "Angel in the House" (1854): "Her disposition is devout/her countenance angelical/The best things that the best believe/are in her face so kindly writ/The faithless, seeing her, conceive/Not only heaven, but hope of it."[22] Or Jules Michelet's description of "woman" in *La Femme* (1860): "She is your nobleness, your own, so raising you above yourself. When you return from the forge, panting, fatigued with labor, she, young and fresh pours over you her youth, brings the sacred wave of life to you and makes you a god again with a kiss."[23] Or Ruskin writing "Of Queens' Gardens" in *Sesame and Lilies* (1865): "Man is eminently the doer, the creator, the discoverer, the defender. His intellect is for speculation and invention . . . . but her intellect is not for invention or creation, but for sweet ordering, ... She must be . . . . incorruptibly good; instinctively, infallibly wise."[24]

The Romantics, here represented by Patmore, Michelet and Ruskin, invoked the divine and the sublime. Women were consequently "angels" ministering to men; however, they were hardly asexual angels in their capacity to revive diminishing male sexual prowess. Clearly these writers fuse morality and sexuality. Like Patmore, Michelet and Ruskin, Mill also thought that women's contribution to civilization was essential, but it was not women's angelic nature, eroticized or not, that would raise men to new heights. Unlike that of the three cited above, Mill's is the voice of reason; he does not confuse the mystical, the religious, and the sexual. Extravagant as his praise of Harriet might have been, he did not make of her a religious idol. "She was the source of... what I hope to effect... for human improvement."(111) Mill understood her value as a force in history. He would have agreed with Fourier, who in 1808 wrote: "the extension of women's privileges is the general principle for all social progress." And, in the same vein, Mill's own father had, in 1817, called "the condition of women... one of the most decisive criterions of the stage of society at which [a nation has] arrived."[25] Echoing both Fourier's and his father's view of women as a barometer of historical progress, he wrote in 1868:

> I am profoundly convinced that the moral and intellectual progress of the male sex runs a great risk of stopping, if not receding, as long as that of the women remains behind, and that, not only because nothing can replace the mother for the education of the child, but also, because the influence upon man himself of the character and ideas of the companion of his life cannot be insignificant; women must either push him forward or hold him back.[26]

There was, moreover, a fundamental difference between Mill and the rest of the Victorian Romantics. They believed womanly qualities to be innate; Mill, like his eighteenth-century British precursors Catharine Macaulay-Graham and Mary Wollstonecraft, understood that these qualities were conditioned.[27] As he claimed in *The Subjection of Women:*

> any of the mental differences supposed to exist between women and men are but the natural effect of the differences in their education and circumstances, and indicate no radical difference, far less radical inferiority, of nature.[28]

Harriet reminded him of Shelley in that her "protests against many things that are still the established constitution of society," resulted, he believed, "not from hard intellect but from noble and elevated feeling"; yet that did not prevent her, as it had not prevented Shelley, from "piercing to the very heart and marrow of the matter . . . the essential idea or principle." (p. 112)

His editor Stillinger felt we must "cringe" at Mill's exaggerated praise of Harriet, but what Stillinger objects to so strongly is exclusively the praise of Harriet's intellect. In this, Mill stands out in contrast to practically all other male authors of his time writing about their own close female connections, or about women in general. To object to Mill's language is to read the book without placing it into the context of mid nineteenth-century male rhetoric on women. I suggest that he occasionally adopted the romantic rhetoric of his day in his description of Harriet—but applied it to the one feature of existence that he most wanted to elucidate in his autobiography: the human mind.

Unlike other major male figures writing at mid-century, however, Mill did not look for opposite poles or complementarity in male and female qualities. In his pathbreaking parliamentary speech advocating woman's suffrage in 1867, Mill put this very succinctly:

> Under the idle notion that the beauties of character of the two sexes are mutually incompatible, men are afraid of manly women; but those who have considered the nature and power of social influences well know, that unless there are manly women, there will not much longer be manly men . . . . the two sexes must now rise or sink together.[29]

As early as 1833 he had expressed his view of androgyny with great clarity in a letter to Carlyle:

> The women, of all I have known, who possessed the highest measure of what are considered feminine qualities, have combined with them more of the highest masculine qualities than I have ever seen in any but one or two men. . . . I suspect it is the second-rate people of the two sexes that are unlike—the first-rate are alike in both . . . but then, in this respect, my position has been and is . . . "a peculiar one."[30]

What Mill considered "peculiar" here has been the ideal for many feminists throughout the nineteenth and twentieth centuries. But what did he understand by "feminine" and "masculine" qualities? I believe he associated tenderness, sympathy, and the expression of feelings, but not passivity, with the feminine; and intellectual rigor with the masculine. Harriet combined both. Throughout the *Autobiography* Mill demonstrated vividly how well Harriet integrated qualities that he considered feminine and masculine in her own person—but what about himself? What of the "feminine" in Mill? The phrase "the first rate are alike in both" is highly significant for appreciating Mill's own striving towards the "first rate," the combination of masculine and feminine as he understood it, in his own character.

Having missed love and tenderness in his childhood and youth, Mill craved and admired those qualities he believed to be feminine—sensitivity and emotional warmth. He deeply resented his father's denigration of passionate emotions (p. 31) and his father's objection to his own tendency to daydream, which the elder Mill called "inattention" (p. 24). He described in lyric terms the grounds of Ford Abbey in Devon, where he spent several years during his early adolescence as "riant and secluded, umbrageous, and full of the sound of falling waters," surroundings that he deemed to be producing "a larger and freer existence and a sort of poetic cultivation" (pp. 35–36). Retrospectively he understood the crisis of despair that he had suffered in his early twenties as caused largely by a lack of familial love and tenderness, and consequently his own inability *to* love. "If I had loved anyone sufficiently . . . I should not have been in the condition I was" (p. 81). He pulled himself out of the crisis when he began to appreciate "states of feeling" and, even more important, the fact that "thought [could be] coloured by feeling" (p. 89). He asserted that "The cultivation of feelings, became one of the cardinal points of my ethical and philosophical creed" (p. 86).

It is profoundly moving to find this man, this reasoning machine, as he called himself, struggling to nurture the growth of emotions and susceptibilities he viewed as feminine. Most importantly, his life-long commitment to justice became infused with fervent emotion. Unlike women in general (according to the received wisdom of his age), he had to *learn* to feel and to express emotion. In this endeavor, first poetry and later Harriet were undeniably his teachers.

In examining the "feminization" of John Stuart Mill, I have used the concept of the "feminine" as Mill himself conceived of it. Since Mill's writing and political activity suffused the thinking about women of his time, and even subsequently, his ideas are a part of the development of progressive thought. His "self-feminization" derived from a conscious attempt to incorporate qualities that he valued. The current discourse on "femininity" and "masculinity," while far more complex, attempts to validate these same qualities and to make them prevalent in the whole society. Our late twentieth-century debate has invented dramatically new "feminine" roles for men as infant caretakers, "househusbands," and nurses. Men are encouraged as never before to express their tender emotions; it is now almost permissible for enlightened men to weep. Mill, then, was not only a man of his time, but a man ahead of his time, not merely politically, as we have long known, but also socially and psychologically.

Chapter Seven

The Literary Standard, Working-Class Autobiography, and Gender[1]

Regenia Gagnier

Introduction

A decade ago in "Working/Women/Writing," Lillian S. Robinson asked that criticism, especially feminist criticism, not uncritically accept the doctrines of individualist aesthetics:

> It is a fundamental precept of bourgeois aesthetics that good art . . . is art that celebrates what is unique and even eccentric in human experience or human personality. Individual achievement and subjective isolation are the norm, whether the achievement and the isolation be that of the artist or the character. It seems to me that this is a far from universal way for people to be or to be perceived, but one that is intimately connected to relationships and values perpetuated by capitalism. For this reason, I would seriously question any aesthetic that not only fails to call that individualism into question, but does so intentionally, in the name of feminism.[2]

Robinson then reads the collection *I Am a Woman Worker* as an act of community indistinguishable from "self-actualization."[3]

In a 1985 essay on imperialism in *Jane Eyre* that attempts to wrench feminists from the mesmerizing focus of Jane's subjectivity, Gayatri Chakravorty Spivak follows Elizabeth Fox-Genovese's characterization of feminism in the West as female access to individualism: "the battle for female individualism plays itself out within the larger theater of the establishment of meritocratic individualism, indexed in the aesthetic field by the ideology of 'the creative imagination'."[4]

At a time when "the creative imagination" has ceased to bear the authority or command the attention it did in bourgeois Victorian culture; when it is found to be as historically embedded and culturally bound as the "normative eye" or "universal vision" referred to by the editors of this volume; and when literary critics forecast "the end of autobiography" and give up generic definitions of autobiography, it is worth considering the relation of autobiography to individualist aesthetics. The first half of this paper will show how individualist aesthetics have been used to disqualify women's and workers' autobiography, and will then propose an alternative rhetorical strategy for considering these works—not, as historians have, as data of varying degrees of reliability reflecting external conditions, but as texts revealing subjective identities embedded in diverse social and material circumstances. The second will turn to the function of gender in working-class writing, with special attention to the ideological effects of the middle-class sex–gender system upon working-class subjects for whom that system was a material impossibility.

The Limits of Individualist Aesthetics

Since the nineteenth century, professional writers and literary critics have attempted generic definitions of autobiography, encouraging readers to take some autobiography as proper autobiography and other as life, perhaps, but not Art. Such determinations were concurrent with developments in literary professionalism. Despite the marketing developments of 1840–1880 that resulted in the institutionalizing of authorship—for example, specialist readers at publishing houses, literary agents, author's royalties, the Society of Authors, and so forth—literary hegemony, or a powerful literary bloc that prevented or limited "Other" discursive blocs, did not operate by way of the institutional infrastructure, rules, and procedures of the ancient professions of law, medicine, and clergy. By, or through developments in, the nineteenth century, those ancient professions effectively exercised monopolies over their professional association, its cognitive base (knowledge and techniques), its institutional training and licensing, its "service" ethos justifying autonomy from the market and collegial control, and the security and respectability differentiating its practitioners from other members of society.[5]

From the second half of the eighteenth century, when the democratic revolution combined with the effects of printing, writers had attempted to "commodify" literary talent in the same way.

In his *Essay on the Manners and Genius of the Literary Character* (1795), Isaac Disraeli makes the literary character independent of local or historical environment, locating the writer's special commodity in his unique psychology.[6] After Disraeli, the so-called Romantic poets, with their unconsciously commodified image of the poet, as in Wordsworth's Preface to the second edition of the *Lyrical Ballads* in 1802, aimed at privileged professional status without the institutional apparatus of the learned professions. In *The Prelude,* subtitled *Growth of a Poet's Mind,* Wordsworth tentatively specified the meticulous—and idiosyncratic—training program of the poetic sensibility, to be legitimated with great bravura in Shelley's poets in "A Defense of Poetry" (1821; pub. 1840)—"the unacknowledged legislators of the world." Mary Jean Corbett has argued that with the sublimation of the poet, the "literary character" sought self-determined valuation rather than subordination to the market; recognition of literature as a specialized and special service offered by the possessor of poetic knowledge for the edification of others; and a measure of social independence and economic security. Like Disraeli, the Romantics felt the need to distinguish "true artists" from the more populous tribe of scribbling tradespeople.[7]

With the exception of Keats, who died young enough to truncate his agonistic relations with a "free market" that granted the poetic "gift" of the son of a stable-keeper no special privilege, the Romantic poets were of sufficient means to enjoy the homely privileges of the gentry amateur. In 1802, eighty percent of the English population lived in villages and farms. Yet by 1851 half the population was urban, and by 1901 eighty percent lived in towns. Within Victorian bourgeois ideology specialized knowledge and services came to be within the public sphere. The person who "worked" at "home," within the private sphere, was either payed very little, as in working-class women's "sweated" homework, or nothing, as in middle-class women's household management. This contradiction for the literary men who worked at home contributed to their fear of "effeminization" within a society that conflated "public" with masculine for the middle class and differentiated this competitive marketplace from the private "feminine" space of the home.

Dickens's work of autobiographical fiction, *The Personal History and Experience of David Copperfield* (1850), did for the middle-class novelist what Wordsworth had done for the poet, and more: it introduced to an extended market—Dickens was the most popular writer of the nineteenth century—the professional author, and it reclaimed and colonized the home as *his* domain. Dickens's competitive product, a "critical" reflective sensibility ("Nature and accident had made me an author," writes David in Chapter 48, entitled "Domestic"), was commodified in *David Copperfield* as *the* autobiography of the self-made author: it showed the buying public who the man writing "really" was. But in contributing to the ideological distinction between mental and manual labor (David vs. the Peggotty family) that oppressed working-class writers in ways that I shall specify below, Dickens also contributed to the division of labor along lines of gender. He showed that behind every David Copperfield writing at home, there was an Agnes Wickfield, a perfect household manager, for whom homemaking was as effortless as writing was for David.[8] David's "progress" to worldly success follows a sequence of relations with unsuitable women, until childlike and incompetent mother and first wife, vulgar nurse, excessively independent aunt, and flirtatious, class-aspiring Little Emily are supplanted by the "good angel" Agnes, who even as a child is introduced as "a little housekeeper" with "a little basket-trifle hanging at her side, with keys in it."[9] Agnes Wickfield Copperfield is the prototypical wife, who cares for the material needs of the writer and who in later times would type the manuscripts. Moreover, the writer David was to be distinguished from lesser "hack" writers like Mr. Micawber (whose wife is disorganized and whose imprudently large family is banished to Australia); Mr. Dick (the "blocked" hysteric who lives with the "divorced" and sterile aunt); and Uriah Heep (the sweaty-palmed charity-school lad who had presumed to compete with David for Agnes).[10]

A vast cultural production relegating women to household management while "authors" wrote made it difficult for middle-class women to write. Men and professionals, especially professional men, worked in the abstract realm of mental labor; women and workers, especially women workers, worked in the immediate, concrete, material. Agnes, as it were, types the manuscripts of David's *oeuvre:* women, like workers, mediate for men between conceptual action and its concrete forms: "lady typewriters" (as late-Victorians called them), Beatrice Webb's "social investigators," Florence Nightingale's nurses, and working-class cooks and cleaners.

In the canonical literary autobiographies, having a woman at home is necessary to the self-conception of authorial men. In John Stuart Mill's *Autobiography* (1873), the great radical retires to Avi-

gnon (to get sufficient distance and perspective upon English society) with his stepdaughter Helen Taylor as secretary. In John
Ruskin's *Praeterita* (1885–1889), the social critic retires to Brant-
wood with "Joanie" Severn and calls his last chapter, before madness silenced him forever, "Joanna's Care." Charles Darwin's
attentive wife and considerate family enabled the scientist to
withdraw for the last forty years of his life from bothersome social
engagements (which made him ill, he says) into secluded work and
domesticity at Down.[11]

In her edition of his *Autobiography,* Darwin's granddaughter
Nora Barlow includes some notes Darwin scribbled in two columns
as he deliberated whether or not to marry. On the plus side, the
advantages of marriage, he listed "constant companion, (friend in
old age), who will feel interested in one, object to be beloved and
played with—better than a dog anyhow—Home, and someone to
take care of house. . . . Imagine living all one's day solitarily in
smoky dirty London House.—Only picture to yourself a nice soft
wife on a sofa with good fire, and books and music perhaps." On
the negative, "Not MARRY" side, he listed, "Perhaps my wife won't
like London; then the sentence is banishment and degradation
with indolent idle fool" and "I never should know French,—or see
the Continent,—or go to America, or go up in a Balloon."[12]

In Samuel Butler's fictive autobiography *The Way of All Flesh*
(1873–1878; pub. 1903), the only woman the narrator approves is a
rich aunt who offers the protagonist a room of his own in which to
develop his aesthetic and muscular interests and then conve-
niently dies, leaving him her fortune. Now if we return to Disraeli
we find a chapter on "The Domestic Life of Genius," in which we
are instructed that "the home of the literary character should be
the abode of repose and of silence" (234), where "the soothing in-
terruptions of the voices of those whom he loves [may] recall him
from his abstractions into social existence" (236). And there are
additional chapters upon "the matrimonial state of literature" and
"a picture of the literary wife" who silently mediates between social and material distractions while the detached and isolated literary character produces abstract thought.

Even reading, which unquestionably empowered men of all
classes, was dangerous for women. In her brilliant autobiographical piece "Cassandra" (1852), Florence Nightingale writes con-
temptuously of the autonomy denied women in the practice of
their being "read aloud to," a practice she compares to forced
feeding.[13] In many working women's autobiographies, reading is

perceived by employers to interfere with their work and consequently often jeopardizes women's jobs. Because of the sexual division of labor, reading and writing threatened rather than
advanced women's work.

Feminist scholars have told the story of middle-class women's
writing. Yet like the historical subjects themselves, they have
rarely questioned the distinctions between mental and manual labor that first excluded women and they have rarely attempted to
demystify the individualist "creative imagination" that women, as
producers of concrete material life, were historically denied.[14]

In one of the most revealing cultural confrontations in modern
British history, Virginia Woolf's 1931 Introduction to the autobiographical accounts of the Women's Co-Operative Guild illustrates
the cross-purposes of individualist aesthetics and other uses of
literacy.[15] Having been asked to write a preface, Woolf begins with
the problem of prefaces for autonomous aesthetics—"Books should
stand on their own feet" (xv)—and solves the problem of introduc-
ing the Co-Operativists' writing by writing not quite a Preface but
rather a personal letter to the editor, another upper-class woman,
Margaret Llewelyn Davies. Woolf wants the Co-Operativists to be
individualists, to develop the self-expression and choices for things
that are ends in themselves like "Mozart and Einstein" and not
things that are means like "baths and money" (xxv–vi). She wants
for them, in short, rooms of their own, private places for private
thoughts, detached, as Bourdieu would say, from the necessities of
the natural and social world.[16] Some working-class women, indeed
many upper domestic servants—the most ideologically "embour-
geoised" workers—did want such pleasures; but the Guild wom-
en's accounts indicate that they wanted something different. They
wanted communality; and distance from the necessities of the natural and social world ("our minds flying free at the end of a short
length of capital," as Woolf puts it [xxv]) had not led middle-class
women to change society in that direction.

Rather, the Co-Operativists are especially grateful to the
Guild for transforming shy nervous women into "public speakers"
(32, 48–49, 65, 100–101, 141): a woman can write forever in a
room of her own without ever learning not to go dry-mouthed and
shaking in public. Woolf writes sympathetically about the production of the Co-Operativists' texts, "a work of labour and difficulty.
The writing has been done in kitchens, at odds and ends of leisure,
in the midst of distractions and obstacles" (xxxix), but confined by
her own aesthetics of individualism and detachment, she cannot

imagine that "the self" can be communal, engaged, and dialogical as well as individual, detached, and introspective. If such a world were possible, she cannot imagine herself within it:

> This force of theirs [the Co-Operativists are tellingly always "they" to Woolf's editorial "we"] this smouldering heat which broke the crust now and then and licked the surface with a hot and fearless flame, is about to break through and melt us together so that life will be richer and books more complex and society will pool its possessions instead of segregating them—all this is going to happen inevitably—but only when we are dead (xxix).

Social historians (not to speak of socialist feminists) have made this point somewhat differently to middle-class feminists. The issue concerns normative dualism, the belief that the especially valuable thing about human beings is their mental capacity and that this capacity is a property of individuals rather than groups ("Mozart and Einstein"), and liberal rationality, the belief that rational behavior is commensurate with the maximization of individual utility.[17] Showing the astonishing "strategies" of married working-class women who lived at or below the poverty line in the late nineteenth and early twentieth centuries—working part- or full-time outside the home, using children's wages, controlling household budgets, using the products of their families' allotments, and borrowing both goods and cash—Elizabeth Roberts writes that she is often asked what women themselves "got" out of their lives:

> It has been remarked that they gave to their families much more than they received in return. These questions and comments would not have been asked nor made by the women themselves. Their own individual concerns were of little importance to them. They appeared to have found their chief satisfaction in running their homes economically and seeing their children grow up. Their major preoccupations were (throughout the period) feeding, clothing and housing their families.[18]

In an article in the same collection, Diana Gittins writes of the three interrelated and often overlapping occupational spheres for working-class women from the mid-nineteenth century through the Second World War—paid work, unpaid domestic work in extended families, and marriage—as "strategies for survival, but survival for the household generally rather than for the individual women."[19] My reading of working women's autobiographies confirms that such strategies for the family household were, again, indistinguishable from self-actualization.

But nonindividualism comes in many forms, and working-class autobiography suggests that that of women at home with their families in nineteenth-century Britain was the least conducive to the constitution of writing subjects. Contrary to the claims on behalf of a room of one's own, workers' autobiographies suggest that writing women were those whose work took them out of the home. Although some working people wrote to understand themselves, producing the kinds of texts I discuss in detail below, most wrote for communicative rather than introspective or aesthetic ends: to record lost experiences for future generations, to raise money, to warn others, to teach others, to relieve or amuse themselves. One functionalist William Tayler, footman to a wealthy London widow in 1837, wrote his autobiographical journal "to improve my handwriting."[20]

Such functionalist uses of literacy contrast markedly with the aesthetic of detached individualism represented by literature (as it is represented in literature departments) in general and by the autobiographical canon in particular. The criteria we may deduce from the canon include a meditative and self-reflective sensibility; a faith in writing as a tool of self-exploration; an attempt to make sense of life as a narrative progressing in time, with a pronounced narrative structured upon parent–child relations and familial development; and a belief in personal creativity, autonomy, and freedom for the future. This is autobiography as the term is usually employed by literary critics, and it is also bourgeois subjectivity, the dominant ideology of the nineteenth and at least the first half of the twentieth century. It adds to assumptions of normative dualism and liberal rationality the assumption of abstract individualism, or the belief that essential human characteristics are properties of individuals independent of their material conditions and social environment.

Modern literary critics have made deviation from this model of autobiography a moral as well as an aesthetic failure. Despite Georges Gusdorf's "discovery" in 1956 that the "self" of modern literary autobiography was limited by culture and history, in 1960 Roy Pascal claimed that "bad" autobiography indicated "a certain falling short in respect to the whole personality . . . an inadequacy in the persons writing, a lack of moral responsibility towards their task."[21] Pascal's stance belongs with that of James Olney in *Meta-*

phors of Self (1972); both were apologists for the primacy of individualism as represented by a literary tradition. Even more recent and properly deconstructive theorists of autobiography in the 1980s, like Paul Jay, Avrom Fleishman, and Michael Sprinker, privilege what they intend to deconstruct by employing such notions as "the end of autobiography."[22] For the organic, self-regarding, typically male and middle-class self of literary autobiography was always only one "self" among others, even before it was dispersed under the conditions of postmodernism. Feminist critics and theorists of women's autobiography, like Estelle C. Jelinek, Sidonie Smith, Shari Benstock, Bella Brodski, Celeste Schenck, Susan Groag Bell, and Marilyn Yalom, have exposed the masculine bias of much of this theory, if often remaining within its class and literary assumptions.[23] Rather than privileging the customary literary associations of autobiography, or honoring the customary distinction between literary autobiography and other "non," "sub," or "extra" literary self-representation, I consider all autobiography as rhetorical projects embedded in concrete material situations.[24]

Discursive production must be understood in terms of the multifarious purposes and projects of specific individuals or groups in specific material circumstances. For example, I have often found it useful to adapt Roberto Mangabeira Unger's spectrum of personality (from longing to be with others to fear of others) to discourse, locating a text between the poles of discursive participation and antagonism with others.[25] All autobiographical "moves" in my sense are "interested," whether or not they are as intentionally political as those of the Guild Co-Operativists or Chartists. All display the features of two contexts, as cultural products in circulation with other cultural products (e.g., some music-hall performers wrote specifically for their writing's exchange value) and as articulations of participatory and antagonistic social relations. Sometimes these articulations are simultaneously participatory and antagonistic. Writers like Annie Kenney in *Memoirs of a Militant* (1924) and William Lovett in *Pursuit of Bread, Knowledge, and Freedom* (1876) are participatory with their respective movements, Suffrage and Chartism, while antagonistic to the hegemonic discourses of sexism and classism—"hegemonic" meaning dominant with respect to other discourses, preventing other discourses their full development and articulation. I read autobiography rhetorically, taking language as realist, not in the sense of metaphysical realism, direct isomorphism with reality (Thomas Nagel's "the view from nowhere"), but realist in the sense of pro-

jecting objectively real articulations of power in particular communities. Like reading itself, writing is a function of specific and
community interactions.[26]

I want to emphasize that when I say "power" I intend its feminist as well as its Foucauldian associations: empowerment,
"power to," as well as "power over." Autobiography is the arena of
empowerment to represent oneself in a discursive cultural field as
well as the arena of subjective disempowerment by the "subject-
ing" discourses of others. In the postmodern world we live in, "autobiography" as bourgeois subjectivity may be dead except in
academic or psychoanalytic circles; but as long as there is society,
even cyborg society, there will be rhetorical projects of participation and antagonism in concrete material situations.[27] It is the responsibility of protectors of speech not to disqualify subhegemonic
articulations, like women's, like workers', by evaluating them out
of the game.

Gendered, Classed Subjects and Cultural Narratives

There is no "typical" Victorian working-class life or autobiography; rather, the forms of autobiography were as multifarious as
the British laboring classes themselves. I have provided an anat-
omy of such writing elsewhere, based largely upon several hundred of the 804 texts indexed in John Burnett, David Vincent, and
John Mayall's important bibliography *The Autobiography of the
Working Class* (1984), but several salient points are worth reiter-
ating here before focussing on gender.[28] First, loose "generic"
groupings may be made according to the rhetorical approach outlined above; these indicate some uniformity in how texts are written, read, and historically assessed in terms of the participatory
modes of value and consensus and the antagonistic modes of resistance, domination, and appropriation. Thus in nineteenth-century
Britain, when working people began to include their occupations
in titles of their work, as in *Memories of a Working Woman, Confessions of a Strolling Player, Narrative of a Factory Cripple, In
Service,* and *Autobiography of a Private Soldier,* "memories" often
came from southern agrarian workers who hoped to preserve local
history for members of the community, or domestic workers whose
trade had declined radically after the First World War; "narratives" from organized northern industrial workers who sought to
empower other workers and compete historically with the bour-

geoisie; and "confessions" from transients like stage performers who hoped to gain cash by giving readers immediate consumable sensation.[29] In other words, socioeconomic status, rhetorical purpose, status of labor, and geography were often heavily significant in the forms the autobiography took.

The second point that must be reiterated is that for working-class autobiographers, whether factory operatives (38% of the working population in 1861), agricultural laborers (18%), miners (4%), or domestic servants (19%—half of the population of women workers), subjectivity—the sense of being a significant agent worthy of the regard of others, a human subject, as well as an individuated "ego" distinct from others—was not a given.[30] In conditions of long work hours, crowded housing, and inadequate light, it was difficult enough for workers to contemplate themselves; as writers, they now had to justify themselves as being worthy of the attention of others. Thus I have written of what I call the "social atom" phenomenon: most working-class autobiography begins not with family lineage or a birthdate (conventional middle-class beginnings), but rather with a statement of its author's ordinariness, encoded in titles such as *One of the Multitude* (1911) by the pseudonymous George Acorn, a linguistically-conscious furniture builder who aspired to grow into an oak. The authors were conscious that to many potential readers they were but "social atoms" making up the undifferentiated "masses." As radical journalist William Adams put it in 1903, "I call myself a Social Atom—a small speck on the surface of society. The term indicates my insignificance. . . . I am just an ordinary person."[31] Depending upon the author's purpose in writing, such rhetorical modesty could signify any point within an affective range extending from defensive self-effacement through defiant irony, as in the "Old Potter" Charles Shaw's splendid, "We were a part of Malthus's 'superfluous population.' "[32] I have examined the sources of this rhetorical modesty in the writers' struggle, as *Homo laborans* rather than *Homo cogitans,* to distinguish themselves from "the masses" in order to present themselves as subjects worthy of the attention of others; their simultaneous resistance to embourgeoisement; and their competition with representations of themselves in middle-class fiction and its implicit, broadly Cartesian, assumptions about the self.

The relevance of gender appears with the structural differences between workers' autobiographies and the classic realist autobiography, in which gender plays a major structuring role. The classic realist autobiography includes such elements as remembered details of childhood, parent–child relations, the subject's formal education, and a progressive developmental narrative of self culminating in material well-being and "fame" within greater or lesser circles (whether the Old Boy's place among Old School fellows or John Stuart Mill's place in the democratic revolution). Most workers' autobiographies deviate from this narrative pattern for fairly obvious reasons: in *A Cornish Waif's Story* discussed below, Emma Smith was born in the workhouse, raised by a child molester, and educated in a penitentiary.

First, most of the writers were working outside the home by the time they were eight years old, so the period of "childhood" is problematic, the remembered details often truncated to the more common "first memory." This first memory is often traumatic; its significant positioning within the first paragraphs of the text operates and resonates differently from the evolutionary narrative of childhood familiar to readers of middle-class autobiography. Second, as will be demonstrated in detail below, parent–child relations among the working class often differed from those in the upper classes. Third, since the subject's formal education competed with the family economy, in most cases it was not limited to a particular period. In many working-class examples, education often continues throughout the book and up to the time of writing. And fourth, most working-class autobiographies do not end with success but rather *in medias res*. In this context it is worth noting that with the exception of political and religious-conversion autobiographies, most working-class texts do not have the crises and recoveries that are common to "literary" autobiography, just as they do not have climaxes. The bourgeois climax-and-resolution/ action-and-interaction model presupposes an active and reactive world not always accessible to working-class writers, who often felt themselves passive victims of economic determinism. Working since the age of nine, Mrs. Wrigley writes a life consisting of a series of jobs, mentioning in the one sentence devoted to her marriage its maternal character and her childlike relations with her employers: "I was sorry to give up such a good home, and they was sorry for me to leave but my young man wanted to get married for he had no mother."[33]

What is "missing" then in much working-class autobiography is the structuring effect, apparent in any middle-class "plot," of gender dimorphism. In Britain, middle-class boys experienced and wrote of an ordered progress from pre-school at home to childhood and youth at school and university, through the Raj, diplomatic corps, or civil service, or through domestic life with equally gen-derized wives and daughters.[34] Middle-class women wrote of early life with fathers and afterlife with husbands. These two pat-terns—as central to the great nineteenth-century realist novels as to Victorian autobiography—represent middle-class gender con-struction of masculinity and femininity, power and domesticity. Whereas boys learned "independence" through extrusion from mothers and nannies and paternalism through elaborate forms of self-government in public schools, middle-class girls, under con-stant supervision by parents and headmistresses, learned to be de-pendent upon and obedient to husbands. (Many, needless to say, also rebelled against this pattern. See especially Cecily Hamilton's trenchant and witty *Marriage As A Trade* [1909], recommended reading for every Victorian and feminist course.) Working-class women, on the other hand—from the time they were old enough to mind younger siblings, to their minding the children of the upper classes, to their noncompanionate (economically-oriented) mar-riages ("because my young man had no mother")—learned to be self-reliant and nurturing, and their husbands learned to be "ma-tronized." "What I needed was a man who was master in his own house," writes Emma Smith, "upon whom I could lean. Instead of this, I always had to take a leading role."[35]

This difference in the practical sex-gender system leads to the major structural difference of working-class autobiography, but there are gender similarities that transcend class differences. Working women refer far more frequently to their husbands or lov-ers and children (their personal relationships) and working men to their jobs or occupations (their social status). Traditionally pre-vented from speaking in public, even women like the Guild Co-Operativists, who write with the explicit purpose of political reform, speak from within a material economic realm; yet politi-cized men, even before they gained full male suffrage in 1885, were accustomed to public speaking (for example, in pubs) and argued within the discourse of national politics.[36] Comparatively isolated within their homes (or others' as domestics), the Co-Operativists learned to internalize rhetorical values acceptable to the middle class, such as the catechism, criticizing personal injustices and in-equalities within marriage and the family. On the other hand, from early experience in public and on the job with others, the men write movingly of specific material deprivations but predom-inantly of the "rights" of workers and the class struggle, explicitly attacking class structure.

This different understanding of injustice—one local and immediate, the other systemic—leads to different formulations of political goals. The Co-Operativists see politics as a forum for domestic demands, such as baths for miners or peace to save the life of one's remaining son. The radical men want what the middle class has. These may not in effect be different goals: what the middle class has is baths and sons comparatively safe from war; but because the women reason from personal example and moral lesson and the men launch discourses articulated within the democratic revolutions of the United States and France, even politically motivated autobiography is often informed differently by women and men.

Such differences, however, arise in the relative isolation of women's labor as the highest paying and most independent employment was consigned to men as principal breadwinners and women were driven from the factories from the 1840s; and they may be dealt with by social historians concerned with the interrelations of gender, "private" and "public" spheres. For the literary or cultural critic, gender in working-class autobiography is most interesting when it shows itself as ideological hegemony—in Antonio Gramsci's sense of popular consent to the political order. Here the game is embourgeoisement. Although the texts to which I now turn by no means represent the majority of working-class autobiographies, there are enough like them to indicate how gender operates as a cultural narrative.

In such texts, one finds the cost of bourgeois familial or gender ideology to women and men who were not permitted bourgeois lives. They were often written by people with lives of unmitigated hardship, for whom writing is a form, more or less successful, of therapy. They are not trying to sell their work so much as to analyze and alleviate their pain; yet their narratives are derived from models, often literary models, more suitable to the conditions of middle-class authors. Unlike other working-class writers, they have also extensively adopted middle-class ideology: they have accepted the value of introspection and writing as tools of self-understanding; they seek to write their lives as middle-class narratives, especially with respect to the development of parent–child relations and material progress; and they believe that writing and self-understanding will help them succeed. Yet although they attempt self-analysis, their experience cannot be analyzed in the terms of their acculturation. This gap between ideology and experience leads not only to the disintegration of the narrative the writer hopes to construct, but, as the analyses below will show, to the disintegration of personality itself.

Discussion of these texts is inescapably reductive, for their characteristic is the authors' layered revisions of their experience, which contribute to an unusual density of signification. Literary readers will find them the most "literary" of working-class writers.[37] Here I shall focus upon the writers' attempts to structure their lives according to middle-class gender ideology.

The struggle between ideology and experience is inscribed, both micrologically and macrologically, in James Burn's *Autobiography of a Beggar Boy* (1855). At nine years old, Burn tracks down his biological father in Ireland, where the boy is humiliated to wear rags, endure lice, and work in isolation. In a fit of humiliation and self-hatred and a parody of primogeniture, he runs away, calling the dirt he associates with his father his patrimony. "I had neither staff, nor scrip, nor money in my pocket. I commenced the world with the old turf-bag. It was my only patrimony. In order that I might sever the only remaining link that bound me to my family, I tore two syllables from my name [i.e., from McBurney, his father's name]."[38] This minute detail of the boy's inability to meet a cultural code—his castration of his father's name as sign of his lack of father and patrimony in a patriarchal and propertied culture—prefigures the larger narrative distortion reflecting the insufficiency of his experience in the face of his society's master narrative of male progress.

When Burn summarizes the lesson of his life for his son at the end of his book (199–200), the summary corresponds to his preceding narrative only up to a point: he writes of his thoughtless wandering until he was 12 years old, of parental neglect ("I had been blessed with three fathers and two mothers, and I was then as comfortably situated as if I never had either one or the other" [106]), and of his lack of social connection for long periods. This summary corresponds to the episodic structure of his preceding story and to the fragmented nature of his childhood as itinerant beggar on the Scots border. Yet then Burn refers to the "grand turning point" of his life, when he learned a trade as hatter's apprentice. In fact, only a nominal change occurred with his apprenticeship: since there was no work, he was permitted to call himself a hatter rather than a beggar while on tramp for fourteen hundred miles (135). He makes much of a change of status from unemployable to employable, although no material change occurs— he remains unemployed. Similarly, he continues to insist upon the great happiness of his domestic life, despite the necessity of living apart from his family for long periods of tramping and the deaths of his wife and twelve of his sixteen children. The summary concludes with the assertion of his relative success in remaining respectable as a debt collector to the poor, a respectability reinforced by the bowdlerized version of 1882, in which he finally obliterated all references to sexual experiences and bodily functions.

This summary male middle-class narrative, beginning with the imaginary "grand turning point" of his trade, occludes, first, Burn's political activity, for which he was well known, and, second, much of his past. With the threat of the General Strike in 1839, he had turned against the Chartists and begun to conceive of his prior activism as "madness." In revising his life, this "madness" is excluded along with earlier madnesses, such as the madness of Scottish and Irish poetry. Due to its link with superstition and supernaturalism—and despite his opinion that English poetry is "dull and lifeless" in comparison—Burn must reject it as irreconcilable with "useful knowledge" (192–198). Similarly, the lively Dickensian style of the first two chapters shows his affection for society on the borders—for its lack of social differentiation and its extreme linguistic diversity. Yet this too disappears from his summary. He is left attempting to reconcile his proprietorship of taverns and spirit cellars with his hysterical temperance, and passing over the details of his job as debt collector to his former Chartist friends. Everything that must be repudiated in the service of class mobility—social tolerance, epistemological pluralism, the aspect of freedom of life on the borders as a beggar boy—is expunged from the summary. Yet in dutifully obliterating or rewriting his past, there is no indication that Burn is comfortable with his present or future. As he puts it, "Amid the universal transformation of things in the moral and physical world, my own condition has been tossed so in the rough blanket of fate, that my identity, if at any time a reality, must have been one which few could venture to swear to" (56); or, "All our antecedents are made up of so many yesterdays, and the morrow never comes" (185).

Moreover, despite the seasonal difficulties of the hatting trade and high unemployment among artisans in Glasgow in the 1830s and 1840s, and despite an active and successful life as spokesperson for hatters in the Glasgow United Committee of Trades Delegates, Burn blames himself for his failure in business. Assuming a liberal and masculine ethic of autonomy and progress, he concludes that he was personally deficient in the struggle to maintain either self or social position, and he therefore believes himself uneducable: "Although my teachers have been as various as my different positions, and much of their instruction forced upon me by the necessities of my condition, yet I have always been a dull dog" (196). Assuming individual responsibility for conditions beyond his control and de-identifying with other workers, he remains merely isolated, neither materially and socially residing in the middle class nor identifying with his own. The disturbing power of the first half of the text, with the boy's mystical worship of his stepfather; the disintegration of the later sections; the emphatic progress and rationality in tension with the obsessive memories of early days; and the mystified transition from anger against a negligent father to guilt as an unworthy native son all contribute to a nightmare of socio-psychic marginality. Nonetheless, the book was received as a gratifying example of self-improvement and respectability among the lower classes.[39] Today we can see it as releasing all the phantoms of an ideology of familialism and progress upon a child who was deprived of a family and a chance. Unlike other working-class writers, Burn attempts to narrate his experience according to upper-class models. The price he pays is narrative and psychological disintegration.

Whereas Burn's story shows the effects of Enlightenment narratives concerning material progress, the pursuit of knowledge, and political emancipation, presumably from his days as a Chartist, and masculine "success" stories combining with familial narrative, women's narratives of this type are correspondingly dominated by familialism and romance. In his *Annals of Labour,* the social historian John Burnett cites Louise Jermy's *Memories of a Working Woman* as an example of a successful transition from a low-paying millinery position into domestic service and, ultimately, marriage.[40] Yet Jermy herself sees her life as a series of episodes failing to conform to her expectations of family and romance. Born in 1877, she is motherless before her second birthday. Her childhood and health are "bartered" by her father and stepmother when she is taken from school to do mangling at home in order for her parents to buy a house. Her adolescence is isolated, "not like other girls," between illness and an apprenticeship at fourteen to a dressmaker in "sweated" conditions (long hours in confined and crowded space, few and short breaks, low pay). Her education is continually frustrated as her stepmother destroys her books, and while in service to a married couple at Birmingham University "anything like deep thinking produced the dreadful headaches" (93).

Jermy's romantic life is also a series of noncorrespondences. A fragile betrothal conflicts with the long hours in service and the nine p.m. curfew of domestic servants, until her fiancé bolts and leaves her in a severe depression that endures two years. Finally she marries a farm laborer in 1911 but, like many husbands described by working-class wives, he is "delicate"; ill every spring, he lives only ten years. Jermy returns to work to raise her two sons.

She suffers from amnesia, ceases in childhood to confide in others, and bears a conviction of her awkwardness and unattractiveness. She leaves the millinery shop not, as Burnett implies, for better wages but in order to leave home; and she wears black—the "decent black" of domestic servants, as Mayhew put it, "no ringlets, followers, or scandals"—on and off the job.[41] While each episode fails to correspond to its middle-class analogue, Jermy nonetheless adopts middle-class standards and conventional narratives as her own. R. H. Mottram introduces *The Memories of a Working Woman* as the first autobiography written by a member of the Women's Institute. Yet Jermy never mentions the Institute: the dominant features of her life, at least prior to the Institute, were perverted familial relations (glorified dead mother, evil stepmother), aborted romance, and pronounced isolation.

In *A Cornish Waif's Story: An Autobiography,* the pseudonymous Emma Smith's life is also a sequence of noncorrespondences to middle-class norms. Born in 1894, Smith was the "illegitimate" daughter of one of the 23 children of a Cornish tin-miner blinded in a mining accident and retired without pension. As a child she is told that her mother is her sister. As accompanist to a hurdy-gurdy player, she is sexually molested by a man she calls "Fagin" and his friend Dusty the Sword Swallower. At eleven, she runs away and is sent to a convent penitentiary, a home for "errant" girls: "I was no more a prostitute than Dickens's Oliver Twist was a thief, if I may draw upon a character of fiction to illustrate what I mean. Yet here I was placed in the category, and indirectly it has affected my whole life" (108).

The convent penitentiary fails to prepare her for her reentry into society, especially for marriage and a family, while it equally denies her a "speakable" past. Upon release, "it was impressed upon me . . . that I was never to talk about the Home or let anyone know where I had come from . . . it was something to be very ashamed of" (133). Working as a servant in a vicarage provides dissonances that are borne out by her own marriage—"Nothing was as I imagined it. The vicar was blessed with an unholy temper. His wife did not get on with her husband and took no pains to hide the fact" (134). Her marriage to a gardener is probably arranged by her employers—"If you have two servants, a man and a woman, the thing to do is to marry them up. Then you have two servants for the price of one" (152)—and she very quickly distances herself as a unique, reflective, psychologically rich self ("a complex piece of machinery") from her husband ("a simple country man"), who, as a transparent product of his class status, fails to fulfill her emotional, intellectual, and romantic aspirations (152–166).

Again echoing Oliver and Agnes, she obsessively attempts to reconcile with her mother (from an external point of view, always a nonexistent dyad), aborts an extramarital romance in Australia, and returns with her husband to Cornwall. Yet rather than a parish girl's progress to financial and domestic stability (she is a successful head laundress with three healthy daughters), Smith's is an "hysterical" narrative indicating her nonadjustment to married life and maternity. She is as unwilling a wife as a waif.

If personal identity is a function of a temporal unification of past, present, and future, Smith was as deprived as Foucault's "Herculine Barbin" (who, raised as a girl in a convent, was legally declared to be male as an adult) of the past she had had to repress, and as unprepared for the future entailed by her gender and family: "I would dream that I was an inmate of a convent . . . I was, or could have been, supremely happy if it were not for the knowledge that somewhere in the background I had a husband and children" (178). After several mental breakdowns, she twice attempts suicide (quietly, like a good servant, with aspirin and sleeping pills), but is finally convinced by her doctor that her responsibility is to live for her family. In her last paragraph Smith once again turns to fictive modes to mediate her experience, this time apparently unconsciously: "I should end my life story on a very happy note if I could honestly record that I have grown so well-balanced mentally that nothing now upsets or worries me. Such, however, is not the case. I am easily worried and upset over certain things, and for this reason as much as for others, I am anxious to find a little cottage somewhere in Cornwall with a bit of ground upon which we can grow vegetables and flowers. It would be a great thrill to me if my dream cottage had a view of both the sun rising and the sunset, for the sun rising fills me with hope, and the sunset fills me with peace" (188). Novel-readers will recognize this image of the rose-covered cottage as the standard ending of Dickens's domestic fiction, including the image and final resting place of the adopted orphan Oliver Twist.

What is common to these texts is the conscious desire on the part of the writers to write their lives according to middle-class narratives and the unconscious distance between those narratives—especially of financial success, familialism, and romance—and the facts of their existence, especially economic determinism, nonfamilialism, aborted romance, and noncompanionate marriage. What these narratives of disintegrated personality tell us about gender is that in circumstances of familial deprivation, familial ideology can only be assumed at great psychic cost.

Yet not all working-class autobiographers assumed familial ideology at such a cost. It was a cultural commonplace that many male radicals—for example, Thomas Hardy, William Lovett, Thomas Cooper, Robert Blatchford, Robert Lowery, James Watson, and Thomas Dunning—had been raised by women alone ("resourceful widows" was the technical term), and they resisted bourgeois ideology as much as Emma Smith suffered from it. Unlike the writers above, the male radicals were engaged in communities with common purpose, and they were engaged in the process of rearticulating their common experience through the progressive narratives of the Enlightenment—as Lovett put it, through their common pursuits of bread, knowledge, and freedom, or material well-being, education, and political status. Emma Smith, Louise Jermy, and the Chartist renegade James Burn, on the other hand, were as isolated, individualistic, or unaffiliated as the middle-class subjects whose ideology they adopted—as isolated but not so autonomous. Smith maintained the forms of middle-class respectability and swallowed her pain like sleeping pills; Jermy was forced to return to work to support her fatherless sons; and as Burn said, whether or not there was work, his children were his "hostage to the State" (132).

Faced with such difficulties, the emotional health, or functional identities, of working-class writers was not dependent upon their politicization in any rigid sense so much as upon their participation in alternative articulations of their common experience. The indomitable Ellen Johnston, known to working people as Scotch Nell the "Factory Girl," could have been a Jermy or a Smith. Abandoned by her father, a stonemason, "tormented" by her stepfather, "deceived" by two lovers, and ostracized as a fallen woman, the power-loom weaver/poet's brief *Autobiography* (1867) is melodramatically modelled on Walter Scott and "those strange romantic ordeals attributed to the imaginary heroines 'of Inglewood Forest' "; her poems show the effects of literary hegemony, although often gender- and class-inverted, as in "Lines to a Young Gentleman of Surpassing Beauty."[42]

Yet Johnston also articulated a common experience of great value to herself and her fellow workers: for every epideictic lyric to a romantic young gentleman there are many more in praise of working men (she writes, she says, to relieve them from the toils of factory life), and her *Autobiography* concludes not with melancholy and melodrama but with her taking her foreman to court, indicating that the Factory Girl has learned to imitate the middle class in more than literary hegemony. She publishes proud poems on her "illegitimate" daughter "bonny Mary Auchinvole"; composes many—including love poems—on behalf of less literate co-workers; includes in her volume addresses and songs written for her from other workers (to which she often composes personal responses); goes international with "Welcome, Garibaldi" and "The Exile of Poland"; and writes with irresistible affection for the material life of the factory, as in "An Address to Napier's Dockyard" and "Kennedy's Dear Mill." "The Factory Girl's Farewell" concludes:

> Farewell to all the works around,
> The flaxmill, foundry, copperage too;
> The old forge, with its blazing mound,
> And Tennant's stalk, farewell to you.
> Your gen'rous masters were so kind,
> Theirs was the gift that did excel;
> Their name around my heart is twined:
> So Gailbraith's bonnie mill, farewell!
>
> Farewell, my honour'd masters two,
> Your mill no more I may traverse;
> I breathe you both a fond adieu;
> Long may you live lords of commerce.
> Farewell unto my native land,
> Land of the thistle and blue-bell;
> Oh! wish me joy with heart and hand;
> So Gailbraith's bonnie mill, farewell! (95)

Johnston participated fully in public life in factories in England, Scotland, and Ireland. Familial and romantic ideology exacted the highest psychic cost to those who lived in isolation. It seems inescapable that the emotional health and flourishing self-image of working-class subjects whose lives did not conform to the patterns of the dominant culture were proportionate to the degree of participatory—as opposed to purely antagonistic—discursive engagement with others beyond the family in the home. The narrative and psychological disintegration of working-class writers who attempted to adopt middle-class narratives of self, and the relatively successful identities of those supported by alternative participatory articulations, indicate the significance of discourse—in this case, of gendered, familial discourse—in human identity, as well as discourse's inability entirely to override nondiscursive material conditions.

Chapter Eight

"Yo Sola Aprendi": Mexican Women's Personal Narratives from Nineteenth-Century California

 *Genaro Padilla*

Desde muy niñita, ántes de venir de Mexico, me habían enseñado á leer. . . . Ya cuando era mujercita en California, yo sola aprendí á escribir, valiéndome para ello de los libros que veía—imitaba las letras en cualquier papel que lograba consequir—tales como cajillas de cigarros vacias, ó cualquier papel blanco que hallaba tirado. Así logré aprender bastante para hacerme entender por escrito cuando necesitaba algo.

(Lorenzana, p. 5)

[When I was a very young girl, before coming from Mexico, I had been taught to read. . . . And so when I was a young woman in California, encouraged by the books I saw, I taught myself to write by copying letters of the alphabet on any piece of paper I could find—such as empty cigarette packets, or any blank sheet of paper I found discarded. In that manner I learned enough to make myself understood in writing when I needed something.]

So Apolinaria Lorenzana remarks in her "Memorias de la Beata" (1878),[1] the account of her life as a nurse and teacher in the mission system of early nineteenth-century California. Doña Lorenzana was one of some forty women whose lives were recorded during the 1870s when Hubert H. Bancroft was collecting personal testimony for his work on California history. She was in her late seventies at the time she collaborated on her "Memorias," feeble in body and therefore discouraged because she felt like a burden to the people around her: poor, dispossessed of large tracts of land she had acquired independently during a lifetime of work and service, completely blind. The world she had known was receding into a past as unrecoverable as her sight. Still, during the late winter of 1878 she was scrawling her mark upon history—I say scrawling because at the end of the narrative, transcribed by Thomas Savage, she literally sealed her life on the last page in a nearly illegible marking of her initials. For an old woman who had lost almost everything, this act of will signified a final utterance of personal identity.

I

In the 1870s Hubert Howe Bancroft, book-dealer, document collector, and professional historian, solicited scores of personal oral testimonies by "Californios," as the native Hispano-Mexicanos called themselves. These narratives undergird his massive *History of California,* published between 1884 and 1889 in seven volumes, as well as *Pastoral California* (1888), a rather ethnocentric[2] and romanticized history of pre-American California society. As Bancroft himself wrote of the project in *Literary Industries,* he and his field assistants collected some "two hundred volumes of original narrative from memory by as many early Californians, native and pioneers, written by themselves or taken down from their lips . . . the vivid narratives of their experiences."[3] There are, from my count, some 150 Hispano personal narratives, of lengths varying from ten pages to a fair number that are hundreds of pages long. I must confess not only my sense of wonder, but my sense of resurrective power at discovering Bancroft's storehouse of California lives; here are scores of disembodied voices, textualized lives stored away for a time when they might be rescued from obscurity: María Inocente Avila, "Cosas de California"; Juan Bernal, "Memoria de un Californio"; Josefa Carrillo de Fitch, "Narración de una Californiana"; Rafael González, "Experiencias de un soldado"; Pío Pico, "Narración histórico"; Vincente Sánchez, "Cartas de un Angelino"; Felipa Osuna de Marron, "Recuerdos del pasado"; Pablo Vejar, "Recuerdos de un viejo."

These personal narratives provide a broad field of information on Hispano-Mexicano life before and immediately after the loss of California and much of northern Mexico to the United States in the war of 1846–1848.[4] Given the kind of information Bancroft wished to elicit, the narratives generally describe the significant historical, political, and social events of the day; manners, customs, and education; the social economy, and early relations with the native Indian people and the American immigrants. In the act of testimonial compliance, many of the narrators present a picture of an idyllic pre-American California. Nostalgia is especially conspicuous in the recollections of the social elite; however, even those narratives left by members of the lower classes, men who were soldiers and women who worked in the mission system, produce an image of a generally stable, self-sufficient society—at least before the American invasion and subsequent social transformation. The nostalgic tendency of the narratives must be understood, it seems to me, as a direct result of sociocultural loss, especially since almost all are characterized by a general sense of malaise, evident in those narrative stretches that describe political, economic, and cultural rupture. Nostalgia and attendant bitterness is actually the product of testimonial compliance, in which the recollected past is always at counterpoint with the present.

It is the disjuncture between a valorized pre-American life and the profound sense of loss after the invasion which provided the autobiographical moment when past and present could be reconsidered, conjoined, reconciled to some degree. Whereas for Bancroft the collection of these personal narratives was foundational research for his *History of California* project, for the narrators themselves it was the critical and perhaps only occasion for recreating the life of the self, together with the world inhabited by that self. The reconstitution of pre-American society was less an escapist activity than a strategy, only vaguely conscious of its means for sustaining order, sanity, and purpose in the face of economic and political dispossession, spiritual fragmentation, sadness, and longing. An established way of life was disintegrating, being rubbed out, erased—even at the moment the life was being narrated, transcribed, textualized.

I read these narratives as legitimate autobiographical enunciations, by individuals whose voices have not been merely forgotten but, like the people themselves, suppressed. Rather than affixing a degree of historical truth-value to their testimony or arguing the merits of their representativeness of Hispano-Mexicano culture, my primary concern is to recover the voices of these ghosts. They make their own claim to resurrection simply because, within the confines of oral testimony meant to subordinate their stories to Bancroft's history, these women and men marked their narratives with well-defined personalities. The narratives bequeathed by these individuals may have been used by Bancroft as social history, but it is the ever-present "I" that transforms them from oral history proper into the genre of life-writing we call autobiography. The subtle disclosure of individual experience and the overlay of individual personality upon the description of external sociopolitical realities, as well as the individuating of external events, mark these narratives with distinct autobiographical authority.

As one might expect, of the one hundred and fifty California narratives in the Bancroft collection, fewer than forty are by women. When Bancroft was collecting personal narratives, men who held public office, military officials, soldiers, or traders were called upon to record their *recuerdos* more often than were women. Women's narratives, moreover, were considered either supplemental to the men's or as sources of information for what Bancroft referred to as the "woman's sphere."[5]

Typical of men's autobiographies in general, the men's narratives reconstruct the powerful public identities the Californio patriarchs enjoyed before they lost everything to the Americans. Juan Bautista Alvarado, Pío Pico, Antonio Coronel, Mariano and Salvador Vallejo, and Manuel Castro, along with scores of other once prominent Californios, collaborated on narratives that reconstituted the period from the late eighteenth to the mid-nineteenth century, an era during which they ruled over a vast expanse of geography, native people, as well as their own families. For example, one of the wealthiest and most influential of these patriarchs was Mariano G. Vallejo, whose "Recuerdos históricos y personales tocante a la álta California" (1875) comprise nearly one thousand manuscript pages of personal, familial, social and cultural history.[6] Aristocratic, socially elitist, manipulative and exploitative, these men made for themselves and their families a world predicated upon their unquestioned authority as fathers and husbands.

In such a patriarchal world, male authority is seen as giving purpose and coherence to the family as well as to the larger social community. Respect for, obedience to, honor of, and deference toward the Patriarch were, for Vallejo, signs of familial and general social well-being before the Americanization; after the displacement of the Patriarch, the children fell away from a well-established code of behavior, and the Californio world collapsed upon itself. Once, young men greeted their fathers in the street with respectful address. Young women, once proud of their ability to administer domestic affairs, were in the 1870s interested—according to Vallejo—only in making an impression at the theater and at dances; Vallejo calls them "muñecas incapaces de dirigir el manejo de sus casas" [dolls/fashionable mannequins incapable of directing the management of their homes]. As he recalls, there were, after the conquest, more "solteronas" [old maids] than ever because men were reluctant to marry, afraid that they would be ruined and dishonored by "mujeres necias y vanidosas" [foolish and vain women] (V.4:336–37).

II

If for men like Vallejo the good old days of patriarchal authority evoke memories of harmonious filial, marital, and social relations, the women's personal narratives provide a markedly different scenario, especially of personal, communal, and gender-related experience. While there is a general affirmation of the Californio way of life, there is also a tendency to expose the constraints placed upon women within the patriarchy. Many of the narratives were composed by women from prominent families whose reminiscences were recorded primarily because of their relationship to certain influential men; yet, although the women may begin their *memorias* speaking about their husbands, fathers, or brothers, almost invariably the men get lost in the narratives. A few of the most memorable were left by working women who claimed for themselves independence and self-sufficiency; men are absent nearly altogether from these stories. My reading suggests that the California women manipulated the interview process whenever they could in order to comment upon gender-related issues, be it tense relations with parents, especially fathers, or with husbands and the patriarchal system in general. In being asked to remember their lives vis-à-vis men, women often subverted the transcription process in order to mark the narratives with their own distinctly gendered autographs.

Aside from the accounts of political intrigues, revolts against various Mexican officials, and the war with the United States that Bancroft wished to elicit from all his informants, from the women he especially wanted "information on manners and customs of the Californians." He prodded the women to remember social events, their favorite dances and songs, their marriages, children's births—in short, their domestic lives as diminutive reflections of the lives of Hispano men. This directive, ironically, meant that memory was pointed back towards women's activities. Providing basic information on the "woman's sphere" created a space in which a woman could remember *herself* and reconstitute her own life. Whenever topical testimony directed by the interviewer gave way to personally significant reminiscence, the narrative became genuinely autobiographical. This point of convergence between obligatory testimony and a consciously individuated narrative is also often marked by feminine affiliations—women remember themselves in relation to other women. In each of the narratives I have read, then, a distinct female identity emerges that will not be dismissed.

María de las Angustias de la Guerra's *Ocurrencias en California* (1878) offers a lively account of political intrigues and upper-class relations in pre-American Santa Barbara. Much of the narrative records the revolts against the various governors appointed from Mexico City, the pirate Bouchard's raid on Monterey when she was a girl, social balls and comical scandals, and memories of her politically influential father and brothers. As a representative of the Mexican landholding class and a member of one of the leading California families, Angustias de la Guerra generally ratifies patriarchal concerns over land, wealth, political and social status. This is as one might expect, since in reaffirming male class prerogatives, she is reaffirming her own privilege. Yet, Angustias de la Guerra is also scathingly critical of the men in power.

When referring to the early incursions of American "adventurers" surveying California, for example, she seizes the moment to issue an unexpected but sustained critique of the Hispano men's handling of the American threat. Referring to events early in the 1840s, she says that it was obvious, at least to the women, that the Americans in the territory were up to no good. When she and other women make their suspicions about a certain Charles Gillespie known to Manuel Castro, a commanding officer, they are chastised. "Castro told us that we were thinking ill of an invalid gentleman, accusing all the women in general of thinking ill of others, much more than the men. We answered that almost always we more often hit the mark" (de la Guerra, pp. 140–141). As it turned out, Gillespie was an American agent who was instrumental in staging the Bear Flag uprising in Sonoma (June 6, 1846) that led to open warfare between Mexico and the United States.

In a related part of the narrative, she charges that "when the hour came to defend the country against foreign invasion" the military command "performed no more service than the figurehead of a ship." Her sarcastic remarks about the officers are counterpointed by the dramatization of her own part in the struggle against the Americans. She describes an incident (1846) in which a *mexicano,* José Antonio Chavez, who was fleeing for his life from the American troops, was concealed in her home at a time when her husband was away. Although the Americans invade her home, rouse her out of bed—one even points a gun at her—she does not flinch in her resolve to hide Chavez, who is lying under a pile of blankets upon which her infant Carolina is sleeping. In fact, in de la Guerra's account it is women alone who are the main saboteurs: María de la Torre, a neighbor; Manuela and Carolina, her daughters; and various maids are all complicit in the concealment of Chavez. Finally, de la Guerra rather casually mentions that she accomplished all of this after "having given birth to a baby girl a few days before"—this at a time when women were confined to bed for up to forty days after delivery.

The preceding Chavez account, together with her criticism of certain other elements of the patriarchy, constitute enunciations that mark the narrative with her own name and feminine identity, not those of either of her husbands. Nor is her distinctive personality lost in the *a posteriori* versions produced by her male editors. Thomas Savage's introductory notes to the narrative he transcribed, as well as those to the 1956 published translation of her memoirs, all but bury her under the weight of men's names and position. Savage wrote: "Mrs. Ord (née Angustias de la Guerra, and whose first husband was Don Manuel Jimeno Casarín, Secretary of State, Senior member of the Assembly, and several times Governor pro tem, of Cal. & c) is well known as a lady of intelligence. . . . " (de la Guerra, p. 1). The editors of the English translation added: "The historical manuscript, Ord (Angustias de la Guerra), *Ocurrencias en California* was related to Thomas Savage by Mrs. Dr. James L. Ord for the Hubert Howe Bancroft Collection of 1878" (Foreword). María de las Angustias de la Guerra survives only parenthetically in these introductory notes, as well as in much of the solicited narrative, precisely because it was "her connections and position," as Savage noted, that "enabled her to inform herself upon Government affairs"—connections and position vis-à-vis influential men. Yet, in the entire narrative there is no mention at all of her husband Dr. James L. Ord and only passing remarks on Don Manuel Jimeno Casarín.

Another narrative in which a woman stakes her claim to personal identity other than that of a wife is Eulalia Perez's "Una Vieja y Sus Recuerdos," the acronical story of a woman reputedly 139 years of age when she relates her life as "partera" [midwife], "cocinera principal" [head cook], and "llavera" [keeper of the keys], as well as "dueña" [supervisor] of various shops at San Gabriel Mission during the first half of the nineteenth century. In recollecting her life history she reenacts the self-empowering process whereby she, some seventy years earlier, appropriated levels of responsibility within the mission system that, as she makes quite clear in her recollections, granted her authority over numerous men. What presumably begins, for the interviewer at least, as a narrative from which information about the operations of the mission system could be elicited, ends up as a story of a woman, alone with five children, who brought the male-dominated world into conjunction with her own will to be self-sufficient.

Like de la Guerra, her immediate autobiographical utterance is an act of toponymic self-identification: "Yo Eulalia Perez, nací en el presidio de Loreto en la Baja California. . . . " of her two husbands' names—neither "Guillen" nor "Mariné"—are noted here or anywhere else in her narrative, except where she concedes her brief marital phases with them; not being present in the text, theirs are names without substance. Eulalia Perez's reappropriation of her given name thus constitutes an act of deliberate self-possession, the willing into textual permanence of her own personal existence. It is as though women like Angustias de la Guerra and Eulalia Perez realized that their identities were in danger of being submerged and even effaced by the men to whom they were related and by whom they were censored. Their response to the threat of obscurity was to seize the opportunity provided by the Bancroft oral history project to reconstitute their own lives. There are strikingly discernible moments in each of the narratives when, in the process of reciting the customs and manners Bancroft wanted to record, they rediscover areas of long evaporated personal experience.

Eulalia Perez's location of a distinct identity outside relationships with husbands points to a particularly critical issue in many of the women's narratives. In a word, they reveal no little resentment about marriage expectations. The entire arrangement, from betrothal at an early age to the actual wedding ceremony, was effected almost exclusively between the fathers. The tradition of marrying girls at a young age—between thirteen and fifteen—was a practice that appears especially vexing in many of the women's narratives and is remembered with some bitterness when other momentous life experiences seem forgotten.

María Inocente Pico de Avila, a member of the wealthy and influential Pico family in Los Angeles, defers to her husband's life early in her narrative—"Cosas de California" (1876)—commenting upon his family genealogy, education, military career, and resistance to the American forces. But when remembering their marriage, she suddenly recalls that like other girls she was only beginning to read, write and do arithmetic when taken from school to begin preparation for her *primary* role in life as a wife. As Avila remembers:

> Muchas niñas no concluían ni esos pocos estudios, porque las quitaban sus madres de la escuela casi siempre para casarlas, porque había la mala costumbre de casar á las niñas muy jovencitas, cuando la pedían. Yo estuve en la escuela solo hasta los 14 años; después me llevó mi madre al rancho para enseñarme a trabajar, y a los 15 años y ocho meses me casé. (Pico de Avila, p. 20)

> [Many girls never even finished these few studies, because their mothers nearly always took them from school to marry them off, because there was the bad custom of marrying girls very young, when they were called for. I only stayed in school until my fourteenth year; then my mother took me to the ranch to prepare me to work, and at 15 years and 8 months of age I was married.]

In the men's narratives, as one might expect, the primacy of marriage and the shaping of domestic consciousness in women is regarded as central to the maintenance of social order. In his "Notas históricas sobre California" (1874), Salvador Vallejo, brother of Mariano, remembers, "we [the patriarchs, of course, with mothers as the enforcers of male dictates] taught our girls to be good housewives in every branch of their business; our wives and daughters superintended the cooking and every other operation performed in the house, the result of the training was cleanliness, good living and economy" (S. Vallejo, p. 99). The women's narratives expose such domestic training and early marriage as forms of sexual coercion and social control. Avila's forceful denunciation of "la mala costumbre de casar a las niñas muy jovencitas" ("mala" here signifying "hateful," "callous," "malign" even "evil") is decisively anti-patriarchal. The autobiographical enunciations of the California women, almost without exception, show that they were conscious of the socio-sexual function of early marriage, or marriage at any age, for that matter. For women like Avila, having their schooling abruptly terminated, or being denied a lettered ed-

ucation altogether because of gender, meant having a vital part of
the self closed off, stunted.

There were women, of course, who refused to be stunted. Apolinaria Lorenzana, to whom I now return, was one such woman.
She had come to Monterey, California, with her mother and a
group of orphaned children before she was seven. Lorenzana remembers that the children were distributed among families "como
perritos" [like puppies], while she remained with her mother and
various other women. Many of the older girls soon married, including her mother, who returned to Mexico with her soldier husband and died soon thereafter. Over a period of seven years, like
the other "perritos," she was passed between several families,
mostly in soldiers' homes. It was during this period, when she was
about fourteen, that she taught herself to write on scraps of paper.

Lorenzana looks back to this moment as the beginning of
her independent life as a nurse and teacher. She not only proudly
describes how she taught herself to write, but how she shared her
knowledge with other young women who were eager to learn in a
society that discouraged women's intellectual development. But,
as she points out, she did not exclude boys from her lessons: "I
taught children of either sex to read at the request of their parents" (MS: 42).

As for marriage, Apolinaria Lorenzana simply chose not to.
Nowhere in her narrative does she express the least regret that
she had no husband or children, never does she complain of having
been lonely. On the contrary, she was highly regarded as a result
of her teaching and general care of children, enough so that she
had nearly two hundred godchildren, an honor bestowed much
more typically upon men, especially *ricos,* than women, especially
solteronas. As for not taking a husband, she has this to say:

> When I was a girl, there was a young man who often entreated me
> to marry him. But I did not feel inclined toward matrimony (know-
> ing full well the requirements of that holy institution), and so I re-
> fused his offer. He then told me that since I wouldn't marry him, he
> was leaving for Mexico. So he left. (Lorenzana, p. 43)

Lorenzana says no more about the matter. She does, however,
have a great deal to say about her work; in fact, much like Eulalia
Perez, whom she knew well, she exults in describing various re-
sponsibilities in the mission chain. She remembers overland journeys along the coast of the mission. She vividly relates a story told

by Doña María de los Angeles, a woman in her care, about an Indian revolt in which her husband was killed and her children kidnapped. Lorenzana's account of this mother's grief is moving: "The miserable mother neither spoke nor cried, for the anguish had crushed her. I tried to console her, and encouraged her to eat, but she was inconsolable . . . and for the rest of her life she suffered terribly, without cheer—at last she died under the weight of her grief" (Lorenzana, p. 41).

One notices here and throughout the "Memorias" just how much Lorenzana's narrative is women-centered. She gives substance to women, making their desire to learn, their illnesses, and their griefs real and memorable. Lorenzana often maintained contact with women from their infancy to adulthood through multiple generations; for instance, she recalls: "I had in my charge, caring for her from the time she was two or three years old, a girl, whose mother was my goddaughter in both baptism and marriage and for whose three children I was also godmother. At any rate, that girl, who was my first charge, I taught to read, pray, sew, among other things, and when the time came she married and is now the mother of her own family" (Lorenzana, p. 43).

In her late seventies Lorenzana still retains a strong sense of respect from the California community. As Thomas Savage points out in his prefatory remarks to the transcription, "many of the native Californians of both sexes spoke of her in the highest terms of praise . . . as la Beata (the pious)." Yet, there is also a sense of pained resignation at the end of her life. In her own words: "aquí me hallo pobre y desvalida, con escasa salud" [Here I find myself poor and destitute, my health broken]. Her anguish, however, is not merely the result of age, blindness, and infirmity, for as Savage mentions she "appears to be a good old soul, cheerful," but rather because like many Californios—both women and men—she felt displaced, and hence confused, embittered, resentful toward a nation that had made her a stranger in her own land. Remember, here was a woman who was not only psychologically and socially independent, but economically independent as well.

During the many years she worked in the mission, she acquired three separate ranches of her own. Two of these were granted to her by the government, a privilege that was almost never extended to women. The other, situated between the two, she purchased outright. Although Savage notes that she "was loath to speak on this subject, assuring me that she didn't want even to think of it" (Preface), she does say enough to convey a strong sense of proprietary interest in her land; she never intended to sell it and is quite clear about the fact that she was swindled out of it, although like many other *mexicanos,* she is not sure precisely how. It is at this point in the narrative, startled by a twenty-five-year-old nightmare, that she says:

> Es una história larga y no quiero ni hablar de ella. Los otros dos ranchos me los quitáron de algun modo. Así es que después de haber trabajado tantos años, de haber poseido bienes, de que no me desposeí por vento ni de otro modo, me encuentro de la mayor pobreza, viviendo de favor de Dios y de los que me dan un bocado de comer. (Lorenzana, p. 30)

> [It is a long story and I don't even want to discuss it. The other two ranches they somehow took from me. So, that's the way it turns out that after working so many years, after having acquired an estate, which I certainly didn't dispose of by selling or any other means, here I find myself in the greatest poverty, living only by the grace of God and through the charity of those who give me a mouthful to eat.]

Lorenzana discloses no self-pity over her decrepit condition, her loss of sight, nor even her poverty. Evidence of dispiritedness takes the form of sociocultural displacement, present in a majority of the California narratives—in both the women's and the men's. Like nearly all the Californios of her generation, she found herself in the 1870s not only near the end of her life, but at the end of a way of life. With anger and pain apparent in her words, Apolinaria Lorenzana literally inscribes her initials on the final page of her "Memorias" not only as a hedge against her own death, but also, it seems to me, as a gesture of defiance against a form of historical and cultural death.

III

The women's narratives remind us of just how tenuous existence was in post-1848 society for a people trying to give purpose to the personal life during a time of immense social, political, and cultural upheaval. Life in a stable social world was difficult enough for women. Their narratives make this plain. But what they also make plain is that the American takeover was a trauma that disrupted life for everyone. Bitterness, a profound sense of loss, confusion, and displacement color the women's personal narratives fully as much as the men's. As Lorenzana said over one hundred years ago, the way *mexicanos* in the latter part of the nineteenth century were dispossessed of their land, livelihood, often their dignity and their very voice constitutes a long and troubling story.

Some of the women were so deeply embittered by the events of 1846 that when asked to comment on the war they spoke through clenched teeth. Rosalia Vallejo de Leese, sister to Mariano and Salvador Vallejo, was still so angry three decades after the war that she refused to give more than a brief narrative; what she does remember of the Bear Flag incident of 1846 ends in these words: "those hated men inspired me with such a large dose of hate against their race, that though twenty-eight years have elapsed since that time, I have not yet forgotten the insults they heaped upon me, and not being desirous of coming in contact with them I have abstained from learning their language."[7] She also forbade her children to speak the language of *los estranjeros* in her presence.

Yes, I know, her words here are presented in English, the language of the enemy, but not of her choice, or mine. The document itself was, for some strange reason, transcribed into English even though most of the Californio narratives were given and remain in their native Spanish.[8] Even those few texts that have recently been translated will require careful re-reading, since there is evidence of frequent mistranslation. I raise this issue here because it is directly gender-related. To elaborate: Angustias de la Guerra's narrative, one of the handful that have been published in English translation, gives the impression at a crucial juncture that women were not troubled by the American occupation. This happens in Francis Price and William Ellison's translation *Occurrences in California* (1956), where de la Guerra is *made* to say that "the conquest of California did not bother the Californians, least of all the women" (59); what she *did* say was "la toma del país no nos gustó nada á los Californios, y menos á las mujeres"—which should be translated as "the taking of the country did not please the Californios one bit, and least of all the women." Contrary to the mistranslation (was it a willed misreading that made for the mistranslation?) of her comments, de la Guerra's *Ocurrencias* must be read as oppositional narrative. In other words, her narrative as well as those of other California women articulate the fact that they did not welcome the Americans.

Although Bancroft solicited women's personal narratives in order to provide general information on the collective "woman's sphere," the women made the testimonies individually self-reflexive. In each of the narratives I have discussed, a substantive individual identity emerges that warrants autobiographical legitimacy. Apolinaria Lorenzana is distinct from Angustias de la Guerra because both constitute themselves distinctly. Moreover, their narrative lives are contextualized by the sociocultural and gender-related moment that contributed to their historical identities. In that respect, the narratives must be seen as the products of a dialectical process. Since they were collected by men who represented the occupying culture, it is reasonable to assume that Mexican women were engaged in a power struggle within the very interview process. Angustias de la Guerra was sought out for interview because she was related to influential men through whom she had apparently informed "herself upon governmental affairs"; yet by the end of her testimony she had appropriated the narrative process for inscribing her own life. And although at the moment of narration she was "Mrs. Dr. James L. Ord," she did not ratify the American occupation, as perhaps the interviewer had expected. Eulalia Perez was surely approached for interview because she was a curiosity—a woman of 139 years, according to local history; yet she did not relate her life story as a wonder of longevity, but as a story of self-reliance.[9] In each of these narratives there is evidence of evasion, redirection of the past, and reconstitution of a "self" that proceeds beyond interrogatory expectations.

As for the dialectic of gender present in the narratives, while it would be inaccurate to make a generalizing claim that women's narratives roundly criticize the Hispano patriarchal system, they do question masculinist controls within a culture that placed constraints upon their intellectual development, excluded them from the networks of sociopolitical hierarchy, and sought to domesticate their desire for self-sufficiency. Hence, intra-cultural and gender-related commentary of a critical bent is more manifest in the women's narratives than in the men's, where patriarchal customs are self-servingly remembered. Again and again one reads narratives by women who were articulate, intellectually inquisitive, "self"-conscious, and undoubtedly capable of fully independent lives, as demonstrated by Eulalia Perez and Apolinaria Lorenzana.

Patriarchal and testimonial forms of containment, in fact, often provided the impulse to reconstruct individual identity and personal experience in a genuinely self-empowering manner. Angustias de la Guerra reconstructs her own heroism against the insolent *americano* soldiers, and thereby levels a critique at the Californio men; Eulalia Perez marks her consciously planned appropriation of authority in an otherwise male domain; Maria Inocente Pico gives tribute to her husband, but also remembers being yanked out of school to undergo domestic "training" for him; Apolinaria Lorenzana recreates her life not only as nurse and teacher, but as property owner who had to contend with swindling Americans. In each of the narratives women push beyond testimonial expectations to discover or invent the narrative space required for reconsidering their lives within a male-controlled domain, for reassessing the social transformation that affected them as much as their male counterparts, and, ultimately, for celebrating their own lives.*

---

*An earlier version of this paper was presented at the Stanford University Conference on Autobiography and Biography: Gender, Text and Context (April 1986). I wish to thank Marilyn Yalom of the Stanford Institute for Research on Women and Gender for suggesting changes and expansion. I am also indebted to the encouragement and criticism of Ann Parsons, Josette Price, Luis Torres.

Chapter Nine

Reconstructing the Person:
The Case of Clara Shortridge Foltz

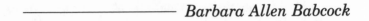 *Barbara Allen Babcock*

Clara Shortridge Foltz (1849–1934) was not a private person. Craving recognition, wealth and power, she publicized herself with uncommon energy and enthusiasm. During her long lifetime, she achieved at least one of her goals: recognition. For many years, her name was familiar to Californians as the state's "first woman"— first woman lawyer; first woman to attend law school; first woman notary public; first woman counsel to a legislative committee; first woman deputy district attorney. She was the first to conceive the idea of a public defender for indigents accused of crime, and worked to implement the concept through legislation in thirty states. The first American Constitutional clauses guaranteeing women access to education and employment were in large part Foltz's achievement. An early feminist, Foltz crusaded for suffrage and founded women's improvement organizations. She also practiced law continuously for fifty years.

Wherever she went—to San Diego during the 1887–1888 real estate boom, where she published a daily paper; to New York in 1895, where she lectured for the Lyceum Bureau, practiced law, and sued a restaurant that refused service to unescorted women; to Denver at the turn of the century, where she specialized in mining law and helped publish a weekly magazine; to Los Angeles for the last third of her life—she was "prominent." That word recurs in contemporary descriptions: a "prominent" Californian, a "prominent" lawyer, a "prominent" suffragist. From her promontory, she ran in 1930 for Governor of California. Naturally, she was the first woman to offer herself for that post.

Foltz wanted her fame to endure. From 1916 to 1918, when she was in her sixties, she wrote "The Struggles and Triumphs of a Woman Lawyer," a serial published in her monthly magazine,

The New American Woman. In each issue of the magazine, she spent a page or two on memories from her lawyer life. She told of her admission to the Bar, of her suit to gain entry to Hastings Law School, and of some cases. Acknowledging that her narrative was "brief and hastily recorded," Foltz wrote that she hoped someday "an inquisitive biographer" would use her scrapbooks and papers to "write the history of the first woman to practice law on the Pacific Coast. Modesty should hardly prevent me from suggesting that my name must necessarily 'go over the top'."[1]

I am that "inquisitive biographer," eager to revive her fame, and to find in her life an example for generations of lawyers, and women, and women lawyers. The task is complicated, however, because although Foltz often spoke of devoting the last years of her life to an autobiography, she never published it, and her papers were apparently discarded at her death.[2] Her biography thus depends upon the public record, which consists of her own publications,[3] newspaper accounts,[4] the papers of contemporaries, legal documents and biographical indexes.[5] Also, Clara Foltz always moved to the action, so that her story is found, for example, in histories of the Western suffrage campaigns, the development of the California oil industry, and Progressive era politics.

In this essay, I offer a sample of how I intend to write about the life of Clara Shortridge Foltz from the public sources. Taking a central event in her life, I can construct with some certainty its outer dimensions: that it occurred, when and how. But I would like also to reconstruct its meaning for her and perhaps for us, and that is more problematic. The event for construction and reconstruction is her divorce from Jeremiah Foltz in 1879.

An immediate obstacle to the task is that Clara Foltz did some reconstructing of her own. As early as 1878, and continuously from 1885 on, she referred to herself as a widow, though Jeremiah was very much alive. She did not drape her story in simple black but added frills, making it one "of her romantic marriage at fifteen, of her widowhood when scarcely out of her teens."[6] And she proclaimed that "it was to enable [women] in some degree to protect themselves and their children when the shadow of death had fallen upon the head of the household that formed the nucleus of my determination to open the way for women in the profession of law in California."[7]

Foltz's reconstruction was quite successful. Almost all newspaper articles and biographical entries in her lifetime, as well as *The New York Times* obituary, record her as a widow. But in the

basement of the San Jose courthouse are the handwritten plead-
ings in *Foltz v. Foltz,* which reveal that she had married in 1864 in
Indiana and was divorced fifteen years later when she was thirty.
There were five children ranging in age from thirteen to three
years old, "who all have been *for the last two years* and are now
under the sole custody and control of the plaintiff."

The two years, 1877 to 1879, were the same ones in which
Clara Foltz turned from obscure housewife and mother into the
renowned "Portia of the Pacific." Is there a connection between her
entry into the legal profession and her divorce? Self-presentation
as a widow prevented people from thinking that her decision to
be a lawyer had destroyed her marriage. The question, of course,
is whether it did. We are thrown upon the public record for the
answer.

From a few newspaper interviews published early in her career, when Foltz spoke about her marriage and even mentioned
her divorce, we learn that Jeremiah Foltz, a young German
farmer, eloped with Clara Shortridge, whose parents did not ap-
prove of the match. One story recounts that "when she had come
to realize the gravity of her course, cherishing as she did the most
childlike devotion to her parents, she resolved to bend all the energies of her young being to the promotion of marital happiness,
not so much for her own sake, as for that of her father and
mother."[8]

In lectures and interviews, Foltz often told of her very early
ambitions to be a lawyer, but "as she drifted into young ladyhood,
her ideas became more romantic, and her dreams were not of ora-
tory, or fame, or political recognition. With a purely feminine
ideal, she dreamed of a handsome noble husband, who would cher-
ish her and keep her sheltered from the unknown world in a
happy little home."[9]

"In the springtime of married life," Clara later wrote, husband and wife "fly to each others' sides like steel to magnet."[10] But
in her own case ardor quickly faded:

> The life of the child-wife was a troubled one. Upon an Iowa farm,
> the greater part of her time which could be spared from the cares
> of maternity was devoted to manual labor, necessitated by family
> needs. Her husband removing to Portland, Oregon, she rejoined him
> there in January, 1872, with a babe of nine weeks. She found him
> clerking at starvation wages, and immediately went to making
> dresses and keeping boarders. She had to bear the entire burden of

her own and her children's maintenance, and barely managed to do
so. Her husband coming to California, she again followed.[11]

Not only Clara, but also her parents and four brothers, moved
to Oregon and then to California. We do not know why Jeremiah
Foltz moved to San Jose, California; perhaps he was drawn by the
large German community there. Nor do we know what he made of
his wife's entire family joining them. Whatever he made of it, the
presence of her family enabled Clara Foltz to do more than keep
house, raise her children and augment their income in traditional
ways. She later credited her father with encouraging her to study
law and her mother assumed much of the child care while Foltz
was busy doing things women did not do.

A few years after the divorce, Clara Foltz described her marriage as a struggle to "maintain not only the little ones that came
so fast, but also the man who should have stood between her and
the great unknown world."[12] In her own and others' later accounts,
the husband drops out entirely. Thus a friend recommending her
to the Governor for an appointment in 1891 wrote of a woman
alone seizing on law study in desperation:

> When I first met Mrs. Foltz she was a dressmaker . . . working her
> life out to support herself and her little family. Recognizing the fu-
> tility of such a struggle against the growing needs of her children
> [he says nothing of the growing number] she determined to fit her-
> self for a more remunerative calling and so devoted herself to the
> study of law with that end in view. . . . [13]

Jeremiah Foltz was an unsuccessful provider. He was also
probably an unfaithful husband. Within two weeks of the divorce
decree, he was remarried to a woman he had met in Oregon, to
whom he apparently made frequent visits during 1878–1879. The
divorce papers state not only that the five children were in the
sole custody of their mother during this period, but also recount,
in the common yet poignant pleading of the time, that as of July
1879, and "for more than a year last past, defendant has willfully
failed and neglected to provide plaintiff with the common neces-
saries of life . . . " and "that she and her said children would have
gone hungry, homeless, unclothed and destitute had it not been for
plaintiff's personal exertions and the assistance of her friends and
relations."

"Plaintiff's personal exertions" during this period while her
marriage was falling apart were extraordinary. First, she read law

with a San Jose attorney; realizing that even if she were admitted
to the Bar she would be unable to practice, she prevailed on a local
state Senator to introduce the Woman Lawyer's Bill, which she
drafted herself. The bill provided that any person of good moral
character might be admitted to the Bar, eliminating the prior re-
striction to "white males." Clara Foltz went to Sacramento, lobbied
the bill through, and then became, in September 1878, the first
woman lawyer in the state.

Foltz and her friend, Laura DeForce Gordon, the second
woman lawyer in California, decided that formal education would
enhance their legal careers. In January 1879, they tried to enter
Hastings College of the Law, California's first law school. When
they were denied admission because they were women, they
brought suit. As a direct result of the women's case and their other
efforts, the California Constitutional Convention of 1879 enacted
two clauses that were unprecedented in the history of American
organic law: one provided access for women to all departments of
the state University and the other that: "No person shall, on account of sex, be disqualified from entering upon or pursuing any
lawful business, vocation or profession."[14]

Aided by the Constitutional provisions whose passage they
had spearheaded, Foltz and Gordon won their case against Hastings in the trial court. Foltz then joined the Bar of the California
Supreme Court and successfully argued the Hastings appeal.[15] As
with her admission to the Bar, there was nationwide publicity.

The measure of Foltz's early achievement was taken a few
years later:

> [I]t was genius only that could step from cradleside into the ranks
> of one of the profoundest professions and without education or
> learning, burdened with the cares of a large family and against the
> prejudice of sex, rise in six short years to the position of a first rate
> lawyer in a metropolitan city.[16]

The spectacular successes that opened her career all occurred
while Foltz's marriage was deteriorating, making it hard for her
to counter the constant contention that women could not, and
should not, be both lawyers and wives. In the grip of a peculiarly
male hysteria, her opponents urged that if women were lawyers
the institutions of marriage and home would be destroyed. Foltz
had, moreover, to contend with the formidable U.S. Supreme Court
precedent denying Myra Bradwell of Illinois the privilege of prac-

ticing law, and in a concurring opinion observing that "the har-
mony of . . . the family institution is repugnant to the idea of a
woman adopting a distinct and independent career from that of
her husband."[17]

Such sentiments defeated Myra Bradwell even though her
husband was at her side encouraging her to practice law. It is not
surprising that Clara Foltz decided, as her career rose and her
marriage declined, to present herself as a widow.[18] A widow left
with five children to support, who has already tried traditional
women's work, does not choose, but is forced into, man's sphere.
Her story as she told it to *The New York Times* in 1897 was that
she "was left a widow while she was still young with five children
to support. She bravely declined offers of aid from her relatives
and declared her intention to study law."[19]

There is evidence in the public record that she did not lightly
don widow's weeds, but made at least one major effort to save her
marriage. In February 1878, Clara Foltz left California while the
Woman Lawyer's Bill was pending in the legislature in order to
see Jeremiah, who was in Portland on one of his frequent and extended trips.[20] An Oregon paper reported that she planned to return and practice law there—surely an optimistic fantasy about
reuniting with Jeremiah, since she would have faced anew in Oregon all the obstacles to joining the Bar, which she had not yet
overcome in California.[21]

She said that she wanted the marriage to survive, and perhaps she meant it. In one of her lady-lawyer interviews, given before the final break, she maintained:

> . . . A great many women have consulted me in regard to getting a
> divorce. They naturally come to me when in trouble of that
> kind. . . . I deem the marriage relation too high and holy to be bro-
> ken except for the very gravest of causes.[22]

Jeremiah Foltz, too, may have made at least one effort to prevent the final split. He was back in San Jose early in 1879 and a
suffrage friend wrote to Laura Gordon: "I am sorry to hear that
Mrs. Foltz's husband is here . . . She will rue the day that she goes
back to him as his submissive slave—for what does he care about
woman's freedom or personal liberty?"[23]

The timing of Jeremiah's return was not good for reestablish-
ing a typical nineteenth-century household. Clara Foltz was in the
midst of her suit against Hastings, and had actually moved for a
few months to San Francisco, taking the older children with her.

The press was following her every move in the suit; among the numerous articles appeared an item in the *Sacramento Record Union* that is summary and portent of the Foltz marriage. It is a letter [on the front page] from an unnamed "Oregon correspondent," with a Portland dateline:

> Seven or eight years ago a young woman with four children already under her wings came to Oregon in search of her husband. She was twenty years of age at that time, and was very self-possessed, besides being rather attractive. Her husband was clerking in a store here . . . [and was unpopular]. The wife proved to be energetic and rather capable. She was a ready advocate of woman suffrage. *The husband was not of much force and whatever became of him I cannot tell.* I see that the woman, Mrs. Carrie S. Foltz, has been admitted to the bar as a practicing attorney in your State. She has no timidity or shrinking delicacy to prevent her success in that profession and, on the contrary, is a ready talker, sharp and quick witted . . . [24]

Clara did not return to Jeremiah, or he to her in March, 1879. Instead he left San Jose to move permanently to Portland and she filed divorce papers.[25] Her emotional state at this time was apparent. Soon after Jeremiah left, a friend wrote "I am a little troubled about our beloved Clara, others will love her, whose love will not blight . . . Well be it if our gentle, magnetic friend is poised against it all."[26]

Three years after the divorce, Clara Foltz explained that "incompatibilities of temperament had rendered their conjugal life unhappy."[27] Forty years later she elaborated:

> I believe that most of the heart-breakings of married life are due to the lack of a common center of thought between husband and wife . . . [A]s years go on indifference creeps over the pleasant surface of their lives, the tender courtesies begin to be forgotten. She is either engrossed with household cares or the gayeties of fashion, and he has a field of thought entirely foreign to either one or the other.
>
> . . . The society of each becomes irksome to the other and they long for different conditions all because there is not common ground between them. If husband and wife would blend in the harmony of a complete union they must pursue some common theme.[28]

Clara Foltz wrote abstractly, yet the account seems close to her own story, except that it was neither the "gayeties of fashion" nor

"household cares" that engrossed her. Rather, she was occupied
with becoming California's "first woman."

This is the reconstruction from the available sources of Clara
Foltz's marriage and divorce. None of the evidence shows directly
that her grand personal ambitions caused the estrangement. Jeremiah might have been an inadequate husband even to a woman
who remained in the domestic sphere. Or perhaps none but the
most unusual nineteenth-century man could have tolerated living
in the shadow of Clara's splendid entrance into the legal profession. Finally, it is possible that her decision to be a lawyer occurred when the marriage was already troubled, and was only one
factor among many that drove them apart. Foltz herself implied
that divorce is the end of a process of degeneration: " . . . the civil
court only gives legal sanction to a decree that nature has already
entered in the hearts."[29]

I believe, however, that there is a causal connection between
the collapse of her marriage and her choice of a career—that
Clara Foltz's story is not simply the old tale of desertion and infidelity. Jeremiah Foltz had married a girl of fifteen. Fifteen years
later he—whose name never appeared in the newspapers—found
himself with a famous wife. She was a person of stunning energy,
force, ambition; he was barely able to make a living. As long as she
supplemented the family income by sewing and taking in board-
ers, the marriage survived. Once she took the dramatic and much
publicized actions that launched her career, Jeremiah defected.
And Clara Foltz argued for the rest of her life that women could be
both laudable lawyers and exemplary wives. The constancy of the
theme is telling, since she had removed herself from criticism on
this point by claiming widowhood. Always, she sounded as if responding to unseen accusers:

> But we are told that if women go into the legal profession, it will
> destroy our homes. Convince me of that and I will assign my cases
> before sunrise and abandon the profession forever; for I realize the
> supreme importance of the institution of home and I will not by
> example or by precept do anything which will in the remotest de-
> gree injure that portion of our social fabric, on which rests the peo-
> ple's happiness and our country's destiny. Think you that
> knowledge of law will destroy our homes?
>
> That is not the legitimate effect of knowledge of any kind. On the
> contrary, a knowledge of the law of our land will make women bet-
> ter mothers, better wives and better citizens.[30]

Clara Foltz never had the opportunity to demonstrate how a knowledge of the law would make her a better wife, nor did she ever openly acknowledge a conflict between marriage–family–home and career. Rather she strove, usually successfully, to present herself as in this typical press portrait: "Here [in 'her beautiful home . . . in San Francisco'], she lives, a standing demonstration that a woman may be a lawyer, an orator, may take an active and earnest interest in her country and the welfare of her people, and not for a moment lose the graces, or sweetness or beauty that crowns and glorifies woman in the home."[31]

Her public treatment of her failed marriage accords with Clara Foltz's character. Romantically, she conceived the death of love as physical, leaving her a widow. Practically, this self-presentation protected her from the recognition by her public, and perhaps even by herself, that she was unable to play devoted wife to a limited man.

Disjunction—between what she said and did, what she aspired to and achieved, and even between what she most fervently proclaimed at one point and another—is typical in Foltz's life. In her speeches and writing, she pledges allegiance to the idea of woman at the center of the home: noble, serene, learned, raising manly sons and virtuous daughters. Yet she saw her own existence as an unending battle on far fields. At the same time, she insisted that her life was exemplary for the "new woman," never hinting at how she or others could be at once in the home and on the field.

Because of her ambivalence about what women should do and be, and because she tried so many things professionally and personally, her life and thought have a fractured, sometimes even frantic, quality that contrasts with the lives of the archetypal figures in the women's movement. She had no overarching sense of mission so pure that it overrode all personal ambition. Nor in Clara Foltz was there some unifying characteristic serving to direct (or now to explain) her thought and action—such as Susan B. Anthony's single-mindedness; Elizabeth Cady Stanton's driving intellect; Carrie Chapman Catt's judgment; Abigail Scott Duniway's certitude. Clara Foltz's life was confused, her vision clouded, her name a misnomer.

The incoherence of her life, as much as the missing papers, may explain her failure before now to attract a biographer. Paradoxically perhaps, the unheroic aspects of her story add to her appeal for a modern chronicler. Refusing to admit either hard choices or mistakes, Clara Foltz pursued professional achievement and recognition, power and wealth, a deeply conceived maternal role, a passionate and beauty-filled life. The degree of confusion and conflict that resulted was unusual in the late nineteenth century; it is familiar today. For the end of the twentieth century, Clara Shortridge Foltz is, at last, a representative heroine.

Chapter Ten

Lorine Niedecker: Composing a Life

 *Glenna Breslin*

Lorine Niedecker (1903–1970) is a fine, but neglected American poet, a second-generation modernist who applied the techniques of the new poetry to her own watery stretch of southeastern Wisconsin with quietly spectacular results. Writing from the 1920s through 1970, Niedecker interpreted surrealist, imagist, and objectivist poetics in unique ways that make her an important part of our literary history. For more than forty years, she published her poems in literary journals and in five collections; after her death, Cid Corman, her literary executor, published a sixth collection. In 1985, her selected poems, *The Granite Pail,* and her collected writings, *From This Condensery,* were published.[1] Now that her work is readily available, more readers are coming to appreciate its beauty and power.

Biographers are aware that, despite their efforts to be objective, their own personalities and experiences influence the way they perceive the life of the other. As Niedecker's biographer, I seek a way out of this dilemma by conceiving my approach to her as a series of encounters, some remote, some close, between two shifting subjectivities. I discover Niedecker through her poems, letters and manuscripts, all of which hold vital clues to her thinking and composing processes. Visits to her home and interviews with people who knew her have brought me closer to her person. And I am guided in my writing of her biography by how she defined herself in relation to what was around her. In this essay I focus on Niedecker's responses to cultural expectations of her as a woman, as revealed through her attitude toward marriage and the personal and literary relationships she established with men she admired. Niedecker learned to work around social conventions for the sake of her poetic development. I will show how Niedecker confronted and transformed her experience of a particular gender role, that of admiring pupil to a powerful male mentor, into a creative source for her art.

As I negotiate between my wish to represent Niedecker accurately and my awareness of my subjective responses to her, I am guided by Niedecker's own experiments in biographical portraiture. Niedecker shared something of the biographer's experience in two projects she undertook in the last decade of her life: an edition of letters written to her by Louis Zukofsky, her "friend and mentor,"[2] and three sequence poems, composed in 1969–1970, based on her readings in the lives and letters of William Morris, Thomas Jefferson, and Charles Darwin. While Niedecker presents these men largely through their own words, she is not simply an admiring recorder. Through her selection, arrangement, and creation of materials, she expresses not only her sense of who they were, but also her idea of who she was. Niedecker's portrait poems subvert conventions of traditional biography and embody her idea of the self as fluid, multiplicitous, and constantly evolving.

Lorine Niedecker felt that her identity grew out of her attachment to the place where she lived. She spent her life in the watery country of Blackhawk Island, where the Rock River empties into Lake Koshkonong in southeastern Wisconsin. River and lake, marsh, woods; the weather and seasons, especially during floodtime; the human and non-human creatures who were her neighbors—all are recurring subjects of her poems. Secretive about her writing in her community and relatively isolated from the literary world, still she ranged widely, connecting to other poets and to a large expanse of geography and history through her correspondence, reading, and imagination. Despite isolation, poverty, and neglect, Niedecker was able to persist and develop as an artist because, first, she was deeply rooted where she lived, finding in her daily observations of the natural world and the human community

> . . . a source
> to sustain her—
> a weedy speech,
> a marshy retainer.[3]

Second, she established at the beginning of her career a relationship with Louis Zukofsky that gave her the encouragement and advice of a fellow poet. Third, she made choices at odds with her culture's expectations of her as a woman in order to free herself as a writer. These three sources of strength come together in "I rose from marsh mud," one of Niedecker's most witty and resonant short poems:

> I rose from marsh mud,
> algae, equisetum, willows,
> sweet green, noisy
> birds and frogs
>
> to see her wed in the rich
> rich silence of the church,
> the little white slave-girl
> in her diamond fronds.
>
> In aisle and arch
> the satin secret collects.
> United for life to serve
> silver. Possessed.[4]

This poem evolved through a series of letters Niedecker wrote to Zukofsky in the spring of 1948, describing walks through woods and marshes, bird-watching, and gardening. One marshy spot seems to her "the primordial swamp" and she a creature with "sea-water in [her] veins." Finally, on a postcard, she juxtaposes her adventures in the swamp and her attendance at a church wedding, with ironic reflections prompted by the conjunction. Niedecker's rejection of conventional marriage as a form of enslavement is inspired by her sense of an autonomous self united with a beloved landscape.[5]

By the time Niedecker wrote this poem, she had experienced two unhappy marriages—her own and that of her parents. In 1928 she had married Frank Hartwig, a local man, but left him and moved back to her parents' home in 1930. One reason for their separation was financial—both lost their jobs and, consequently, the house they were buying. Frank Hartwig returned to his family's farm, taking over its management (his father had died in 1929). Perhaps Niedecker refused to join him there because she did not see herself in the role of farm-wife. As a schoolgirl she had defiantly proclaimed herself "a girl/ who couldn't bake."[6] She would not repeat her mother's life as household drudge: "Hatch, patch and scratch,/ that's all a woman's for," she quotes her mother in one poem.[7] Daisy Niedecker was deaf, morose, embittered by Henry's infidelities with a neighbor whose husband encouraged the affair in order to get Henry to sign over property on the Island to his wife.

Because she was poor and her mother was dependent on her, Niedecker lived with her estranged parents, but she established a life of her own through her reading and writing. Her most important literary friendship began when she read the February 1931 issue of *Poetry* magazine featuring the objectivists, for which Zukofsky was visiting editor. It took her six months, she recalled later, to get up enough nerve to write him, initiating a correspondence that lasted until her death in 1970.[8] Looking back in 1966 she said,

> I feel that without [that issue of *Poetry*] I'd never have developed as a poet—I literally went to school to William Carlos Williams and Louis Zukofsky and have had the good fortune to call the latter friend and mentor.[9]

By 1931 Niedecker had determined to live simply so as to conserve her energies for writing. She had published just three poems, but she knew enough about herself as a writer to greet the objectivists' issue of *Poetry* as a dramatic confirmation: "I saw it and knew here was the center of literature in this country and in the world."[10] Her habit of scrupulous attention to the particulars of her immediate environment must have drawn her to Zukofsky's description of the objectivists' art. Precise articulation of details, attention to form, a desire to balance natural speech and song— these are strong impulses in Niedecker's work; she would have recognized them in the poems by Williams, Zukofsky, Oppen, Bunting and Reznikoff, among others Zukofsky included. From her island home in rural Wisconsin, this isolated poet—"on the periphery of the objectivist movement," as she later described herself—found connection to the "center."[11]

At this time, Zukofsky, just six months younger than Niedecker, was far more advanced in his career. Promoted by Pound and Williams, he had the confidence to act as spokesman for the objectivists. In New York, he was close to other artists, to performances and publishers, all of which offered stimulation and contacts lacking in Niedecker's environment.

Given Niedecker's isolation and characteristic modesty, we might expect her to assume the conventional role of the woman pupil in relation to a male mentor: admiring, deferential, eager to serve and anxious about his criticism. The danger for the woman in this role is that she may lose her sense of self, her confidence in her own decisions about the direction her work should take; she may even become an imitator of her mentor's work. While Niedecker admired Zukofsky, learned from his critiques of her manuscripts and depended on his advice about publication, she was not an imitator. As I will show later on, Niedecker found ways to use their friendship to enhance her independent development as a writer.

The relationship between the two poets was complicated after Niedecker and Zukofsky met for the first time in the winter of 1933–1934, when she travelled to New York to see him. Although her only contact with Zukofsky had been through letters, apparently Niedecker arrived intending to stay. Her bold act attests to her passionate desire to find not only a literary, but also an emotional connection to that "center" she had greeted with such joy in the objectivists' issue of *Poetry*. Friends who knew them during that winter in New York recall that Niedecker and Zukofsky lived together for some months in his single room, spending part of each day at work on their writing, he at his desk and she at a kitchen table. With Zukofsky and his friends, Niedecker explored New York's neighborhoods, museums, and libraries. For the first time in her life, she experienced the stimulating companionship of a group of educated, creative, permissive people. Then she became pregnant. No one seems to know how she felt about the pregnancy, except that she wanted to keep the child. Zukofsky's distress was intense—his life at that time precluded such responsibility. Niedecker was willing to remain unmarried and return to her parents to have the child, but Zukofsky persuaded her against this plan and she borrowed money from her father for an abortion. In the end, Niedecker returned to Blackhawk Island because she sensed Zukofsky wished her to leave.[12] Even if she had wanted to stay in New York on her own, jobs were scarce; she had no way to support herself and no family or close friends in the community to supply a home base.

Years later, Niedecker wrote to Zukofsky: "In after years if they ever talk about me and ask 'was she ever in love' they'll have to say, 'yes, she was in love with Zukofsky's words.'"[13] Her playful remark masks the difficult process by which she reconceived the relationship. Niedecker had literally fallen in love with Zukofsky's words—his essays and poems in *Poetry* and his subsequent letters to her. Wanting more than his words, she went to New York, but after living with Zukofsky, she came to realize that only through words—an exchange of letters and manuscripts—was a union possible.

I believe it is wrong to interpret Niedecker's role in the story I have just recounted as that of a "rejected woman." After she left her husband, Niedecker sought an alternative to marriage, not a substitute male to help her fulfill that scenario. Her primary devotion was not to a man, but to her writing, and Zukofsky helped confirm her in this vocation. She took the initiative in making contact with him and continued through the rest of her life to cultivate this connection—at a distance. Her correspondence with Zukofsky played an important part in her composing of an alternative life-script, and when she undertook in 1965 to prepare an edition of his letters to her, she was gratifying herself as much as she was honoring him.

Niedecker's relationships with living men, in particular with Zukofsky, help us understand the literary relationships she established with men who are dead and famous. The friendship between Niedecker and Zukofsky, and the extent to which they influenced each other's writing, offer challenging subjects for lengthy study. I will touch briefly on the issue of Niedecker's dependence on Zukofsky as preliminary to my analysis of how the relationship bears upon her later experiments in biographical portraiture.

During the first fifteen years of their friendship, Niedecker and Zukofsky corresponded "at least once a week," exchanging manuscripts and personal news.[14] In the early letters, Zukofsky offers some instruction concerning the handling of rhythm and lineation; he suggests readings for Niedecker, introduces her to editors and publishers. As she gains confidence in her powers, Niedecker rejects Zukofsky's suggested revisions and critiques his manuscripts. Both poets found the correspondence stimulated creativity, and they quote from each other's letters in their poems. One of Niedecker's major works in the early 1950s is a collection titled "For Paul," based in part on Zukofsky's letters about his son's childhood.

Other evidence shows Niedecker playing the conventional role of protégé. She aided Zukofsky by typing some of his manuscripts and by publishing a review of *A Test of Poetry* (1948) and an essay, "The Poetry of Louis Zukofsky" (1956), to help him gain wider recognition.[15] In 1956 she deferred to him by withdrawing her manuscript from Jonathan Williams, telling Williams that he should get Zukofsky's manuscript printed first.[16] When Zukofsky refused in 1966 to write either introduction or blurb for *T&G*, her first major collection, she was hurt, but eschewed pressure and complaint.[17] Despite such disappointments, her attitude remained grateful and admiring, even "adoring," or so it seemed to Carl Rakosi when he met Niedecker for the first time in 1969. Rakosi recalls the following exchange, which took place soon after his arrival at Niedecker's home. As if she were anxious to establish essential verities from the beginning, she asked: "Don't you think Louis is the greatest poet writing today?"—to which the startled Rakosi replied, "Why, no." When Rakosi asked her, "What does Louis say about your poems?" she replied, "Oh, he says the cruelest things, tears them to pieces," and yet she continued to "adore" him.[18]

Despite such indications of emotional dependence, in her literary career Niedecker proved her independence. She survived a potentially harmful association with a powerful male mentor by paying close attention to her own voice and surroundings as materials for her poetry and by finding ways to use her friendship with Zukofsky for her own creative purposes.

In 1965, Niedecker undertook an edition of Zukofsky's letters to her—by then, more than thirty years' worth. Her intention, she told Cid Corman, was to present "just the essences, tincture of Z!, a drop to a page, that constant, deep-in spot in his being."[19] She cut up his letters and arranged the fragments without annotations, trusting that what would emerge would not be a jumble, because all came from a self she felt she understood intimately. When she came, in 1969–1970, to write the poems about Morris, Jefferson, and Darwin, she drew on this experience of selecting and arranging fragments of a life to generate a dynamic portrait.

Zukofsky gave Niedecker permission to edit his letters to her, but when she sent the 370-page manuscript to him for approval, he refused to let her seek a publisher and demanded the carbon copy.[20] Niedecker never fully understood Zukofsky's refusal. Sharing his desire for privacy, she argued (to Corman, not to Zukofsky) that her edition was not biography, but "chunks of beautiful literature, something he wrote not just for me but the world. And while we live."[21] But her own descriptions of the project reveal a conflicting motive. If her selection presents "the essences, tincture of Z," then Niedecker *is* making a biographer's claim: her choice and arrangement of the fragments of letters written to her constitute an insider's portrait of the poet and man. Admiration fuels her project, but so does a desire to appropriate; Niedecker asserts her possession of the essential "Z."

Niedecker's last poems, the three sequences based on her readings in the lives and letters of Morris, Jefferson, and Darwin, resemble her edition of Zukofsky's letters in that each is a portrait composed as a collage of quotations and references with no overt explanations linking the selections. Although the poet's choice and arrangement of her materials does, of course, constitute interpretation, Niedecker's aim is not primarily to shed "new light" on a famous man. One clue to her motives is her remark in a letter written while she was working on her Morris poem: "How I love the letters of big people," she exclaimed.[22] At first glance, the remark may seem self-deprecating. Are we to see Niedecker's last poems as hymns of praise to famous men? Did she submerge her creativity in making arrangements of quotations from their writings?

When she completed her "Thomas Jefferson" sequence, Niedecker wrote to a friend:

> My Thomas Jefferson written and sent out. Up very early mornings—nearly killed myself—and all that reading beforehand (until I realized what am I doing?—writing a biography or history?? no, all I could do is fill the subconscious and let it lie and fish up later).[23]

Not biography, not history, but food for the unconscious. During the composition of "Darwin," Niedecker wrote to another friend:

> After the heat subsides I'll let you know the day I make noodles so if you wish, come up and observe the masterchef as she putters.

> At the moment this noodle drops a few lines of Darwin's *Formation of Vegetable Mould, through the Action of Worms, with Observations of Their Habits* into the soup-conscious.[24]

Clearly, Niedecker saw her reading and note-taking as part of the creative process. Presumably mingling in the kettle with bits of Darwin's writing and events from his life were Niedecker's own experiences and memories. Even in these poems which seem largely about the lives of others, Niedecker was expressing her personality and preoccupations.

One reason she was attracted to these particular men is that they were experimenters, like herself, subverters of fixed ideas and repressive systems. Morris worked as a socialist to restore an

ideal of craftsmanship to industrial Victorian England; Jefferson
helped overthrow a monarchy; Darwin's discoveries challenged the
Biblical version of creation and the supremacy of humans over
other creatures. Niedecker's work is a series of experiments with
language and form that place her, as she expressed it, "with the
persons/ on the edge."[25]

Another attraction of these men was that each left a considerable body of informal writing. One reason Niedecker loved the letters of "big people," as well as their diaries and journals, was that
letters often reveal the freshness and confusion of thoughts-
in-process, quirky and spontaneous. Moreover, letters convey the
drama of relationship—the person is "'talking to someone, not just
talking.'"[26] Niedecker's aim as a poet was always to catch the voice
of the individual creature, whether sora-rail or Founding Father.
"I'm a different character in a different drama with almost every
poem I write," she said.[27]

While Niedecker genuinely admires Morris, Jefferson, and
Darwin, she is not intimidated by their stature. She is an active,
not a passive reader of their texts, selecting, arranging, and con-
densing. In her poems, Niedecker's verbal and formal strategies
subvert the conventions and assumptions of the "great man" portrait. Drawing on the private writings of these men, she catches
them out of the formal dress of public discourse, exposing their
doubts, unhappiness, yearnings, and affections. She takes liberties
with them—cuts up their writings into fragments and condenses
their long and well-documented lives into short lines. She even
goes so far as to alter their words in quotations without indicating
that she has done so. If we think about the conventional treat-
ments of the lives of great men, the chronological accounts of their
progress, the judicious weighing of achievements and failures, the
exhaustive documentation, the striving to be "definitive," we see
that Niedecker's idea of a portrait is radically different. She ig-
nores chronology and levels hierarchies, giving prominence to details often slighted by biographers. Because she does not link her
references and quotations with explanations or overt interpretations, she leaves open many possibilities of connection, creating
space for the reader to act imaginatively on the fragments. Her
treatment undercuts the notion of the unitary self, implying instead that identity is multiple and fluid.

Obviously, Niedecker's poems about famous men are not "biographies." However, the comparison is useful in speculating about
her motives for undertaking these projects. Like the biographer,

Niedecker avidly reads and researches; her aim is to incorporate the material residue of another's life. Like the biographer, she inscribes herself in the portrait she creates through her selection and arrangement of biographical materials. Niedecker's experiments may have been motivated by her desire to master through writing her connection to men she admired, to carve out a place for herself and assert her right to authorship in the patriarchal culture they represented.

A look at the first three stanzas of "Darwin" will show how her selection and arrangement of fragments generates a dynamic portrait.

> His holy
> > slowly
> > > mulled over
> > matter
>
> not all 'delirium
> > of delight'
> > > as were the forests
> > of Brazil
>
> 'Species are not
> > (it is like confessing
> > > a murder)
> > immutable'[28]

Stanza one is entirely Niedecker's creation. Boldly naming Darwin's "matter" "holy," she cuts through the conflict Darwin was never able to resolve for himself between the claims of physical science and religious dogma. "Mulled over/matter" also links the physical and ideal, comparing the action of pulverizing, or grinding down, as of rocks, to the patient, painstaking thought processes of the scientist. "Mulled" also suggests an action of being steeped, or long immersed, whether of spices in wine or facts in the mind. Niedecker's description of Darwin's thinking resembles her own creative processes. Her long poems and sequences evolved from copious research and note-taking, followed by exacting reduction of these materials to extract "essences."

In the second and third stanzas, Niedecker dramatically juxtaposes quotations from letters written twelve years apart. She selects the phrase "delirium of delight" from a three-page outpouring of the young Darwin's raptures over the lush tropical forests he saw for the first time in 1832, early in the voyage of *The Beagle*.[29] In sharp contrast, Niedecker records in stanza three Darwin's reluctant acknowledgement of the conclusions he had resisted as a young man. "At last gleams of light have come," he wrote in 1844, "and I am almost convinced (quite contrary to the opinion I started with) that species are not (it is like confessing a murder) immutable."[30] Niedecker's dramatic powers and her ear for memorable and revealing speech are evident. Intense emotions spark off each other—"delirium of delight" and the guilt of the self-appointed murderer. In Section III of her poem, Niedecker portrays yet another patriarch unsettled by Darwin's discoveries, Fitzroy, the Captain of *The Beagle,* whose dogmatic adherence to the Biblical account of creation in arguments with the young scientist probably aided Darwin's formulation of his revolutionary theories.

In the last stanzas of this five-part poem, Niedecker finishes with a quotation from a letter in which Darwin attempted to clarify his ideas about religion.[31] Darwin undermined authority, spent "Years . . . balancing/ probabilities," only to end in uncertainty.

> Darwin
>
> sailed out
>   of Good Success Bay
>   to carcass-
> conclusions
>
> the universe
>   not built by brute force
>   but designed by laws
> The details left
>
> to the working of chance
>   'Let each man hope
>   and believe
> what he can'[32]

Distilling "essences" from Darwin's life and writings, Niedecker arranged them to express her belief in individuals who, like the universe, are open-ended and constantly evolving.

Through her portrait poems, Niedecker reminds us that a self, finally, is a mystery. A sobering thought for a biographer. We can know this or that about a person's life, but what do we really know

with certainty? Niedecker's brief portrait of Mary Shelley is a
haunting reminder that what we think we know about the biographical subject, even one of our own gender and vocation, is often little more than conjecture.

> Who was Mary Shelley?
> What was her name
> before she married?
>
> She eloped with this Shelley
> she rode a donkey
> till the donkey had to be carried.
>
> Mary was Frankenstein's creator
> his yellow eye
> before her husband was to drown
>
> Created the monster nights
> after Byron, Shelley
> talked the candle down.
>
> Who was Mary Shelley?
> She read Greek, Italian
> She bore a child
>
> Who died
> and yet another child
> who died[33]

Niedecker's poem may be read as a paradigm of the biographer's dilemma; her opening question speaks to the general difficulties of understanding another's life. The second, more specific,
is obviously ironic; Niedecker knew who Mary Shelley's famous
parents were. But raising the question of name points to the fact
that in marriage, Mary's husband's name erased hers. In the next
stanza, Niedecker's offhand reference to "this Shelley" (juxtaposed
against the donkey anecdote) seems slyly dismissive of that famous husband, whose reputation eclipsed his wife's. Perhaps these
stanzas derive from Niedecker's awareness of a parallel to her own
relationship with Zukofsky, the writer whose reputation out-
stripped hers. But the real emotional center of the poem is the
following evocation of Mary the woman writer, alone and inspired,
working through the night while the men talk in another room.
Drawing on Mary Shelley's own dramatic account of the circumstances in which she began to compose her novel, Niedecker an-

swers the question, "Who was Mary Shelley?" by identifying her as "Mary . . . Frankenstein's creator." The last two stanzas suggest that Mary Shelley's lasting achievements were creative, rather than procreative . . . as in Niedecker's own case.

Although the poem begins and ends with losses and reminders that we can recover little of another's life, its dominant tone is positive. Despite her personal losses, Mary Shelley persisted and triumphed; her "hideous progeny"[34] outlived her babies and continues to compel readers' imaginations. Niedecker's portrait of Mary Shelley compels the imagination because it derives from an affinity between the two women. How could she know this other? Because she knew who she was, she could touch the elusive one and appropriate, for artistic usage, the other's essence.

Chapter Eleven

Postmodernism and the Biographer

 *Diane Wood Middlebrook*

"Postmodern" is a term that was routinely applied in the 1980s to all manner of contemporary arts. Eclectic architecture, minimalist fiction, computer-generated music, deconstructive criticism, video installations: these might be on anyone's general list of "Postmodern Art." Strictly speaking, "postmodern" is a Western concept referring to an era in culture: American and European culture after World War II. But in usage it has become a handy label for whatever disturbs our expectations by disrupting and recombining traditional elements, achieving effects of discontinuity.

Biography, with its time-honored goals of setting out descriptions and interpretations of individual lives, would seem to be a bastion of humanism safe from encroachment by the spirit of postmodernism. Yet a number of recent biographies indicate that cultural critiques developed under postmodernism have trickled into the way biographers too must now conceive the modes of representation conventional to their genre. These critiques condense to three fundamental questions. The first: what is an Author? The second: what is a Reader? The third: what is a Subject?

I stumbled into these questions and problems in the course of a several-year metamorphosis from English professor into biographer of the American poet Anne Sexton (1928–1974). One day late in September 1980, I went to the office of a literary agent in New York. I had come to sign a contract that had been discussed for two months by the lawyers of all concerned. The other party in the contract was the Executor of the Estate of Anne Sexton. Sexton's papers had just been sold to The Harry Ransom Humanities Research Center at the University of Texas, Austin. The issues under deliberation were movie rights, period of exclusivity of access to unpublished material, relationship of the subject's family to the finished manuscript, and other details pertaining to ownership.

The family's authority had been vested in the literary agent, and when I had signed the contract I thought I would ask a question that had been on my mind for some time: "Do you think *I* need an agent?" The agent was amused. "Well, no. What you have signed is a good contract, for an English professor. But when you have finished the book, you will be a biographer. Then you will need an agent."

What is an author? From the contractual point of view, authorship can be seen as less an activity than a social position, established only after a work is complete. Writing the biography, you are an English professor—or, maybe, a housewife, a journalist, a surviving spouse. An author is the "person" deduced from the point of view in the text, created by the process of writing and publishing the book.

To whom are the author's words supposedly addressed? The biographer as biographer has many rationales for what "he" is doing, but in the background of every book is a contract which places it in the medium of the marketplace. For the "professor," that marketplace is both financial and intellectual. In addition to royalties paid for sales of the book, a traditional value is assigned biography, to which the professor by definition more or less subscribes. That is the belief that reading biography improves and civilizes people. Thus, the author of a biography is supposed to be that improving and civilizing point of view, the voice that points out the exemplary character of the subject's actions and thoughts and productions. The reader is theorized as a receptive, judicious, well-trained human being capable of tracking the hermeneutic horizon of an argument and profiting morally from doing so.

The climate of postmodernism, though, is skeptical about how far any point of view—either that of author or reader—can be generalized. For example, it obviously generalizes a point of view to call all authors and readers "he." It is an acceptable convention, to conservatives: conveying the assumption that decisionmaking, judiciousness, gatekeeping are still regarded as culturally "masculine" operations, no matter who performs them.

Now, neither author nor subject in a biography is uninfluenced by points of view that structure the cultures that fostered them. Of great significance are ideas about gender difference so fundamental in any culture that they seem natural. What makes a man "manly," a woman "womanly"? How does a man become what Emerson could comfortably call a "Representative Man," and what happens to the category if it is filled by a female?

In the past ten years most of us have grown accustomed to acknowledging the illegitimacy of Emerson's easy elision of the Human into Man. We "solve" the problem by reminding ourselves and others to say "he or she."

Yet a same-but-different problem arises from saying "he or she." This locution conveys two assumptions. One is that biological sex is the ground of a specific, generalizable social identity: Woman. The other is that it is socially valuable to keep that difference before us as Difference. Women gain social recognition in the conventions of usage only to have their presence reinforced there in an "or." In English, there is no genderless pronoun for the singular third person, so gendered is our consciousness of others; and postmodern feminism has put that issue on the intellectual agenda in a way that affects the writing of biography. The very idea of the author as a "universal" point of view generalized as "he," "Man," "Woman," "the human," along with the very idea of a disinterested, ideology-free system of production generalized as "the humanities"—these are the very ideas that postmodernism has, to use a postmodern term for the process—"called into question." And no biographer, no English professor, can work today without sharing the anxiety of having the enterprise itself interrogated by such central questions as What *is* an author? And who is assumed to be *the* reader of the book underway? And what difference does gender difference make in her/his point of view on the (gendered) subject of the biography?

The archive of Anne Sexton is peculiarly fraught with objects and issues that raise all of these questions. I want to mention only a few instances, before I go on to discuss briefly some examples of recent biographies that seem to offer cunning strategies of response to the intellectual climate of postmodernism.

Let me introduce Anne Sexton in two lattices of facts.

The first positions her in a domestic, or so-called "private" world. Anne Gray Harvey Sexton was born in 1928 in Newton, Massachusetts, and lived her whole life in the suburbs of Boston. Her father owned a wool factory and was its principal salesman. The first world war made him rich; the second world war made him very rich, selling blanket and uniform cloth to the U.S. Army.

Sexton eloped at age nineteen, and had two daughters. Her husband worked for her father, as a wool salesman. After the birth of her second child she had a nervous breakdown and attempted suicide.

She was treated in psychotherapy for eighteen years, and was hospitalized twenty-two times. At age forty-five she committed suicide by carbon monoxide poisoning.

That can be called a sketch of the Sextons' private life. Let me now briefly characterize her career, or public life.

Sexton began writing poetry in psychotherapy after her first suicide attempt. She published her first book of poems, titled *To Bedlam and Part Way Back,* only three and a half years later.

In her eighteen-year career, she published eight books of poetry and wrote a play that was produced off Broadway at the American Place Theatre.

Though she never went to college, she was awarded three honorary doctorates for her poetry, and at the time of her death was full professor of creative writing at Boston University. During her brief lifetime she received most of the honors available to American poets—to name only a few, a Guggenheim Foundation grant, a Ford Foundation grant, a Pulitzer Prize.

Those are the facts of Sexton's life, the chronological outline that must or might underlie any biography. It is probably clear from these details that Sexton's history embraces many of the themes and issues central to the era of postmodernism: growing up affluent in the suburbs, in the consumer culture of the 1950s; rising to prominence in a field charged with gender politics; doubly marginalized by her situation as a woman and as a person disabled by mental illness. Yet as a poet Sexton's relationship to all these issues was fundamentally creative. She cannot be reduced to a historical or psychological "case," or statistic, for she was an author herself, and her poetry reflects an acute critical intelligence—a fully *postmodern* intelligence—about living in her female body, in her profession, in her world. Moreover, the world she lived in is pretty much *this* world, not distanced by much time and change.

However, Anne Sexton the person exists no more. Now she exists as an enormous, boundless archive, some of which is housed in the memory of her friends and enemies, but most of which is located at the Humanities Research Center at the University of Texas at Austin, where she never set foot. This archive includes— in addition to a staggering quantity of paper—a film, sixty or so audiotape recordings of interviews and readings, four reel-to-reel tapes of sessions with her psychiatrist, hundreds of newspaper clippings, her typewriter, spectacles, and three teenage scrapbooks full of swizzle sticks from Manhattan nightclubs and rotting, worm-infested corsages.

Postmodern culture is fiendishly self-documenting, as the sheer amount of detritus in this archive suggests. Yet the documentation of Sexton's life is woefully incomplete—there is no way to retrieve her innumerable phone calls. Biographers have always been dependent on the written records they could retrieve; the development of electronic technologies in postmodern culture challenges the priority of written language. Moreover, the consumer culture treats artistic personalities as commodities. During their lives now most major poets are filmed, videotaped, broadcast on radio, interviewed on talk shows, taped live at readings. This adds not only another source of material to be interpreted but another form of authorship to be decoded. When a poet is the guest star on a talk show, is a poet talking or a star?

Further, the very genre of biography requires that there be a person, a consistently represented self at the center of the book. Yet as the discipline of semiotics so compellingly demonstrates, language is fundamentally non-representational: the materials of a biography are not life, but documents, and all documents refer within systems of language, within different discourses. (Is a poet talking, or a star?) And documents exist in the realm of public life, the realm of the political. This is true of even the most intimate love letters, and notes made in private journals. Thanks largely to the influential thinking of feminists, these days it is a tenet of current criticism that the personal *is* political; and contemporary theories of discourse from Barthes to Bakhtin begin with the same premises about how language itself works to shape the ways it is possible to express anything at all about oneself or others.

But in any case, the biography never has functioned simply as an arrangement of facts; it is a narrative, with a point of view. No matter how subtly the biographer inserts herself into the text, she will have to be there behind the scenes, managing the chronology, not just documenting it. When a person has as fundamentally sensational or soap-operatic a life as Anne Sexton, the biographer who wishes not to foreground the sensational will have to find strategies of decompression. Otherwise the story will be orchestrated by twenty-two hospitalizations for mental illness, and will have to culminate in suicide. But in what conceptual space may Anne Sexton's biographer stand to avoid shaping a biography along the chronology of her life? What is a subject?

Further, Sexton during her lifetime suffered a number of kinds of sexual and physical traumas that have since her death undergone highly politicized analysis. Incest, child abuse, the sexual exploitation of female patients by psychiatrists—all these are current topics in many arenas of public discourse, from the sensationalist press to electoral politics to women's studies. What controlling authorial point of view can absorb this kind of material? Where does the author situate herself to interpret a life that has so many weighted dimensions? How is the author going to express authority?

Many questions of this kind form the unfinished business of my own current writing. However, to pursue their implications, I want to look briefly at a few recent biographies in which issues of authorial voice seem to have been handled in a variety of ways, from the traditional to the self-conscious. I will limit myself to opening sentences from the first paragraph of each book, to illustrate how rapidly the author of a biography takes center stage in the form of a man or a woman, and a controlling point of view.

My first example comes from a book published in 1982, written by an Englishman. It is stylistically the most traditional of the three books. The author is Ian Hamilton; the subject is Robert Lowell. Hamilton begins with a quotation from Lowell's autobiography.[1]

> Like Henry Adams, I was born under the shadow of the Dome of the Boston State House, and under Pisces, the Fish, on the first of March, 1917. America was entering the First World War and was about to play her part in the downfall of five empires.

> The setting for this ominous nativity was a brownstone high on Boston's Beacon Hill, the town house of Arthur Winslow, Robert Lowell's maternal grandfather. The house was fronted by two pillars copied from the Temple of Kings at Memphis, and every afternoon Grandfather Winslow, "a stiff-necked, luxurious ramrod of a man," would station himself between these "loutish" props and survey his social gains. On the afternoon of March 1, 1917, he was probably well pleased. This new child—first son of the union between two celebrated Boston names—would surely prove another asset. Certainly, it was hard to see how such a flawless pedigree could engender positive embarrassment.

Many biographies begin with the birth of the subject. Hamilton's biography of Lowell begins with the subject's account of his birth. An aperture is thus immediately opened in the text, between fact and interpretation; it is an aperture elbowed wider by an ironic and well-placed adjective: "this *ominous* nativity . . . " It is a light touch, picking up on Lowell's metaphors, but it indicates that Hamilton is not going to take Lowell at his word; Hamilton is going to make Lowell accountable for his own grandiose view of himself. At least, that is what seems to me the consistent accomplishment of Hamilton's biography. "It was hard to see," this paragraph concludes, "how such a flawless pedigree could engender positive embarrassment." Hamilton sets up the grandfather at once as one of the many elders, the respectable family members that Robert Lowell will begin to embarrass prodigiously as soon as he is able. But Hamilton does more, as well. One of the themes of Hamilton's book will be how many ways the notion of the "flawless pedigree" influenced Lowell's own sense of himself, and how hard it was for Lowell to see the ways in which he engendered harm. Beset by a chronic mental illness, Lowell every year or so took manic flight into gibbering conviction that he was a superman on the scale of Hitler, Achilles, Caligula, Christ. Even when sane, Lowell was enormously a snob. Yet his own terrific achievement as perhaps the foremost poet of his time, certainly the foremost poet of Boston, did indeed add new luster to the venerable family name.

Hamilton's play with the conventions of biography, his appropriation of Lowell's metaphors, the flickering consciousness of double meanings that announce themselves in Hamilton's prose—none of this is performed in a spirit of condescension. Hamilton knows his subject well, and writes with engaged fascination, even affection, certainly respect. Nonetheless, from that first page on we are reminded of how completely language *constructs* its subject. Behind Hamilton's choice of an opening to the book lies the old question "What's in a name?" He deftly reveals to us how much of Lowell's sense of himself had to do with being "a Lowell": the shadow of the Dome of the Boston State House! and the fall of five empires? Just by quoting them Hamilton picks up the images and sets them along a bias where the anxious subtext of such masculine self-affirmation begins to glow into relevance. The book is begun in a graceful verbal gesture that decenters the subject even as it erects him for examination. It represents, I think, a man looking at a man.

My second example represents the opposite extreme of Hamilton's urbane authorial voice, for it comes from a biography with no authorial voice in it at all. The book is Peter Manso's *Mailer: His Life and Times.*[2] It begins, paradoxically, in a woman's voice:

FANNY SCHNEIDER MAILER The family? My father—Norman's grandfather—was a rabbi, and the family ran a grocery store in Long Branch, New Jersey. My father couldn't speak English very well, and once, when we were given a summons for keeping the store open on Sunday, I went in his place to court, shaking in my boots. I was sixteen. I had to come up on the stand and explain it wasn't a "subterfuge." The man who was questioning thought I wouldn't understand, but I did, and I told him we had a separate meat department that was closed completely on Saturdays, and that we were open on Sundays but just in the morning, and even so, with the shades drawn. I told him that we were religious and that our clientele had to be served. I said we were most certainly not in "flagrant disregard" of the law. My father wasn't there, my mother wasn't there, it was just me, the champion, to represent my family. I had a lot of spunk, I guess, and they let us stay open.

Manso preserves the convention of opening the biography with an account of the family, but not the convention of performing as an omniscient point of view. *Mailer: His Life and Times* is composed exclusively of excerpts from taped interviews; until the page of acknowledgments—which is conspicuously placed at the end of the biography—the author never says a word in this book. Yet how complete a *character* Fanny Mailer emerges in these first few sentences. Can she really have positioned herself so aptly in the stylistic gene-pool of Mailer's prose? By mid-paragraph, at age sixteen, she had seized authority like Mailer's "White Negro" from "the man who was questioning [and] thought I wouldn't understand; but I did." By the end of the paragraph she has arrived at a self-definition that owes much to Mailer's well-publicized pugilism: "it was just me, the champion . . . I had a lot of spunk, I guess." It is as if the son's distinctive prose has provided the terms on which his origins must be articulated; Mailer himself has given birth to the mother who speaks in these pages. And for my ear, at least, that little tag "I guess" feminizes the rhetoric, giving it the voice of a Mom. Yet the author of this page is certainly not Fanny Mailer. It is the selective editorial ear of her transcriber, present everywhere in the book as a sly, manipulating Absence.

My final example comes from an author who enters the biography in the first person in the first sentence.[3]

JOSEPHINE HERBST was dead four years before I heard of her, a handful of ash in an Iowa cemetery, her grave not yet marked. Her exit *was noted by The New York Times* and *The New York Review of Books,* which is more than you could say about her existence much of the time, but blaming the reviewers would be too simple, for if she was not among the saved in the literary sense, she was in the personal, and there they were by her bedside, the cast of characters of several disastrous decades, distinguished critics of culture and art, writers great and small, radicals and former radicals of every degree of hope and despair, as awed by the spirit of her dying as they had been by the spirit of her life. Toward the end she wasn't writing very much. She kept her memoirs with her at all times, and even as late as the last few days she liked to think she would finish them at last, but by then it was as much the memories for their own sakes as it was the achievement she was after, and there were readier avenues to memory than the exhausting struggle with art. Her past drifted across her consciousness and occasionally across her lips. She had spent the last few weeks even physically surrounded by the past, preparing her personal papers for the university archives that now seemed her likeliest guarantor of posterity and settling a number of old scores via marginal comment as she did so. Every now and then an opinion or two escaped her. Frightened as she was by the ordeal of her body, from the outside she looked almost as impressive as ever. Propped up in bed, hair combed by a friend, a nineteenth-century novel resting heavily on her frail chest, she dictated a letter to a distant relation who had sent his final greetings to the hospital. "I cannot pretend any of this is easy, nor that I know the outcome," she began, in the tone of apparent confession she had brought to perfection in her later writings, but the outcome was as certain as nature. It was 1969, she was seventy-seven years old, and she had seen very many people die before her. I was much younger than that, I had seen very little, and I knew nothing whatever about it at the time.

Josephine Herbst, by Elinor Langer, is a most artful work. The first paragraph rewinds a reel of images back across the boundary of the grave to a dramatic moment in the subject's life: a deathbed scene, Last Words (actually if you fast-forward to the end of the book you see that these are penultimate words: the actual last words come in a brilliant re-run of this scene in Chapter 30). The rush of syntax along with the emphatic multiplicity of detail signals an intention to capture the spirit as well as the data of this life: in this book, we are going to get the real thing.

And yet this scene is not the work of an eyewitness. "Dead four years before I heard of her ... her grave not yet marked ... I was much younger ... I had seen very little ... I knew nothing whatever about it at the time." The first and last sentences of the

paragraph enclose the subject, a handful of ash, in the subjectivity
of another human being. At the outset of the biography's time/
space, neither one of them exists: one is dead, the other unborn as
author. A profound sense of personal, womanly destiny enlivens
this wonderful book. The encounter with the remains of Josephine
Herbst becomes for Langer a quest for intellectual, political, and
emotional maturity, a quest that takes some completely unpredict-
able turns reflected in Langer's style, which from a baseline trans-
parency becomes by turns meditative, catechistical, badgering,
comic. Few contemporary biographies take such enormous risks,
for the "I" is constantly calling herself into question, expressing
doubts about her own powers of objectivity as she uncovers data
that baffle, embarrass, and enrage. At the heart of the work is
Elinor Langer's desire for a heroine, a role model; and she reveals
to us how often she is disappointed. And yet, despite the personal
inflections, Langer's effect is finally one of enormous control. The
authorial presence in *Josephine Herbst* is on close analysis a flex-
ible position from which to coax us into interest in the subject's
long life, with its repetitious jealousies and the long boring
stretches of silence while Herbst is at her desk day and night, at
work.

What all three of these biographies have in common is the
postmodern era of their composition, when the author cannot assume that "he" speaks from a secure center of culture, from the
apex of the intellectual pyramid that provides the most trustworthy view of reality. The name of that pyramid used to be "tradition;" it used to be captured in a metaphor as a shelf of "great
works." A humanist entered history by absorbing these works and
recreating their wisdom for "his" age; in the process he was, as
T. S. Eliot put it, purged of "personality."

The era of postmodern society—"information society"—has revealed the unplanned obsolescence of this metaphor of the five-foot
shelf of books and a universal mind. Sophisticated retrieval systems now make possible, for the biographer along with everyone
else, a preposterously wide range of sources, and extravagant
means of searching them. Documentation must now be understood
to include not only all types of print but all types of electronic me-
dia, including holographic computer-generated models of totalities
that flow from only a few statistics.

In this upheaval the biographies I have glanced at here stand
as models of de-centered subjectivity. All are marked by what I
have labelled the postmodern anxiety about authorship: aware-

ness that both author and subject in a biography are hostages to the universes of discourse that inhabit them. Among the most important of such universes are the distinctions separating "masculine" from "feminine." Gender relations are embedded at the very root of the subject–object split that postmodernism has foregrounded as its special territory. What meanings in these terms most influence the thinking of the author approaching her or his subject? What ideas about gender most influenced the sense of selfhood exhibited by the subject? The postmodern era has produced rich sources of criticism on the salience of gendered relations in understanding human lives. The question of gender, once opened, cannot be closed; it can only be pursued.

Chapter Twelve

The Mother Tongue of Paul Celan: Translation into Biography

John Felstiner

I

Start with the mother tongue (as we all do anyway)—*Muttersprache* in German, *mameloshn* in Yiddish—start with the "mother tongue," and you can see a tense interplay within the East European poet, Paul Celan: between his mother, murdered in a Nazi labor camp when he was scarcely 22, and his native tongue, turned murderers' tongue as well. "Within reach, close and not lost," Celan told a German audience some years after the war, trying to say what had survived the European Jewish catastrophe— "Within reach, close and not lost, there remained in the midst of the losses this one thing: language," *dies eine: die Sprache.*[1] And then he says it to them again, focusing in on language, *die Sprache,* almost as if that word's gender identified it with his mother: *Sie, die Sprache,* he says, doubling the feminine pronoun and article *sie* and *die—Sie, die Sprache, blieb unverloren, ja, trotz allem,* "She"—I want to say, "the language, was not lost but remained, yes, in spite of everything."

Celan's youthful, traumatic sunderance from his mother, along with his drastic hold on the mother tongue, seem to bear out a theory of loss and language. Certainly his poems, even where his mother does not epitomize the Jewish dead, seek in varying ways a kind of primal at-oneness—with a place, a time, a people—that symbolic language inevitably misspeaks, misnames. And then two things complicate Celan's case. First, he lost his mother not in the natural course of things but by violent rupture. Second, his German language inhabited not the symbolic world of the father, whom Nazis also murdered, but the world of the murderers themselves. How then could Celan dwell within the mother tongue, his

167

only medium of return and restitution, when it had muted his mother's tongue?

Language and loss: a word, especially within the charged field of lyric speech, abruptly displaces and replaces what it points to, at once revealing and redeeming an absence, standing yet covering for something lost. As the poet Robert Hass puts it, "A word is elegy to what it signifies."[2] When what is lost, what the word replaces, is not just the immediate presence and actuality of things, but the person herself at whose lips a poet first got his words, then that abstract dialectic between language and loss becomes grounded in the pathos of a child's thwarted return to the mother, an exile's endlessly voided nostalgia—what Celan once called "the No of my longing."[3] And when the poet is a Jew and the language in question is mid-twentieth-century German, whose users could fashion the term *judenrein* ("Jew-free, pure of Jews"), then that radically abused language, as George Steiner has claimed, may no longer serve as it served Goethe, Hölderlin, Rilke, to convey a sacred or supernatural or even secular wholeness.[4]

Now the translator of a writer such as Paul Celan engages with these complex workings of language and loss in an especially revealing way. For translation, particularly verse translation, can be seen as the specific art of loss. "Poetry," Robert Frost reportedly said, "is what gets lost in translation," and Celan might have agreed, though his own often-brilliant renderings of Shakespeare, Emily Dickinson, Osip Mandelstam, and others argue against Frost's absolute dictum. At the same time, Celan's famous image (adapted from Mandelstam) of a poem as "a message in a bottle, cast out in the (not always greatly hopeful) belief that it may somewhere and sometime wash up on land, on heartland perhaps"—this image suggests that the translator of such a poet may be effecting a kind of rescue or restitution.[5]

What complicates Celan's case is his being stranded, as orphan and exile—his being thrown solely upon the resources of a mother tongue that had passed, he said, "through the thousand darknesses of deathbringing speech."[6] To translate Celan's German into English would seem to displace the orphan and exile yet again from his mother and native tongue. Still I do sense, in translating him, a responsive and partly restitutive potential. For one thing, my father was born in a city not far from Celan's homeland, and heard German before he heard English. Engaging with "his" language reknits my own affiliation. And in another dimension, as a translator I remain acutely mindful that Paul Celan, who never healed from the catastrophe my family was spared, took his own life at the age of 49, in 1970. Cutting off his voice that way, he leaves his translator obligated to find a complementary voice, in a sense a continuing voice. And because Celan with an extraordinary insistence found his reality in the language of poems, translating them can turn into an unusual sort of biographical (and autobiographical) practice. Not only should the act of translation emerge from biographical and historical grounding; the art of it also gives voice to someone, discovers a self.

Celan's complex, tragic relation to the German mother tongue gives his personal loss (and thus the loss entailed by translation) an extra turn of the screw. For him, the elegiac or redemptive virtue of lyric speech risks vitiating itself in the very act of utterance.

> Whichever word you speak—
> you owe
> to destruction,

Celan wrote.[7] And in another poem he wrote this:

> To a mouth
> it was a thousandword for—
> lost,
> I lost a word that was left me:
> sister.
>
> To
> polygoddedness
> I lost a word that sought me:
> *Kaddish.*[8]

"Thousandword," like "polygoddedness," may allude to the so-called Thousand-Year Reich. As an only child, Celan missed a sister and may have sought her in the mother he also missed, or in a beloved. His late poem *Mandelnde,* "Almonding Woman," addressed to a Jewish friend, ends with the Hebrew word *Hachnissini* ("Bring me in"), which is also the first word of a 1905 lyric by Bialik: "Bring me in under your wing, / and be mother and sister to me."[9] And *Kaddish* is the Jewish prayer for the dead, often spoken for one's parents. So these stanzas, more explicitly than most, bind loss and language into each other.

Or take this lyric, worth quoting in full for its purposefulness
and for an accident in translation that points up that purpose:

The Travel Companion

Your mother's soul hovers ahead.
Your mother's soul helps sail around night, reef upon reef.
Your mother's soul lashes the sharks on before you.

This word is your mother's ward.
Your mother's ward shares your couch, stone upon stone.
Your mother's ward stoops for the crumb of light.[10]

In the German, rhythm and alliteration link *Mutter* to *Mündel*,
"mother" to "ward": the mother remains, even after her death, a
protective guardian to the speech she fostered. In translation, English finds near-homonyms for *Wort* and *Mündel*, "word" and
"ward." These clinch the mother's muse-like role—"This word is
your mother's ward"—even if "this word," meaning any word Celan
wants to utter in a poem, must stoop for crumbs of light. Celan's
mother tongue had "to pass through the thousand darknesses of
deathbringing speech": he could hardly use it, yet could not help
using it to summon the mother who stood for all those lost.

II

It seems as if Paul Celan, long before he might have articulated any theory of loss and language, had one caustically inscribed on his own person. Born in 1920 in Czernowitz, Bukovina,
the eastern outpost of the Austrian Empire until World War I, he
grew up speaking German at home, then learned Rumanian at
school.[11] Paul's father had an Orthodox upbringing and emphasized the Judaic education of his son, who studied Hebrew for
three years until he became Bar Mitzvah. The mother, we're told,
considered "the German language more important, and all her life
she took care that a correct literary German should be spoken at
home," as distinct from the impure German otherwise current in
Czernowitz.[12] She "especially liked to read the German classics,
and in later years she vied with her son in quoting their favorite
authors." It would falsify the dynamics of a middle-class, Central
European Jewish household to say that this child exclusively associated a secular German language with his mother and a religious

Hebrew with his father. The family sabbath, for example, would have been celebrated by both parents together, in both German and Hebrew. But the boy does seem to have grown up resisting his father's Zionist leanings, and decisively closer to his mother, Fritzi Schrager. As a girl, she had lost her own mother early and had taken on the care of her younger siblings. She was—to judge from a photo that her only child Paul kept by him—a comely, soft-featured, warm-spirited person. Paul's father reportedly maintained discipline and distance.

Given these discrepant affiliations to his mother and father, Celan appears kindred with certain other European Jewish writers: with Proust; with Freud, whose father evoked Oedipal instincts as against the mother's less threatening presence; with Buber, who from the age of three felt keenly his mother's absence; with Elias Canetti; with Kafka—Celan once told a friend that Kafka's *Letter to His Father* had to be written over and over again in Jewish homes;[13] and above all with Osip Mandelstam, who also felt a merchant father's "Judaic chaos" but remembered his mother's sonorous Russian speech.[14] Yet none of these writers suffered the wrenching, overnight loss that was to come upon Celan.

Of course it did not take the Third Reich's war against the Jews to bond Paul Celan to his mother. In a recent edition of his earliest poems, we find a sonnet dated "Mother's Day 1938."[15] These lines, with their share of overwrought language, present a delicate task for translation: to expose palpably, but not to parody, the sentiments of a teenager. His first quatrain speaks of "scattered homesickness at night" and "clasping prayers anxious for your face"; the second tells her that her "soft solicitude braided with light" keeps us from turbulent dreams. The sonnet ends:

> You've naught to do with those who flee from rest,
> where motley crowds are swarming, thick and cheap—
> For you are stillness, mother, shimmer from the deep.

Celan's long final line extends the pentameter by an extra foot, as if the word *Mutter* had risen up into the midst of things—*Denn du bist Ruhe, Mutter, Schimmer aus dem Grund.* Opening up at its center to evoke his mother, this line has found both the poem's and the poet's point of balance. She is serene yet vibrant, and fundamental to him. Celan also echoes here one of Schubert's most cherished lieder, *"Du bist die Ruh',"* infusing its romantic serenity into his image of motherly love.

For Mother's Day a year later, May 1939, Celan wrote another sonnet.[16] This time he was away from home, in France studying medicine; the *Kristallnacht* pogroms had occurred, and war was imminent:

> The mother, healing noiselessly, and near,
> whose tender evening fingers brush our skin,
> clears precious space for us, as for the deer
> who draws in welcome breaths of morning wind.
>
> We pick our steps into the stream of things
> and she must be there, cleansing like a death
> that holds the nighttimes off for us and brings
> journeys home sooner, when thunder's a threat.

I feel slightly chagrined at leaving an imperfect rhyme in each quatrain—"skin" with "wind," "death" with "threat"—but maybe in English that effect can suggest Celan's own straining after rhymes. Really troubling is his image of the mother "cleansing like a death." Celan's sonnet betrays an ominous sense of absence even before his mother was taken off.

In July, two months after writing this Mother's Day poem, Celan returned home from France on vacation. Germany invaded Poland in September 1939; in June 1940 the Red Army occupied Czernowitz; a year later, Nazi and Rumanian troops entered the city and ravaged the Jewish population. When in June 1942, in a special *Aktion,* an S.S. *Einsatzkommando* set about rounding up and deporting Jews to Transnistria, Celan evidently urged his parents to hide out with him. But his mother is said to have taken a fatalistic view: "There are already lots of Jews living in Transnistria."[17] Transported eastward into the Ukraine and brutally exhausted in a stone quarry, both parents—first his father, in the fall, then in the winter his mother—were killed as *"arbeitsunfähig,"* incapable of work. How much guilt Celan may have felt that he should have saved them, or at least stayed by them, he never said.

Meanwhile, Celan was spending 18 months at forced labor in various Rumanian camps, and sending home to a woman friend occasional poems and translations from Shakespeare sonnets. Sometime in late 1942 or early 1943, possibly while in a camp, he wrote a poem and called it "Winter."[18] In these quatrains, several rhymes and figures still seem forced, but something has intervened—the years of Soviet occupation and Nazi persecution, the

irrevocable loss of his parents, the writing of many more poems—
to give to this lyric moments of intensity, even of ironic intensity,
not attained in the Mother's Day sonnets. In translating, more
than before I feel stretched to find adequate language—I feel committed, in effect, beyond what reading or analysis entails, to find
words for a ghastly labor camp. And here, for perhaps the first
time, Celan's traditional verse form is forced to admit something
more disruptive than the *Weltschmerz* of German Romantic melancholy. This poem begins, *Es fällt nun, Mutter, Schnee in der
Ukraine,*

> Snow's falling, Mother, now in the Ukraine:
> the Savior's crown a thousand grains of grief . . .
> Here all my tears reach out to you in vain;
> one proud mute glance is all of my relief . . .
>
> We're dying now: why won't you sleep, you huts?
> Even this wind slinks round in frightened rags . . .
> *Are* these the ones, freezing in slag-choked ruts—
> whose arms are candlesticks, whose hearts are flags?
>
> I stayed the same in darknesses forlorn:
> will days heal softly, will they cut too sharp?
> Among my stars are drifting only torn
> strings of a strident and discordant harp . . .
>
> On it at times a rose-filled hour is tuned.
> Expiring: One. Just one, again . . .
> What would come, mother: growing or a wound—
> if I too sank in snows of the Ukraine?

Here again, as in the 1938 sonnet, Celan sets off *Mutter* at the
heart of a key line—of two key lines, in fact, at the beginning and
end of this poem. What is new here, among other things, is the
harp, which evokes Jewish exile—"By the rivers of Babylon there
we sat down, yea, we wept, when we remembered Zion. We hanged
our harps upon the willows . . . " (Psalm 137)—and also figures the
poet as psalmist, suffering yet voicing his mother's loss. In Celan's
sudden orphanhood, it is *Wachstum oder Wunde,* "growing or a
wound," the one barely counterpoising the other in a hazardous
but necessary dynamic.

The question animating Celan's winter elegy—not a question,
really, but a paradox: growth *and* wounding—shows up in another
poem from 1943 concerning his mother, *Schwarze Flocken.*[19]

"Black Flakes" recalls (or re-creates, or perhaps imagines) the moment of receiving a letter from her, letting him know of his father's
death. The son's voice begins, then the mother's takes over, then
the son concludes:

> Snow has fallen, with no light. A month
> has gone by now or two, since autumn in its monkish cowl
> brought tidings my way, a leaf from Ukrainian slopes:
>
> "Remember, it's wintry here too, for the thousandth time now
> in the land where the broadest torrent flows:
> Jacob's heavenly blood, blessed by axes . . .
> O ice of unearthly red—their Hetman wades with all
> his troop into darkening suns . . . Oh for a cloth, child,
> to wrap myself in when it's flashing with helmets,
> when the rosy floe bursts, when snowdrift sifts your father's
> bones, hooves crushing
> the Song of the Cedar . . .
> A cloth, just a small scrap of cloth, so I hold
> by my side, now you're learning to weep,
> the straits of this world that will never turn green,
>   my child, for your child!"
>
> Autumn bled all away, mother, snow's burned me through:
> I sought out my heart so it might weep, I found—
>   oh the summer's breath,
> it was like you.
> Then came my tears. I wove the cloth.

Many things in this poem draw deeply on the resources, both literary and emotional, of translation as it turns into biography. For
one thing, the poem plays off against a traditional theme of love
counteracting winter, as in the sixteenth-century German folksong
"The snow has fallen," where a lover complains of his cold little
room and begs his beloved to take pity and wrap him in her arms
to banish winter. No such familiar consolation—Celan admits by
echoing this song—will dispel the winter of 1943. The form of his
poem also plays ironically against the folk song's reassuringly
rhymed quatrains. Apparently his first published free verse,
"Black Flakes" takes that freedom to modulate from a narrative,
framing voice into his mother's words and then back into his own
direct address to her. The time of the poem ranges from the
present to months before, to the past, to the ancient past. What's

more, only this once and never again a poem of Celan's mentions his father, and even then it does so only through his mother's agency. Within this unusual design, embedding her letter in the text, Celan also conveys a Judaic influx—Jacob, the Song of the Cedar—not in his own words but by way of his mother's.

Now the translator's specific and peculiar challenge and privilege may well occur, it seems to me, in small ways no less than large—small turns of phrase that shape a poem's voice. For instance, where the German says "autumn in its monkish cowl/ brought news to me," I've revised "news" to "tidings" to catch the familiar Gospel sense of *Botschaft*. There and in autumn's "monkish cowl" I hear an edge to the voice, I see a glance at the Christian folk who stood by or abetted the "Final Solution"—especially in the western Ukraine, here rendered idyllic by Celan's "leaf from Ukrainian slopes."

This *Blatt* (leaf or sheet of writing) forms a textual layering that makes present—by translating—the voice of someone not only absent but most likely dead. A "moon" or a "month has gone by now or two," Celan says, to frame what will come, to expose the tidings. Then his mother's letter says, *Denk, dass es wintert auch hier,* "Remember, it's wintry here too." I choose "remember" for *Denk,* rather than simply "think," to bring out the way she reminds him of millennial Jewish suffering—"for the thousandth time now." Under the duress of loss and exile, Celan finds in his mother Mnemosyne, muse of memory and mother of the muses.

Of course this letter comes only putatively from his mother; through her it is himself the poet really reminds of "Jacob's heavenly blood, blessed by axes." Two things from this line can hardly come through in translation. Celan surprisingly uses a Hebraicized spelling of Jacob, with two a's: *Jaakob*—could the English say "Yaakov"? And the blessing of Jacob's blood is couched in a heavily Christian term *benedeiet,* which not only sharpens the sarcasm of "axes" but calls up the most famous occurrence of *benedeiet* in the German Bible, after the Annunciation: "Blessed art thou among women, and blessed is the fruit of thy womb." Within this poem, the Immaculate Conception skews painfully for a moment across the voice of a Jewish mother.

Celan's next line then adds another layer to the history he has his mother transmit. To typify the persecutor, she might have said Amalek or Pharaoh or Haman, but Hetman ("headman") is more specific—the Cossack Khmelnitsky, whose massacres in 1648 decimated East European Jewry. From Jacob to the 17th century to World War II: to make this linkage, to get this grasp of persecution and endurance, Celan has to enter his mother's voice.

But at our own remove, how enter the mind of an orphan who must route the news of his father's murder through his exiled mother's words? Well, perhaps only by way of translation, specifically the art of loss. The passage containing her news pushed me to a more risky invention than anywhere else. "Oh for a cloth, child, / to wrap myself in," she says, *wenn schneeig stäubt das Gebein / deines Vaters*—"when snowdrift sifts your father's / bones." If only because the word "father" occurs here and nowhere else in Celan's poetry, these lines make a particular demand on the translator. I've sent my version of this poem to a friend, a German devoted to Celan. She says I have that phrase wrong: *stäuben* does not connote sifting but dust flying up. I know that, and also that no "drift" appears this time in Celan's German. But somehow the poem's saddest pitch wants the richest music: "when the rosy floe bursts, when snowdrift sifts your father's bones."

Translating Paul Celan draws me at times to look further into certain words than the actual rendition of them requires. When his mother's letter speaks of "hooves crushing / the Song of the Cedar," the line break gives *das Lied von der Zeder* a verse and a life of its own. This, the most specific term in Celan's poem, refers not so much to the Biblical cedars of Lebanon as to the anthem of the First Zionist Congress in 1897: "There where the slender cedar kisses the skies . . . there on the blue sea's shore my homeland lies."[20] Celan had resisted his father's Orthodox and Zionist persuasion, and it would be decades before he ventured to that "homeland." When he wrote *Schwarze Flocken,* there was no knowing whether the Song of the Cedar was irreparably crushed or not.

III

In late 1943, Celan barely escaped death in a labor camp and eventually returned to Czernowitz, now made alien again under Soviet occupation. Not long after his return and still during wartime, he wrote a brief lyric called "Nearness of Graves," whose rolling ballad-like meter and firmly recurrent rhymes I feel bound to try for in translation, because those conventions—familiar in

Rumanian as well as German folksong—gave the poet something to hold onto as he reached out for his mother after her death near the Ukrainian Bug River:

> Still do the southerly Bug waters know,
> Mother, the wave whose blows wounded you so?
> . . .
> Can none of the aspens and none of the willows
> allow you their solace, remove all your sorrows?
> . . .
> And can you bear, Mother, as once on a time,
> the gentle, the German, the pain-laden rhyme?[21]

Here yet again, as at the end of "Black Flakes" and elsewhere, Celan calls out directly to his mother, voicing her name as the verse opens up to her—*Mutter*. But my version, in adhering to Celan's metrical impulse, has dropped something vital from that last couplet, which reads:

> *Und duldest du, Mutter, wie einst, ach, daheim,*
> *den leisen, den deutschen, den schmerzlichen Reim?*

I must have thought Celan's desperate exclamation *ach, daheim* would sound schmaltzy in English—"oh, at home"—and would anyway splay out the four-beat line I mean to respect. Still it is a shame to edit a nostalgia that orients Celan's verse toward the place where folk songs were first sung to him in the *Muttersprache,* songs whose cadences these very verses may be echoing:

> And can you bear, mother, as—oh, at home—once on a time,
> the gentle, the German, the pain-laden rhyme?

That question, uttered with a resonant rhyme in German, the very language at issue, the poet never could answer and never ceased asking.

Just after the war, to someone who wondered how he could go on in the murderers' language, Celan reportedly said: "Only in the mother tongue can one speak one's own truth; in a foreign tongue the poet lies."[22] At the urging of some friends, he did write a few Rumanian poems in Bucharest, after abandoning Soviet-occupied Czernowitz in 1945.[23] But he fled Rumania in 1947, tried living for a while in Vienna, then settled in Paris. Although Rumanian, the state-imposed language of his childhood, would recur to him nostalgically in his exile, Celan never really composed in that tongue, or in the virtually perfect French of his Parisian existence. He held to the mother tongue. Yet during the postwar decades, Celan's writing revealed more and more strain in accommodating "the German, the pain-laden rhyme" to speak his "own truth"—a truth spoken only through what he later called a "radical calling-into-question of art."[24]

Paul Celan's questioning of "the German, the pain-laden rhyme" reaches out as well to touch the poet's translator, and paradoxically so. For Celan's translator must turn both to and away from the German tongue. On the one hand, a translator must take Celan at his word, must take his word for things—must, as George Steiner puts it, wholly trust the poet's language.[25] On the other hand, rendering Celan into English displaces him, conveys him out of the mother tongue. So that much-lamented, generic infidelity of poetic translation—"Translator: Traitor," the Italians say—cuts even deeper in Paul Celan's case, where the (murderously abused) mother tongue was all he had left, the one thing not lost. I feel bound almost filially, I feel entailed to try for the closest equivalent that will work in English, so as to carry over Celan's voice into a time and place he himself cannot reach. At the same time, a verse translation, however sensitive, can only act to estrange the son who says to himself, *Dieses Wort ist deiner Mutter Mündel,* "This word is your mother's ward."

Celan never ceased speaking to his mother, enacting in poems something of the I–Thou relation he had found expressed by Martin Buber. A decade after her death, Celan wrote the poem "In Front of a Candle":

> Out of bossed gold, just
> as you bade me, mother,
> I formed the candlestick—from this
> she darkens up to me among
> splintering hours:
> your
> being-dead's daughter.[26]

From the memory of a mother blessing Sabbath candles, as I take it, Celan's highly unusual locution, *deines Totseins Tochter,* "your being-dead's daughter," summons a mother arrested in time, uncannily becoming as young as her son—becoming, as he hints elsewhere, an only child's lost sister. She rises up, we hear in the next stanza, to the *Scheitel des Jetzt,* the "peak" or "crown of Now"— except that *Scheitel* also denotes the wig worn by orthodox Jewish women, and here translation cannot erupt the way this double meaning can. The poem ends:

> You stay, and stay, and stay
> a dead woman's child,
> consecrated to the No of my longing,
> wedded to a fissure in time
> that the motherword led me to,
> so that just once
> the hand might tremble
> that goes on and on grasping my heart!

Here the "motherword" leads him, not around the reefs of night as in an earlier poem, but to a crevasse, a break in time whose impassability may have something to do with the fact that Celan wrote this poem shortly after he and his wife lost their first child at birth.

Another decade later, almost 20 years after his mother was taken off, Celan wrote *Radix, Matrix* ("Root, Womb"), which begins this way—or at least to my ear it begins this way:

> As one speaks to stone, as
> you
> from the abyss to me, from
> a homeland en-
> Sistered, here
> Hurled, you,
> you of old to me,
> you in a night's nothingness to me,
> you in anew-night en-
> Countered, you
> Anew-You—:[27]

No diary or letter or conversation exists—Celan was highly reticent about his early years—that might reveal him as exactingly as this baffled, probing, reiterated, unanswered invocation. So the translator's efforts at locating "you" and "me" along the lines of an English sentence fragment, or at shaping a credible idiom through ruptured words and phrases, or at finding the term "en-Sistered" to match Celan's sense that his mother, caught young at the moment of her death, is becoming the sister he never had—such efforts must help reveal an emerging document of filial longing, a dialect of postwar orphanhood and exile.

IV

Because "there remained in the midst of the losses this one thing: language," as Paul Celan said, and because the losses centered in the poet's mother, destroyed by speakers of that language, a paradoxical charge attaches to the task of translating out of the "mother tongue," out of a German language at once treasured and traumatic. Celan could evoke his mother only in the *Muttersprache;* so translating his words ("This word is your mother's ward") is tantamount to effacing his mother herself.

Yet translate we do. Something of what Celan's poems do for his mother, by giving voice and presence to her, I hope I may attempt to do for Celan. After all, any decent translation regenerates an otherwise inaudible or possibly forgotten voice. When I make my English version adhere to Celan's prosodic impulse in the elegies to his mother, I am mimicking a voice; that is, re-creating the timbre, rhythm, and idiom evoked by a life-determining event. At their most engaged, my English versions of Celan seem to me almost to fuse the translator with the poet: not only do I speak for him, as it were, but he speaks for me—whether in the strain of postwar Diaspora existence, the thwarted yearning for Zion, the reaching out to a lost parent, or simply the need to make something of a language heard in one's childhood. It can become a presumptuous kind of reverse ventriloquism, this sliding of the voice from poet to translator. But doesn't a thoroughgoing translator feel answerable at some level for what the poet says? And *mustn't* the translator feel that way, in order to generate an authentic voice? With Paul Celan, after nine years immersed in the to-and-fro between his words and mine, at times I feel not merely obsessed but possessed by this lonely Jew. At readings, when I speak aloud my versions of his work, they have come to seem just that—versions or revisions, the old theme scored for a later voice.

To close this essay in translation, I would go back to *Schwarze Flocken* ("Black Flakes," 1943), the first time Celan found his muse in his mother. After the poem's central section, in which she asks for a scrap of cloth to hold against "this world that will never turn green," the son's voice concludes:

> Autumn bled all away, mother, snow's burned me through:
> I sought out my heart so it might weep, I found
>   —oh the summer's breath,
> it was like you.
> Then came my tears. I wove the cloth.

Perhaps, after all, love or remembrance of love can counteract winter, as the old songs would have it. This lyric does not stop there, but aligns its own making with the unmaking force of grief— aligns, as in the earlier poem "Winter," growing with a wound. *Kam mir die Träne. Webt ich das Tüchlein,* runs Celan's last line. At first I tried for the five syllables of those identically stressed statements: "Tears came to my eyes. I knitted the cloth." But *Webt ich* does not mean "I knitted," it means "I wove." Now, as the poet's first person shades invisibly into the translator's, I have found a more compact measure to balance the advent of tears with the weaving of a shawl: "Then came my tears. I wove the cloth." Answering loss with language, translation too may make a text, or a textile—something woven against the winter.

    Schwarze Flocken, "Black Flakes," holds in a single vision the European Jewish catastrophe, Celan's own loss, and his mandate as poet. His mother asked for a scrap of cloth; he wrote a poem, restoring to her something, at least, in the mother tongue.

Chapter Thirteen

Engendering an Autobiography in Art: Charlotte Salomon's "Life? or Theater?"

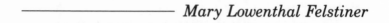 *Mary Lowenthal Felstiner*

Searching for Jews in a southern French town, the Gestapo passed over a large package holding a thousand vivid watercolors. What the package preserved through World War II has stood alone, without antecedents and so far without descendants: an autobiography in art.

In 1941 and 1942 Charlotte Salomon, an artist twenty-four years old, was painting her past while living as a German-Jewish refugee on the Riviera, a strip of Europe not occupied by Nazis for the first years of the war. After 1945, Charlotte's father and stepmother brought her autobiographical work to Amsterdam where they had survived the war, and where its 1325 paintings now reside in the Jewish Historical Museum. Of these, 769 have been beautifully reproduced and usefully introduced in *Charlotte: Life or Theater?* (1981)[1]; several hundred have been exhibited in museums throughout the world; a film, a play, a catalogue, and a documentary have expanded Charlotte Salomon's reputation. But so far no study has been published about her work, perhaps because it resists placement in traditional genres. As autobiography and as artwork, there is nothing quite like it.

In this extended sequence of paintings we see a person coming of age as a woman, a Jew, and an artist in Nazi Germany. We see her father taken to a concentration camp, her stepmother denied an operatic career, herself wrenched away from family, lover, and home into exile. We see the displacement and peril of wartime refugees in France. And we see another life-threatening theme in the personal milieu of her family—the presence of suicide.

Given these conditions, what is striking about this autobiography is that it exists at all. Granted, it matches the efforts of other German-speaking refugees to tell stories of their former and

present lives. But while some, such as Anna Seghers, Franz Schoen-
berner, or Stefan Zweig, counted on an audience, in Charlotte
Salomon's case, such anticipation would have been misplaced. The
mystery is why an unknown artist would undertake such an original project of self-presentation. The project was designed as a visual drama, with over a thousand scenarios, accompanied by
written captions indicating musical cues, textual narrations, solil-
oquies, and dialogue. Introduced by the title *Life? or Theater?: An
Operetta* and divided into acts and scenes, these autobiographical
paintings comprise an elaborate play.

Why did Charlotte Salomon undertake such an intricate con-
struction in such an inauspicious context? Was the genesis of this
peculiar autobiography in some degree linked to the gender of the
autobiographer?

To answer these questions, I will focus on the last section of
the work, the hundred-odd scenes that describe Charlotte's attempts to save her own grandmother from suicide. These scenes
are set in Villefranche, a village near Nice in Southern France,
where her grandparents settled soon after Hitler came to power in
1933 and where Charlotte was sent for safety in 1939. While the
manifest content of this last section is Charlotte's effort to rescue
her grandmother, the underlying intent is the artist's effort to recreate her self.

Though the circumstances at its source seem virtually unique,
Life? or Theater? makes plain a contradiction common among
women's autobiographies. Autobiography, as we know it in the
modern Western world, presupposes an autonomous self, differentiated from others and depicted as unique. Noticing how the social
liabilities of women undermine autonomy and differentiation,
feminist theorists have energetically discussed the distinctness of
women's autobiographies.[2] Some have asserted that as they represent their lives, women allow boundaries to blur between themselves and others; and that this tendency derives in part from
interdependence between mothers and daughters. These assertions
can be specified and extended by analyzing Charlotte Salomon's
visual–verbal narrative. Though Salomon had no conceivable audience, being a semi-concealed refugee from Nazism, she designed
her autobiography as a public spectacle. Showy, self-conscious, and
at the same time private and uncensored, this work lends itself to
interpretation of both psyche and style. From such interpretation,
the following implications emerge for feminist theory: that the
blurring of boundaries between self and other, the *identification*

between women, is a major theme of female self-representation; that such identification is pursued even at the risk of life; that it derives not only from direct mother-daughter transmissions but from the elective affinities between grandmothers and grand-daughters; and finally, that an autobiography, engendered under conditions of historical and emotional dependency, hazards the very self re-created there. What needs further consideration in feminist theory is the *process* whereby hazarding and re-creating a female self end up generating autobiographical work.

Life? or Theater? provides clues to the question: what impels women to record their lives in autobiography? Its last section stages a relationship between a young woman and her grand-mother, playing out their progress from feuding to fusion. Char-lotte Salomon's grandmother—an emigré from Nazi Berlin— seems to have impressed her fellow emigrés in Villefranche as a person of remarkable "intellectual energy, artistic and scholarly interest."[3] But if impressing was one side of her personality, sup-pressing was the other. What counts here is that the artist chose to expose only the hidden side, the grandmother's psychic dread, conveyed through a recurring image of her with arms around knees, head between, defending herself against transmissions from her radio and her memory. From the radio: "Frightful excesses against Jews in Germany."[4] From her memory: the suicides of her two daughters. One daughter, Charlotte's aunt and namesake, took her life before Charlotte was born. The other—Charlotte's mother—killed herself when Charlotte was only eight years old.

Elsewhere I have discussed the actual causes of these suicides and the causes Charlotte attributed to them.[5] But here my con-cern is the way Charlotte's discovery of female suicide generated and shaped her autobiography in art. The family had kept its sui-cides secret for years, from 1926, when Charlotte's mother took her life, until the grandmother's attempt in 1940. Not until Char-lotte was twenty-three and a refugee did she face this life-threatening legacy from women. For the first time, she learned that the grandmother's mind had been accumulating despair for years. As the grandfather finally explained: after the suicides of two children, "your grandmother came to the end of her rope. She had no desire to go on living."[6] In Charlotte's portrayal, whenever the grandmother walks, her hands reach protectively for her pock-ets; when she sits, one hand and foot shield the other.[7] She looks petrified, while Charlotte portrays herself as an activist, always in the process of painting. The autobiographer seems anxious to es-

tablish the tensions and differences between the two. In one painting the grandmother studies Charlotte with disdain: "Are you here
in the world only to paint? ... Look at her. Isn't she a case study
in melancholia? Look at her. She needs a man."[8] When the grandmother imposes this conventional view on Charlotte, that "young
girls ... need men," Charlotte turns red in rage and begs her
"once and for all to spare me that topic."[9] The collision over
"that topic" symbolized irremediable breaches between an older
and younger woman. Their "open conflict" was described by an
emigré who knew them well: "not only conflict of generations,
but deep differences in being, grounded in disposition, upbringing
and thinking."[10]

Considering these deep differences, one would expect Charlotte to distance herself entirely from her grandmother. A young
person trying to maintain morale through hard times might well
feel at odds with an old woman's bitter and despondent presence.
But something besides antagonism shows through. In the very
scenes that pass judgment on the grandmother, Charlotte lets the
older woman judge her in turn. In fact, their conflicts revolve
around their common qualities: their tendency toward depression,
their uselessness, their loneliness. Sharing a perilous situation,
Charlotte perceived in her grandmother's mind something she
found in her own—an inability to separate personal from political
stress. One caption to a painting of her grandmother reads:

> The heavy pain that pursued her through life, till now somewhat
> submerged in her depths, seems called up by the raging war, and
> appears fully before her mind, so that she feels her sharp intelli-
> gence and her self-control—what made her life worth living—
> breaking to pieces against a greater force.[11]

The greater force belonged to Germany. Germany imposed ter-
rifying questions that made possible Charlotte's empathy with her
grandmother. Women withered from transplantation—and not always in the same way as men. For example, access to officials,
which proved crucial for emigrés, had traditionally been denied to
women. Moreover, women were only ten percent of the refugees
reaching France in 1933 when Charlotte's grandmother arrived,
and by 1936 only twenty percent.[12] Exiles such as Charlotte and
her grandmother had to learn survival in a men's community in a
foreign country.

When that country had to face German invaders in the fall of
1939, the grandmother tried to hang herself. This attempt, as re-

corded two years later in Charlotte's autobiography, initiates a
forty-six-painting sequence which could be called a rescue drama.
It unfolds in theatrical scenes set inside the grandmother's bed-
room. In the dialogues, Charlotte's utterances appear in large
script, as if voiced with authority, whereas the grandmother's responses come out small and shaky. The sequence starts with the
character of Charlotte holding her grandmother in her arms, re-
suscitating her after a suicide attempt, while the shrunken figure
begs: "Please, let me die." Even though Charlotte wants to disen-
tangle herself, moaning "Oh God, I feel sick," instead, "she forces
herself to go completely out of herself and become engaged only
with her grandmother," with the woman who keeps pleading "Oh
let me die, Oh let me die, for I feel it, I cannot live longer."[13]

Whether in real life Charlotte turned from antagonism to at-
tentiveness, there is no way of knowing. But in autobiography she
constructed a story whose central character, with consequences as
yet unknown, resolves on rescue. The character undertakes a kind
of antiphonal therapy, in order to prove that something outside
the self can make up for human emptiness. Here is a characteristic dialogue:

(Charlotte): Grandma, look at the sun, how it's shining.

(Grandmother): I see the sun shining.

(Charlotte): Look at the flowers on the meadow. So much beauty, so
much joy.

(Grandmother): I see the flowers in bloom, so much beauty in the
meadow.[14]

The granddaughter also tries spiritual inspiration, singing the
chorale of Beethoven's Ninth Symphony, set to Schiller's "Ode to
Joy": *"Freude Schöner Götterfunken Tochter aus Elysium"*: "Joy,
thou spark from flame immortal, Daughter of Elysium. We shall
enter, drunk with fire, Heavenly One, Your holy realm."[15] The
grandmother is drawn right up from her bed by Charlotte's rising
arm and voice. These voice-and-response methods begin to erase
the boundaries between the two women.

What made Charlotte assume the responsibility of rescuing
her grandmother? Her decision "to go completely out of herself and
become engaged only with her grandmother" was largely shaped by
circumstances peculiar to her life *as a woman*—the vulnerability

of women in exile, the family pattern of female suicide, and the affinity women find with each other in a gender-divided world. In Charlotte's mind, the suicide attempt of her closest female relative generated a profound crisis. In the throes of the grandmother's attempt, the grandfather divulged the truth, after thirteen years of secrecy: the women in Charlotte's family, all of them, had killed themselves. Her great-grandmother had attempted suicide for years, her mother's sister had drowned herself, her mother had thrown herself from a window, her grandmother had long ago lost the will to live. In the scene where her grandfather discloses all this, Charlotte barely retains her own sense of identity; she reduces herself to two colors and an outline, undistinguished by clothing or features.[16] Like a blank page to be inscribed, she bares herself to the matrilineal legacy. From then on, step by step, she lets herself become her grandmother's double.

At the beginning of the rescue sequence, as Charlotte tries to inspirit her grandmother, bare backgrounds separate the two women. But as the series progresses, the younger figure merges with the older one, till they are hard to tell apart: a single brushstroke does for both their bodies. As scene after scene fuses one woman with the other, the meaning at the heart of the sequence becomes clear: for Charlotte, keeping her grandmother alive has become the same as saving herself. The doubling process, far from submerging Charlotte, allows her to discover and present a "proposition [that] is going to heal you."

> Instead of taking your life in such a dreadful way, you could apply the same powers to describing your life.... There will surely be something to interest you, something that oppresses you, and as you write it down, you free yourself and maybe even render a service to the world.[17]

Finally, the artwork created two characters so interchangeable that the "you" in "you could apply the same powers to describing your life" means *both of them*. Assimilating the grandmother's potential fate allowed Charlotte to experiment with a potential remedy. The uses of "describing your life" that she charted for her grandmother set her moving toward her own autobiography.

But why do all the paintings of one woman ministering to another revert to elemental forms—flat swatches of color, brief outlines without features, simple tones like orange on brown or blue on blue, a predominance of words over images, evacuated backgrounds? Nothing seems situated, nothing rests on anything else. Most other paintings in *Life? or Theater?* are filled with figures and objects and action. This sequence transmits an atmosphere of suspension, as if the experience will not come to rest in a two-fold rescue; the dialogues too sound like premonitions.

(Charlotte): A frightful ending is on the way and my powers are no longer strong enough for it.

(Grandfather): I'm going out for a moment of air.

(Charlotte): All right, I'll go in to her right away.[18]

Between his sentence and hers, the grandmother springs to the window. Charlotte, alone, witnesses the bloodied distorted body fallen from the window to the ground. The grandfather, returning from his morning walk with flowers for his wife, can only say: "So she has done it in spite of everything" and "That is the fate of this family. . . . Most likely I will live to see even the one in the next room lay hands upon herself."[19]

In the next room, Charlotte is crying out: "DEAR GOD, JUST DO NOT LET ME GO MAD," *"Lieber Gott, lass mich bloss nicht wahnsinnig werden."*[20] These words emerge deep ochre from an incinerating orange background. *"GOTT"* stands out against a chaos of unfilled borders. *"WAHNSINNIG,"* "insane," just manages to constrain itself within the boundaries of the painting. On one side the figure of Charlotte stiffens, on the other the window beckons. Only the drawing pad on Charlotte's knees stands between the window's lure and the woman's life. From that moment on, Charlotte "found herself face to face with the question of whether to take her own life or undertake something mad and most unusual":[21] something incorporating madness but pre-empting its destructive power—an autobiography in art.

What I have called the rescue sequence is more than a record of the grandmother's suicidal impulses, or of Charlotte's own. The sequence is an autobiographical drama *about the creation of an autobiographical drama*. It moves forward in a coherent narrative from rescuing the grandmother to rescuing oneself. After the grandmother's suicide attempt and Charlotte's recognition that the family history could persist in her, antagonism changes into engagement; then engagement turns into identification, to such an extent that the grandmother's suicide threatens Charlotte's own sanity. Finally, the central character poses "the question of whether to take her own life or undertake something mad and un-usual." In other words, the autobiographer imposes on this pro-gression an either-or conclusion that justifies her two-year commitment to autobiography: after all, it saved her life. The res-cue sequence would demonstrate the therapeutic benefits of the work she was about to complete. By its last sheets, the very exist-ence of *Life? or Theater?* would have proven why "she did not have to kill herself like her ancestors."[22]

There is a triumph in this conclusion, given the conditions of suicide and exile weighing so heavily against Charlotte. But we have to remember that this autobiography is not a mirror but a script. There are hints that autobiography did not fulfill the therapeutic potential recommended to her grandmother, that it did not dispel the suicidal impulses left in Charlotte. After all, the grandmother had followed Charlotte's advice, had even worked on writing an autobiography; yet it failed to save her.[23] Though the rescue se-quence ostensibly balances the creation of autobiography against the destruction of suicide, the two never quite come off as opposites; rather they join symbiotically in Charlotte's mind and language.

> My life *commenced* when my grandmother wanted *to take her life,* when I found out that my mother had taken hers, as had her entire family—when I found out that I was the only survivor and when deep within me I felt the same inclination, the urge toward despair and dying.
>
> One can be *resurrected*—in fact, in order to love life still more, one should once have *died.* [my emphasis added].[24]

To "once have died" meant, in the autobiographical script, to have identified fully with her mother and her grandmother; to "once have died" *with them* made her eligible to be "resurrected"—to dis-cover that "instead of taking your life, you can apply the same powers to describing your life."[25] To read Charlotte's private writ-ings (found on unnumbered sheets she did not include in *Life? or Theater?*) is to see the discrepancy between an artistic vision of resurrection and an unresolved personal experience. In the very process of applying her powers to describing her life, she was writing privately: "My happiness was at an end." "I was in despair." "My old despair . . . threw me back into a slow death-like lethargy: if I can't find any joy in my life and in my work I will kill myself."[26]

Painting her life deflected her from taking her life. But in the long run, Charlotte had the same problem as her grandmother: to keep one's inner self alive was to inhabit an outer world one could not bear. At a nexus of private and general distress, Charlotte blocks off her mouth with her hands, as if the character dares not voice the autobiographer's thought: *"I cannot bear this life. I cannot take these times."*[27] In reality, suicide threatened to overtake Charlotte the more her family's history intersected the history of France. The grandmother had committed suicide in March 1940. Only two months later, before Charlotte had time to recover, the German Army defeated the French. Though France's Riviera was not occupied for several years by the Germans and remained relatively safe, French police were known to round up Jews. The duress of this historical situation lies behind Charlotte's paintings of her personal trials.

Even the exercise of memory becomes disheartening in the context of exile. Exile makes literal what most autobiographies leave metaphorical: you can never go back to the setting or the safety of the past. *Life? or Theater?* intends to project the sustaining powers of autobiography but ends up conveying its limitations. Given the conditions outside Charlotte's will, choosing autobiography promised only a temporary reprieve. What would happen to Charlotte when the reprieve expired, when she brought the autobiography to a close?

Perhaps that is why she did not bring it to a close, not in any traditional sense. The last pages offer not a stopping place but a setting out, a journey of risk and an archetypal motif of rescue and renewal. If, as she says at the very end, "she did not have to kill herself like her ancestors," it is because "she remembered Orpheus,"[28] whose descent to the region of death called up those who were lost, including one's former self, yet revived no one and promised no certain return. Orpheus is her symbol for memory amid exile, for resurrection amid suicide, for self-discovery from subterranean sources. The autobiography ends with these words:

She knew: she must disappear for a time from the surface of life and make every sacrifice to bring forth her world anew out of the depths.

And from there came LIFE OR THEATER?[29]

Charlotte Salomon ends the story of her life right then, with the very moment of re-creating herself out of her matrilineal legacy, the moment of embarking on autobiography. The end of *Life? or Theater?* is far from final, for the whole work folds back on itself. Her lived experience of exile and suicide prompts the drama that rotates back to the lived experience.

Few autobiographies puncture the pretense of realism, as Charlotte's did, by insisting on its own theatricality. Facing an imminent menace of effacement, the artist created a conclusion that offers the protagonist a fail-safe sense of control: the project she sets for herself at the end she has already finished. She does not locate herself at an endpoint in real time, which would imply that events not in the script could overtake her later. The final resolution is a continual relay between autobiographer and character, between life and theater. Charlotte the autobiographer finds a reprieve while telling her story; at its end she grants Charlotte the character yet another reprieve, to create the work of art. Culminating a life history with the decision to dramatize it prolongs it indefinitely. This is a script for perpetual recurrence.

When the artist at age twenty-five brought the work full circle, when she hid it with a friend, what she said of it then suggests that she had collapsed her living history into her painting of it: "Keep this safe," she said: *"It is my whole life."*[30]

Late in 1943, the Gestapo moved into the region and took Charlotte Salomon. But her "whole life" stays on: what she lived of it, 1917–1939, in Germany; what she painted of it, 1940–1942, in France; what she lost of it, 1943, at Auschwitz.

Chapter Fourteen

"Father Books":
Memoirs of the Children of Fascist Fathers

——————————————— *Susan G. Figge*

Since the early 1970s, fathers have populated the German-language book market in a series of some twenty-five autobiographical memoirs, which represent a remarkable intersection of autobiography and biography, fiction and nonfiction, family and political history, documentary and diary. Pastor, doctor, military officer, policeman, lawyer, poet, bureaucrat, landed gentleman, dramatist, veterinarian—what these fathers have in common, in addition to being dead, is the experience of fascism. They also share middle-aged sons and daughters who have literary credentials, personal psychic pain, and many unanswered questions.[1]

The autobiographical father memoirs are indeed about Nazi fathers, or about fathers who compromised or collaborated or looked the other way. But they are also about fathers and their children in the psycho-sociocultural setting of the postwar family. The sons' and daughters' need to understand the father's role in the Third Reich is connected to their personal experience of his often arbitrarily authoritarian and emotionally meager parenting and to his own silence about or distortion of his past. The biographical inquiry into the father's life and his child's autobiographical inquiry into the origins of the self are linked together in this new German sub-genre of literature, which focuses on gendered authority in the family and its personal and political consequences.

The significance of the autobiographical/biographical project can be located in the figure of the father himself. For in these texts the father appears not just as a particular domestic tyrant with a questionable if not monstrous political past. Rather, his authority in the family is textually connected to a set of social and cultural traditions of fatherly/male authority which persisted through the Wilhelmine era and which the Nazis were able to exploit.

In her 1979 memoir *The Man in The Pulpit: Questions to a Father,*[2] Ruth Rehmann recalls her pastor father's study in the early days of the Weimar Republic. As a setting for confrontations with his children and for ministering to his flock, the room displayed a system of political and metaphysical father images which upheld this old style clergyman and paternalistic family man in his political conservatism, his class snobbery, and his unconscious sexism. On the desk was a photograph of Rehmann's grandfather—also a pastor and family patriarch. A bust of the old Kaiser and King of Prussia surmounted the bookcase. Dedicated family man and loving father to his people, the Kaiser was a model for every pastor and every father. Thorwald's painting of Christ embodying God the father and son, legitimized in turn the authority of king, pastor and parent. As a child standing in this room, Rehmann saw herself surrounded by a hierarchy of symbolic fathers who served as paradigms for each other, and invested in her own father tremendous moral and spiritual authority. In the course of the memoir Rehmann shows how her father's unquestioning adherence to these symbolic authority figures blinded him both to the harm he inflicted on his wife and daughter and to the evil of Nazism as it erupted in his own congregation.

The grotesque Nazi variation of this patriarchal culture text is a thematic concern in Peter Hartling's 1980 memoir *Love in Arrears.*[3] Hartling tells of his adolescent rage at his non-Nazi father—a sensitive, weak, and anxious man who sympathized with his Jewish clients, practiced a kind of inner political emigration, and tolerated his wife's love affair. Intoxicated by what he describes as the Nazi "man's world," Hartling joined the Jungvolk and condemned his father as a coward. "I wanted a hero for a father, one who participated, who lived up to the warlike phrases . . ." (p. 17). As the teenage Hartling understood the Nazi ideology of masculinity, all authority was invested in the image of the dominating, uncompromising male, conquering hero of the master race and indisputable master of his own family.[4]

The majority of the father books deal with the legacy of this gendered authority in the postwar family, where acceptance of the father's word, no matter how arbitrary, cruel or unfair, was law. The children had nothing to say and the mother very little, and a nineteenth-century Prussian pedagogy supported an immense need to uphold bourgeois standards of cleanliness, order, and the appearance of respectability.[5] Damaged by what psychiatrists Alexander and Margarete Mitscherlich have called "the inability to mourn"—the psychological rigidity and emotional emptiness resulting from denial of guilt and repression of past experience—the surviving fathers, according to their sons and daughters, used their cultural authority precisely to suppress their children's inquiry into the past.[6] The postwar injunction to silence permeated all of German society. The father books show its origins and results in the family, which was in turn a stronghold for the remnants of a patriarchal system that finally had not served either men or women well.

In these memoirs, a major feature of the father's continuing authority is his appearance as the culturally legitimized arbiter of language and story—in short, of narrative. Narration involves principles of selection and ordering which generate and perpetuate the conceptual and cultural patterns by which we live. In retelling their fathers' lives and their own, in trying to uncover old patterns and invent new ones, the sons and daughters must confront the father's authoritarian insistence on his own narratives and his injunction to their narrative silence.

I will look at the theme of gendered narrative power in two of the father books. Sigfrid Gauch's 1979 *Father Tracks*[7] and Ingeborg Day's 1980 *Ghost Waltz*,[8] both of which deal with Nazi fathers in postwar families. I want to suggest how the father's role as narrative authority is thematically and structurally dismantled in these texts and how the daughters, in contrast to the sons, deal with the challenge of narrating the father.

Sigfrid Gauch's father Hermann—medical doctor, early and enthusiastic member of the Nazi party, and Himmler's Adjutant for Cultural Politics—appears throughout the memoir in narrative situations, telling the stories through which he has interpreted his experience. His repertoire includes ancient Germanic sagas, the family tale of his own father's loss of valuable diamond mine holdings to dishonest Jews, and the legend of the Gauch family descent from the German nobility, all related to his children on postwar Sunday excursions when they are forced to visit every castle ruin in the district. At best these stories embarrass and bore young Sigfrid; at worst they provide a kind of conceptual structure which enables the father to originate a mythology of Aryan superiority and race hatred, which he upheld until his death in the 1970s. Named in the Eichmann trial as the intellectual originator of theories of Jewish inferiority, Hermann Gauch was the author of books on race that served as a justification for the Nazi politics of genocide.

In the memoir, the father's stories are seen also as the tools he uses to preserve his own self-delusions. Sigfrid Gauch inserts into the text a manuscript fragment written by his father shortly after his graduation from medical school in the early twenties. Here Hermann Gauch portrays himself as an idealistic young doctor arbitrating between troops of youthful Red Guards and Nazis skirmishing in the Rhineland. In a bombastic rhetorical style, he persuades the warring factions that they are all exploited by Jews and wealthy landowners and that rather than killing each other, they should join forces to fight the French. Sigfrid Gauch shows how the combination of extreme idealism and self-aggrandizement captured in this narrative carried Hermann Gauch intellectually unscathed through the Third Reich, confident to the end of his life that whatever use was made of his racist theories was all for the good. He published "proof" that statistics about extermination of Jews were exaggerated, and continued to believe that neo-Nazis would seize power and the Germanic peoples yet prove their superiority. His son describes this conceptual world as "a closed system of thought. Actually a kind of logical world of wholeness, in which one could feel comfortable, in which one could see meaning, which one did not need to doubt." The father used his narratives to keep that world intact.[9]

It is not simply the content or the function of the father's stories that is at stake in the memoir. Several episodes suggest that he attempted as well to control his son's own language and narrative ability. During Sigfrid's boarding-school days in the fifties, his father rented a room nearby and used his son's spare time to drill him relentlessly in Latin and Greek vocabulary, as if to rob him of all language not authorized by the father. When essays were assigned, the elder Gauch told him how to organize them and what to say. Continuing to write poetry in celebration of home and fatherland, Hermann Gauch published it in the local newspapers under his son's name. These efforts to pass on literally the father's narrative voice and ideas to the son were resisted by the young Sigfrid, who forgot the classical vocabulary the moment he was out of his father's sight; who secretly wrote his own essays for school, and who told fans of "his" poetry that in fact his father had written it.

The memoir itself is, of course, the son's ultimate form of narrative resistance. Here Sigfrid Gauch assumes his father's function—he becomes the recorder of family history; but while his father's unchanging monologic stories bolstered his apparently hermetically sealed world view, Gauch's own narrative structures show him constantly reevaluating his material. His memoir is based on childhood memories, conversations, documents, letters, and reports from his father's friends and relatives. Sections in which grateful patients remember his father's kindness are undercut by childhood memories of his father's whimsical cruelties. His father's own tales of military exploits and meetings with Himmler jostle against Gauch's recollections of his father's childish and demanding old age. Multiple perspectives vie for validity. Gauch calls this technique "letting a mosaic picture of my father's personality appear in a series of chapters and counter chapters, in corresponding episodes."[10] Its end effect is to engage the reader's own critical capacities; to leave room for alternative interpretations.

In contrast to his father's efforts at wielding narrative control, Gauch practices a narrative art that borders on conversation. Addressing his father directly as "du," he leaves his conjectures about him in the subjunctive, as though these were still open questions. His own attempts at explaining, at justifying his father's life, are always presented in the text as if they were being heard by an unreceptive listener, so that they too are relativized. Gauch's persistent ambivalence not only invites the reader's critical reflection, it finally enables the son to accept his own mixed feelings about his father, freeing him both to judge and to love. Gauch calls his memoir an "Erzählung," a story, rather than a documentary, allowing him to frame his narrative as a fiction and to use the storytelling process as a tool to explore the motives and purposes that informed his father's life—insights of which the father, trapped in his own unchanging mythology, was incapable.[11]

In confronting their fathers' control of narrative, the daughters remembering their fathers formulate a yet more complex and radical critique.[12] While the sons locate narrative authority in the person of the father, implicitly raising the question of gender, the daughters explicitly contrast the father's narrative power with the mother's silence—with her verbal disenfranchisement. If we ask the question, who tells the stories by which we live and interpret our lives, the sons answer "the father." The daughters answer, "the father and not the mother."

The son is the natural legatee of his father's narrative power. Sigfrid Gauch recognizes that his father is trying to force his narrative authority and understandings on to his son, and Gauch in fact assumes his father's storytelling function, albeit in a much altered form. In contrast, the daughters understand the voicelessness of the mother and the devaluing of her experience as their common textual legacy. The father—partly through direct injunction to silence, partly through omission—has denied his daughter a language and history of her own, and thereby any claim to narrative authority.

In her 1980 memoir *Ghost Waltz,*[13] expatriate Austrian writer and journalist Ingeborg Day reconstructs her parents' Nazi past, out of her need to love them and at the same time to understand them as the origin of her own inexplicable anti-Semitism. An Austrian peasant by birth, her father had joined the army out of desperation for work in the twenties and had become an early and enthusiastic Nazi, a policeman, and a member of the S.S. Growing up in postwar Austria, Day knew her father as rigid and inflexible, tyrannical and arbitrary. She sees the sources of that personality in his impoverished boyhood, which left him with the need to believe or blame absolutely. The Nazi Party embodied his hopes for a better life for people like himself. In his postwar despair he refused to accept any other creed, and lapsed instead into political apathy and finally into silence altogether. Day's attempts to ask her father about the past are met with his threat to disown her if she perseveres with such questions. Years later he stops speaking to her entirely, after she goes through with a divorce against his wishes.

In the memoir, Day links her father's demand for her silence (like his demand that she continue to be a wife) to his view of loyal and obedient daughterhood. Her mother sees it as his fatherly prerogative: "If your father chooses not to talk about something, *that is a right.* You have no right whatsoever. *He is your father.*" (p. 23) Day's mother's own silence is of a piece with her sense of wifely duty; it is also connected to her lost past. She does not disagree or argue with her husband's most rigid decisions. She does not protest when he engages in numerous affairs. She never speaks about her youth—the eleven years when she had left her family's farm and lived in Vienna by means her daughter can never determine. There are no official registration records, no letters, no pictures. Her father's refusal to answer her questions, her mother's silent acquiescence and missing story, deny Day access to family and female history and leave her with no authoritative female voice. In her search for the past, she must go to radical narrative lengths to overcome her silenced daughterhood.

She begins by learning a new language. English, at first a useful tool for getting along in a foreign country, becomes the only linguistic code in which she can ask questions and pursue answers about her parents. To create a voice for asking and telling, she must operate in a medium not tied to her father's injunction to silence, not tied to her mother's voicelessness. " . . . I could not write about my parents or my childhood in German. My knight in shining armor, my saving-grace shield, is English." (p. 182).

But even in her new "mother tongue" there are narrative pitfalls. As a middle-aged adult in New York, Day watches a late-night talk show featuring interviews with women who have written books about being a mistress. While the moderator sneers and leers his way through this segment dealing with women's experience, he becomes instantly serious in a second segment when the mistresses are replaced by a group of male theoreticians—historians, writers, economists, journalists, who discuss the origins of the Holocaust. The male scholars fight it out, each one trying to gain assent for his own particular version of history.

For Day the message of this episode is clearly that women's narrating of their experience is not to be taken seriously and that legitimized access to the past is through channels of scholarly theory, even though the experts cannot agree among themselves. Listening to the historians, she hears no answer relevant to her questions, and she must construct her own explanation. "Hitler got as far as he did for one reason, a simple one. It all happened because my mother did and felt whatever my father did and felt, and enormous masses of people did and felt as my parents did and felt. And a comprehensive crisis of a capitalist economy it may well have been, and a lot of other things too, but that's neither here nor there for me." (p. 7).

Day's own historical research and narrative practice contrast markedly to that of the talk show guests. In critiquing and supplementing the scholarly establishment, she juxtaposes chapters on Austrian history with segments of her father's personal biography, using them to refine and illuminate each other. She inserts into this material an account of her own narrative methods, emphasizing the legitimacy and importance of individual experience for historical explanation, such as her report of her mother's and grandmother's lives, and refusing to pretend to authorial omniscience.[14]

Her open narrative with its revelation of her thought in progress also breaks the pattern of her father's rigid mentality. He lived with "an inability to see any matter from another person's point of view, not a refusal, an inability. An extreme world, none of the nuances of a more evolved manner of dealing with one's life's events, no shades of gray or mauve. Clear-cut, and the crippling cost in pain accepted as inevitable. All depths of disappointment can be suffered, all measure of loneliness endured, a man keeps his word. That's what he died with, all those kept words." (p. 39)

The often negative scholarly and journalistic German reception of the father books has dealt in charges of confusion of documentary and fiction, irrelevant subjectivity and (particularly female) narcissism, and Oedipal revenge.[15] Yet encoded in the child's relationship to the father is the issue of the individual's relationship to authority, the perception of gender roles, and the assumption of personal agency, with their immense private and political implications. Nor do these texts function simply as "human interest history"—one family's story in the midst of catastrophic events.[16] In particular, Day's memoir—with its themes of the family heritage of anti-Semitism, of suppression of the past, and of women's silence—calls into question the postwar patriarchal father–mother–child triad as a social and cultural institution capable of nourishing healthy persons and of transmitting humane values.

My emphasis here on the thematic and structural importance of narrative in these memoirs is not an arbitrary one. The authors of the father books clearly see narrative power as one feature in the complex familial transmission of fascist psychosocial patterns.[17] The father's narratives reveal his private fantasies and mythologies, the grounds of his action or inaction. That these can have devastating consequences is clear in the case of Hermann Gauch, who used textual elaborations as justification and vehicle to project a whole range of resentments and insecurities onto a group of outsiders—the Jews. Just as important is the father as a culturally legitimized narrator, who uses story and silence to manipulate his children; to perpetuate within them the repression of feelings, the need to dominate others, and lack of self worth; and to suppress his own and his children's effective coming to terms with the Nazi past.

Like the other daughters, Ingeborg Day draws radical narrative consequences from her confrontation with her father, involving for her the abandonment of her father's language, as well as his house and country. She rejects as well the abstract answers of "authorized" male commentators to her most urgent questions about the past, and intertwines the personal history of her family with male-authored "legitimate" history—sometimes calling its theses into question, sometimes correcting its omission of women, always showing its inadequacy to communicate the texture of individual lived experience.

The narrative act itself in these autobiographical memoirs points toward a flexibility, an openness to critique, a self always in process, while the fathers as omniscient narrators are trapped in their own rigid texts.[18] As a genre of literature confronting the German past, the father books embody not their authors' self pity and need for personal revenge, but rather their quest for a usable past in the service of a responsible private and political life in the present.

Notes

Introduction

1. This generally humanistic view runs counter to the position of those scholars who altogether deny the concept of the authorial subject and consequently predict the demise of autobiography as a genre. See, for example, Michael Sprinker's apocalyptic essay, "Fictions of the Self: The End of Autobiography," in James Olney, *Essays Theoretical and Critical* (Princeton, NJ: Princeton University Press, 1980), pp. 321–342, and Paul John Eakin's discussion of the threat to autobiography implied in the French-inspired transatlantic discourse on the ontological status of the self, in his *Fictions in Autobiography: Studies in the Art of Self-Invention* (Princeton, NJ: Princeton University Press, 1985), pp. 181–191.

2. Estelle C. Jelinek, *Women's Autobiography* (Bloomington, IN: Indiana University Press, 1980) and Jelinek, *The Tradition of Women's Autobiography: From Antiquity to the Present* (Boston, MA: Twayne Publishers, 1986); Domna C. Stanton, ed., *The Female Autograph* (New York, NY: Literary Forum, 1984); Sidonie Smith, *A Poetics of Women's Autobiography: Marginality and the Fictions of Self-Representation* (Bloomington and Indianapolis, IN: Indiana University Press, 1987); Shari Benstock, ed., *The Private Self: Theory and Practice of Women's Autobiographical Writings* (Chapel Hill, NC: University of North Carolina Press, 1988); Bella Brodzki and Celeste Schenck, eds., *Life/Lines: Theorizing Women's Autobiography* (Ithaca, NY: Cornell University Press, 1988); Carolyn Heilbrun, *Writing a Woman's Life* (New York, NY: W. W. Norton, 1988); Valerie Sanders, *The Private Lives of Victorian Women: Autobiography in Nineteenth-century England* (New York, NY: St. Martin's Press, 1989). See also Dale Spender, ed., "Personal Chronicles: Women's Autobiographical Writings," Special Issue, *Women's Studies International Forum*, Vol. 10, No. 1, 1987; Margaret A. Lourie, Domna Stanton, Martha Vicinus, eds., "Women and Memory," Special Issue, *Michigan Quarterly Review* (Ann Arbor, MI: University of Michigan Press, 1987).

See also: Linda Anderson, "At the Threshold of the Self: Women and Autobiography," in Moira Monteith, ed., *Women's Writing: A Challenge to Theory* (Sussex, UK: Harvester Press; New York, NY: St. Martin's Press, 1986).

For specific bibliographies of women's autobiographical writings see: Patricia K. Addis, *Through a Woman's I: An Annotated Bibliography of American Women's Autobiographical Writings, 1946–1976* (Metuchen, NJ and London: The Scarecrow Press Inc., 1983); Lynn A. Bloom and Mary Briscoe, *A Bibliography of American Women's Autobiographies 1945– present* (Madison, WI: University of Wisconsin Press, 1983); Marilyn Yalom, "Women's Autobiography in French 1793–1939: A Select Bibliography," *French Literature Series* (Columbia, SC: The University of South Carolina: Vol. XII, 1985), pp. 197–205; Barbara Kanner, *Women in English Social History 1800–1914*, Vol. III, "Autobiographical Writings" (New York, NY: Garland, 1987), and Suzanne L. Bunkers, "Self-Reflexivity in Women's Autobiography: A Select Bibliography," *a[b Auto/Biography Studies* (Fall 1988), pp. 57–63.

3. Philippe Lejeune, *Moi Aussi* (Paris: Editions du Seuil, 1986).

4. Albert Stone, *Autobiographical Occasions and Original Acts* (Philadelphia, PA: University of Pennsylvania Press, 1982), p. 19. Cited by Herbert Leibowitz, *Fabricating Lives: Explorations in American Autobiography* (New York: Alfred A. Knopf, 1989), p. xviii.

5. See, for example, Paul de Man, *The Rhetoric of Romanticism* (New Haven, CT: Yale University Press, 1984) and Paul Jay, *Being in the Text: Self-Presentation from Wordsworth to Barthes* (Ithaca, NY: Cornell University Press, 1984). See also William C. Spengemann, *The Forms of Autobiography: A Collection of Critical Essays* (Englewood Cliffs, NJ: Prentice-Hall, 1981).

6. Domna Stanton, *The Female Autograph, op. cit.*, p. vii.

7. Blanche Wiesen Cook, "Biographer and Subject: A Critical Connection," in Carol Ascher, Louise de Salvo, Sara Ruddick, eds., *Between Women: Biographers, Novelists, Critics, Teachers and Artists Write about their Work on Women* (Boston, MA: Beacon Press, 1984), p. 397.

8. Paul Mariani, "William Carlos Williams," in Jeffrey Meyers, ed., *The Craft of Literary Biography* (London and Basingstoke, UK: Macmillan, 1985), p. 134.

9. Belle Gale Chevigny, "Daughters Writing: Toward a Theory of Women's Biography," *Feminist Studies* 9 (Spring 1983), pp. 79–102. Also in Ascher et al., *op. cit.*, pp. 357–379.

10. Michèle Sarde, *Colette*, trans. Richard Miller (New York, NY: William Morrow and Company Inc., 1980), pp. 7–9.

11. Paul John Eakin, *Fictions in Autobiography: Studies in the Art of Self-Invention, op. cit.*, p. 3.

12. Philippe Lejeune, *Le Pacte autobiographique* (Paris: Editions du Seuil, 1975). A selection of Lejeune's works in English is available in *On Autobiography* (Minneapolis, MN: University of Minnesota Press, 1988).

For a discussion of Lejeune's work, see Paul John Eakin, "Philippe Lejeune and the Study of Autobiography," *Romance Studies* (Summer 1986); and Marilyn Yalom's review of *Moi Aussi* in *a[b Auto/Biography Studies* (Spring 1987), pp. 25–27. Eakin acknowledges the lead of Roy Pascal who, a generation earlier, explored the use of past and present materials to serve the needs of the autobiographer's present reality. Roy Pascal, *Design and Truth in Autobiography* (Cambridge, MA: Harvard University Press, 1960).

13. Georges May, *L'Autobiographie* (Paris: Presses Universitaires de France, 1979).

14. Nancy K. Miller, "Writing Fictions: Women's Autobiography in France," in Brodzki and Schenck, *op. cit.*, p. 59.

15. For a cogent discussion of these issues, see Jane Flax, "Postmodernism and Gender Relations in Feminist Theory," *SIGNS: Journal of Women in Culture and Society,* Vol. 12 No. 4 (Summer 1987), pp. 621–43.

16. Deborah Rhode, ed., *Theoretical Perspectives on Sexual Difference* (New Haven, CT: Yale University Press, 1990).

17. Robert Stoller, *Presentations of Gender* (New Haven, CT: Yale University Press, 1985); J. Money, J. G. Hampson, and J. L. Hampson, "Imprinting and the Establishment of Gender Role," *Archives of Neurological Psychiatry,* No. 77, 1957; Juliet Mitchell and Jacqueline Rose, eds., *Feminine Sexuality: Jacques Lacan and the école freudienne* (New York, N.Y. and London: W. W. Norton, 1985). For a general feminist exposition of gender, see also Suzanne J. Kessler and Wendy McKenna, *Gender: An Ethnomethodological Approach* (Chicago, IL: University of Chicago Press, 1985).

18. Maya Angelou, *I Know Why the Caged Bird Sings* (New York, NY: Random House, 1970); Maxine Hong Kingston, *The Woman Warrior: Memoirs of a Childhood among Ghosts* (New York, NY: Vintage, 1975); Kim Chernin, *In My Mother's House* (New York, NY: Harper/Colophon, 1983).

19. Philip Wylie, *A Generation of Vipers* (Marietta, GA: Larlin Corporation, 1979), reprint of 1942 edition.

20. Jeffrey Meyers, ed., *The Craft of Literary Biography* (London and Basingstoke, UK: Macmillan, 1985); Marc Pachter, ed., *Telling Lives* (Washington, DC: New Republic Books, 1979); Dennis Petrie, *Untimely Fiction: Design in Modern American Literary Biography* (West Lafayette, IN: Purdue University Press, 1981); Eric Homberger and John Charmely, eds., *The Troubled Face of Biography* (New York, NY: St. Martin's Press, 1988).

21. Jean Strouse, *Alice James, A Biography* (Boston, MA: Houghton Mifflin, 1980); Phyllis Rose, *Parallel Lives* (New York, NY: Alfred A. Knopf, 1983).

22. Simone de Beauvoir, *The Second Sex,* translated and edited by H. M. Parshley (New York, NY: Alfred A. Knopf, 1952), p. 133.

23. Sidonie Smith, *op. cit.*

24. For an even more specific gender analysis of the Holocaust as documented in self-reflexive texts, see Mollie Schwartz Rosenhan's unpublished manuscript "Diaries of Adolescent Victims of the Holocaust."

Chapter One

1. This is not to imply that there are not also many more autobiographies by men than by women. However autobiography traditionally has been a more "accepted" genre for women than has biography. In other words, biography and autobiography have tended to be gender-inflected genres.

2. See for example, Paul John Eakin, *Fictions in Autobiography: Studies in the Art of Self-Invention* (Princeton, NJ: Princeton University Press, 1985) and Sidonie Smith, *A Poetics of Women's Autobiography: Marginality and the Fictions of Self-Representation* (Bloomington, IN: Indiana University Press, 1987).

3. My interest in the German women romantics in general and Bettina von Arnim in particular arises out of my work on Christa Wolf. Wolf was instrumental in recouping the writings of Karoline von Günderode (1780–1806) and in reassessing both Günderode's *oeuvre* and von Arnim's *Die Günderode.* The groundwork for my reading of *Christa T.,* and to a lesser degree *Die Günderode,* was developed in my monograph: *Christa Wolf's Utopian Vision: From Marxism to Feminism* (Cambridge, UK: Cambridge University Press, 1988), especially pp. 51–95. I am indebted to Cambridge University Press for granting me permission to draw on my previously published work.

4. See also for example Shari Benstock, ed., *The Private Self: Theory and Practice of Women's Autobiographical Writings* (Chapel Hill, NC/London: University of North Carolina Press, 1988); Bella Brodzki and Celeste Schenck, eds., *Life/Lines: Theorizing Women's Autobiography* (Ithaca, NY: Cornell University Press, 1988) and Sidonie Smith, *op. cit.*

5. Christa T.'s fatal illness has been read by some critics as a suicidal retreat into death. See for example Fritz J. Raddatz, "Mein Name sei Tonio Kröger" in *Der Spiegel* 23 (1969): 153–154, and Marcel Reich-Ranicki, "Christa Wolfs unruhige Elegie," in *Die Zeit,* 25 May 1969. In the overstated words of Reich-Ranicki: "Christa T. dies of leukemia, but her real illness is the GDR."

6. In her recent book Katherine Goodman reads *Die Günderode* as autobiography. See *Dis/Closures: Women's Autobiography in Germany Be-*

tween 1790 and 1914 (New York, NY: Lang, 1986), pp. 73–120; especially 93–105.

7. In *Bettine von Arnim and the Politics of Romantic Conversation* (Columbia, SC: Camden House, 1988) Edith Waldstein reads *Die Günderode* as an epistolary novel. The discrepancy between her reading of von Arnim's text and Katherine Goodman's 1986 reading of *Die Günderode* as autobiography indicates critics' ambivalence regarding the generic categorization of this text.

8. In *Christa T.* Wolf creates a sense of community between characters in the text and readers. She includes readers by shifting between the second-person singular familiar (du), the familiar plural (ihr), and the inclusive plural "we" forms of address. While this technique is not as fully developed in *Die Günderode,* the epistolary form does foster a sense of inclusion through its consistent use of the "Du."

9. See for example Elizabeth Abel, Marianne Hirsch, and Elizabeth Langland, eds., *The Voyage In: Fictions of Female Development* (Hanover, NH/London: University Press of New England, 1983) and Rachel Blau DuPlessis, *Writing Beyond the Ending: Narrative Strategies of Twentieth-Century Women Writers* (Bloomington, IN: Indiana University Press, 1985).

10. This expression is used by DuPlessis to identify the narrative techniques used by modern women writers in order to delegitimate conventional mythic narratives about women and thereby to circumvent the conventional marriage / suicide / madness endings of traditional romance plots.

11. That assessment no longer obtains. In the interim, *Christa T.* has assumed the stature of a classic in the GDR.

12. Christa Wolf, "Interview with Myself," in *The Reader and the Writer: Essays, Sketches, Memories,* translated by Joan Becker (New York, NY: International Publishers, 1977), pp. 75–76.

13. I use the term "alterity" in Simone de Beauvoir's gender-specific sense (as articulated in *The Second Sex*), namely as the positing of Woman as Other in Western thought and culture.

14. According to Freud, mourning, as distinct from melancholia, allows one to experience a sense of impoverishment at the loss of a loved one or ego-ideal without a concomitant sense of diminution of self-regard. See Sigmund Freud, "Mourning and Melancholia," in James Strachey, ed., *The Complete Psychological Works of Sigmund Freud,* Vol. XIV (London: Hogarth Press, 1957), pp. 243–58.

15. "The Reader and the Writer" in *The Reader and the Writer: Essays, Sketches, Memories,* pp. 177–212.

16. "Die Dimension des Autors," in *Fortgesetzter Versuch. Aufsätze, Gespräche, Essays* (Leipzig: Reclam, 1982), p. 83. My translation.

17. Christa Wolf, "Unruhe und Betroffenheit: Ein Gespräch mit Joachim Walther (1972)," in *Fortgesetzter Versuch,* p. 65.

18. There has been much critical debate concerning the precise relationship among Christa T., the first-person narrator, and Christa Wolf. Some critics conclude that Christa T. is identical with Christa Wolf; others read Christa T. as the narrator's alter ego. See Christa Thomassen, *Der lange Weg zu uns selbst. Christa Wolfs Roman "Nachdenken über Christa T." als Erfahrungs- und Handlungsmuster* (Kronberg: Scriptor, 1977), pp. 20–33 for a detailed analysis of the question of author-narrator identification.

19. "The Reader and the Writer," pp. 190–91.

20. James Olney, "Some Versions of Memory/Some Versions of *Bios:* The Ontology of Autobiography," in Olney, ed., *Autobiography: Essays Theoretical and Critical* (Princeton, NJ: Princeton University Press, 1980), p. 254.

21. Georges Gusdorf, "Conditions and Limitations of Autobiography," in Olney, ed., *Autobiography,* p. 39.

22. Mary G. Mason, "Autobiographies of Women Writers," in Olney, ed., *Autobiography,* p. 210.

23. For a discussion of female mirroring see Elisabeth Lenk, "Die sich selbst verdoppelnde Frau," *Ästhetik und Kommunikation: Beiträge zur politischen Erziehung* 25 (September 1976), pp. 84–87.

24. Wolf consciously plays with the notion of authenticity both in the text and in essays that illuminate *Christa T.* See especially her "Interview with Myself."

25. "Really existing socialism *(der realexistierende Sozialismus)*" is the term used to refer to the praxis of socialism in East-bloc countries. In the GDR's early self-understanding, the term was often viewed as coterminous with the Marxist ideal of socialism. Much of Christa Wolf's work concerns itself with the discrepancy between the theory and praxis of socialism.

26. Andreas Huyssen, "Auf den Spuren Ernst Blochs" in Klaus Sauer, ed., *Christa Wolf Materialienbuch,* second revised edition (Darmstadt/Neuwied: Luchterhand, 1983), pp. 99–115. The many parallels Huyssen draws between Wolf's works and Bloch's principle of hope are all the more remarkable in light of the recent revelation that Wolf did not become familiar with Ernst Bloch's philosophy until long after the completion of *Christa T.* See editor's note, footnote 13, p. 115, second, revised edition of the *Materialienbuch.*

27. Ernst Bloch, *Das Prinzip Hoffnung* (Frankfurt: Suhrkamp, 1959), p. 16.

28. Elizabeth Abel has discussed the fluidity between Christa T. and the narrator/ author within the context of preoedipal female psychological development. Using object relations theory (specifically Nancy Chodorow's analysis of the mother-daughter relationship), Abel extends the mother–daughter paradigm to the broader phenomenon of female bonding and develops a psychoanalytic model for female writing based on the commonality/complementarity of female friendship. "(E)Merging Identities: The Dynamic of Female Friendship in Contemporary Fiction by Women," *Signs* 6/3 (1981), pp. 413–435.

29. I am particularly indebted to Wolfgang Iser, *The Implied Reader* (Baltimore, MD: John Hopkins University Press, 1974) and *The Act of Reading* (Baltimore, MD: John Hopkins University Press, 1978).

30. In *New German Critique* 16 (Winter 1979), pp. 31–53.

31. See Sara Lennox, "Trends in Literary Theory: The Female Aesthetic and German Women's Writing," in *German Quarterly* (1981), pp. 63–75, for an excellent, concise overview of the French feminist appropriation of deconstructionist theory.

32. Love, p. 34.

33. Ibid, p. 35.

34. The original draft of this essay was written in 1985. At that time I subscribed to Love's terminology. In fact, I drew on it and read *Christa T.* and *Die Günderode* as examples of antipatriarchal writing.

35. Thus Wolf's text conforms to Mikhail Bakhtin's notion of "heteroglossia" as outlined in *The Dialogic Imagination*. See in particular "Discourse in the Novel," in *The Dialogic Imagination,* translated by Caryl Emerson and Michael Holquist (Austin, TX/London: University of Texas Press, 1981), pp. 259–422.

36. A note on orthography: the original spelling of the family name Günderrode was with two *r*s. However, for a long time, it was spelled with only one *r*. Thus Bettina von Arnim's text is called *Die Günderode*. Christa Wolf insists on the original orthography: in her essays on the romantic poet, she spells the surname "Günderrode." The historical von Arnim was known as Bettina. In *Die Günderode,* however, she signed her letters Bettine, her preferred spelling of her name. Christa Wolf adheres to Bettine's preferred spelling as does Edith Waldstein in her study of *Bettine von Arnim and the Politics of Romantic Conversation.*

37. While it found its most obvious expression in the salon, *Geselligkeit* was also operable in letters written at the time, many of which

were by women. For a discussion of romantic *Geselligkeit,* see Gisela Dischner, *Bettina von Arnim: Eine weibliche Sozialbiographie aus dem 19. Jahrhundert* (Berlin: Wagenbach, 1984), pp. 25–33.

38. The German intelligentsia's response to the French Revolution is a fascinating chapter of intellectual history. Generally speaking, an initial enthusiasm gave way to revulsion as the Revolution passed into its Thermidor phase. Revulsion in turn gave way to cynicism as first Napoleon and then Louis Philippe replaced the Sun King on the world stage.

39. Passed in 1819, the Carlsbad Degrees called for 1. censorship of any written text under twenty pages; 2. the outlawing of *Burschenschaften* (student fraternities); 3. close surveillance of the universities; 4. dismissal of faculty with leftist leanings.

40. Christa Wolf, "Der Schatten eines Traumes" (The Shadow of a Dream), in *Fortgesetzter Versuch: Aufsätze, Gespräche, Essays* (Leipzig: Reclam, 1982), p. 135. My translation.

41. Writers such as Georg Büchner *(Woyzeck)* and Heinrich Heine were also loosely connected to the Young Germans.

42. Waldstein, especially pp. 51–57.

43. Christa Wolf, "Der Schatten eines Traumes," in *Fortgesetzter Versuch,* p. 351.

44. Personal letter to author dated 13 January 1986.

45. "Der Schatten eines Traumes," in *Fortgesetzter Versuch,* p. 351. This statement is, of course, also directly applicable to *Christa T.*

46. Of the two, Bettina is clearly the more strongly female-identified character. Ironically, the historical Günderode's male-identification proved to be the cause of her death. The failure of her ill-fated love affair with Friedrich Creuzer, a married man, ostensibly prompted her suicide. In "Der Schatten eines Traumes" Christa Wolf takes issue with this explanation of Günderode's death.

47. Christa Wolf was the first to do so in her essay on Günderode, "Der Schatten eines Traumes" and on Bettina, "Nun ja! Das nächste Leben geht aber heute an!" (Well, the future starts today), in *Fortgesetzter Versuch,* pp. 325–376 and 377–409 respectively. Gisela Dischner's study on Bettina is indebted to Wolf. A recent interpretation of *Die Günderode* as a female utopia, by Elke Frederiksen and Monika Shafi, discusses the work as an example of *écriture féminine:* " 'Sich im Unbekannten suchen gehen': Bettina von Arnims *Die Günderode* als weibliche Utopie," in *Frauensprache-Frauenliteratur?: Für und Wider einer Psychoanalyse literarischer Werke, Proceedings of the VII. International Conference of Germanic Studies* (Tübingen: Niemeyer), Vol. 6, pp. 54–61. Frederiksen and Shafi's paper was the impetus for my piece.

48. Frederiksen and Shafi also consider *Die Günderode* to be an example of a concrete utopia, p. 56.

49. Dischner, p. 20.

50. See Sigrid Weigel, "Schreiben des Mangels als Produktion von Utopie" (Writing the Lack as Production of Utopia), in Marianne Burkhardt and Edith Waldstein, eds., in *Women in German Yearbook 1: Feminist Studies and German Culture* (Lanham, MD: University Press of America, 1985), pp. 29–38.

51. Bettina rejects the notion of an "angebildet Wesen." Bettina von Arnim, *Die Günderode* (Frankfurt/Main: Insel, 1982). All further quotations will refer to this edition, be in my translation, and be indicated by page numbers in the text.

52. The original reads "jeder soll neugierig sein auf sich selber und soll sich zutage fördern wie aus der Tiefe ein Stück Erz oder ein Quell, die ganze Bildung soll darauf ausgehen, daß wir den Geist ans Licht hervorlassen" (p. 173).

53. Caren Kaplan, "Deterritorializations: The Rewriting of Home and Exile in Western Feminist Discourse," in *Cultural Critique* 6 (Spring 1987), pp. 187–198; here p. 187.

Chapter Two

1. E. V. Lucas, *The Life of Charles Lamb* (London: Methuen, 1905), ii, p. 253.

2. See Winifred F. Courtney, *Young Charles Lamb: 1775–1802* (London and Basingstoke, UK: Macmillan, 1982), p. 370.

3. To Maria Fryer, 14 February 1834. E. V. Lucas, ed., *The Letters of Charles and Mary Lamb* (London: Dent and Methuen, 1935), iii, p. 401.

4. For an account of the transition from the point of view of women writers, see Mary Poovey, *The Proper Lady and the Woman Writer: Ideology and Style in the Works of Mary Wollstonecraft, Mary Shelley, and Jane Austen* (Chicago, IL: University of Chicago Press, 1984), pp. 3–47.

5. See S. T. Coleridge, *On the Constitution of the Church and State*, edited by John Colmer in Kathleen Coburn, ed., *The Collected Works of Samuel Taylor Coleridge* (Princeton, NJ: Princeton University Press, 1976), x, pp. 41 and 72–6. For a detailed account of the relation of paternalism to the English Romantic poets, see David Roberts, *Paternalism in Early Victorian England* (London: Croom Helm, 1979), pp. 25–74.

6. E. V. Lucas, ed., *The Works of Charles and Mary Lamb* (London: Methuen, 1903–5), ii, p. 247. All subsequent references in the text to the Lambs' works are from this edition.

212 *Notes*

7. See Joseph E. Riehl, *Charles Lamb's Children's Literature* (Salzburg: Universität Salzburg Press, 1980), p. 103.

8. To Barbara Betham, 2 November 1814. Edwin W. Marrs, Jr., ed., *The Letters of Charles and Mary Anne Lamb* (Ithaca, NY and London: Cornell University Press, 1978), iii, p. 116. (Marrs is still in the process of publishing a new and definitive edition of the Lamb letters, hence the references to two editions).

9. See Nancy Chodorow, *The Reproduction of Mothering: Psychoanalysis and the Sociology of Gender* (Berkeley, CA: University of California Press, 1978).

10. To Bernard Barton, 1 December 1824. Lucas, ed., *Letters*, ii, p. 447.

11. See, for example, the Elia essay "Mackerey End in Hertfordshire": "I have obligations to Bridget [Mary Lamb], extending beyond the period of memory" (ii, p. 75).

12. See Thomas S. Weisner, "Sibling Interdependence and Child Caretaking: A Cross-Cultural View," in Michael E. Lamb and Brian Sutton-Smith, eds., *Sibling Relationships: Their Nature and Significance Across the Lifespan* (Englewood Cliffs, NJ: Lawrence Erlbaum Associates, 1983), pp. 305–327.

13. See "Appendix IV: John Lamb's Poetical Pieces" to Lucas, *The Life of Charles Lamb*, ii, p. 337, for an indication of John Lamb's habitual mildness. A poem entitled "Matrimony" reads: "At home let's be chearful, good-natur'd, and kind,/When troubles attend us, be ever resign'd."

14. Marrs, ed., *Letters*, i, p. 52.

15. See Courtney, *Young Charles Lamb: 1775–1802*, pp. 22–4, and Lucas, *The Life of Charles Lamb*, i, pp. 14 and 20–27.

16. See the letter to Coleridge of 27 May 1796, Marrs, ed., *Letters*, i, p. 4.

17. See Edith J. Morley, ed., *Henry Crabb Robinson on Books and their Writers* (London: Dent, 1938), i, p. 156, for an entry in Crabb Robinson's diary for 11 December 1814 in which he records Mary's distress and the fact that she found writing "a most painful occupation."

18. For further discussion of the effect upon Mary's writings of her parents' social status as servants, see my article " 'On Needle-Work': Protest and Contradiction in Mary Lamb's Essay" in Anne K. Mellor, ed., *Romanticism and Feminism* (Bloomington and Indianapolis, IN: Indiana University Press, 1988), pp. 179–80.

19. See Thomas Noon Talfourd, *Final Memorials of Charles Lamb* (London: Moxon, 1848), ii, pp. 226–8, for an account of Mary's customary

reticence when well and loquacity during her illnesses. His description, and a further discussion of Mary's madness, is given in my article " 'On Needle-Work'," p. 175.

20. F. V. Morley, in *Lamb before Elia* (London: Jonathan Cape, 1932), manages to present both ideas in the same account (pp. 146 and 246).

21. See the series of letters to Coleridge on the tragedy, Marrs, ed., *Letters*, i, pp. 44–64.

22. Marrs, ed., *Letters*, i, p. 202.

23. To Sarah Stoddart, 21 September 1803. Marrs, ed., *Letters*, ii, p. 124.

24. For an account of such an act of his, see B. W. Procter (pseud. "Barry Cornwall"), *Charles Lamb: A Memoir* (London: Moxon, 1866), p. 113, in which Charles is described as taking a kettle from the fire and placing it for a moment on Mary's headdress, "in order to startle her into recollection."

25. See Simone de Beauvoir, *The Second Sex*, translated by H. M. Parshley (Harmondsworth, Middlesex: Penguin, 1972), pp. 94 ff., for an account of women's immersion in the immanent as opposed to men's more transcendent sphere; and D. W. Winnicott, *Playing and Reality* (Harmondsworth, Middlesex: Penguin, 1974), pp. 95–7, for an account of the female element of "being" as opposed to the male element of "doing" in human development.

Chapter Three

1. Domna C. Stanton, "Autogynography: Is the Subject Different?" in *The Female Autograph* (Chicago, IL: University of Chicago Press [paperback] 1987), p. 15. The collection also includes "My Childhood Years" (my translation). For a more specific discussion of *The Cavalry Maiden*'s place among autobiographies by Russian women, see: Barbara Heldt, *Terrible Perfection: Women and Russian Literature* (Bloomington, IN: Indiana University Press, 1987). For Durova's life in retirement, literary career, and reputation in Russia, see the introduction to my translation of the text: *The Cavalry Maiden* (Bloomington, IN: Indiana University Press, 1988). All the quotations and chapter citations in this article are from that edition.

2. The manuscripts have not survived. Before World War I, Colonel A. A. Saks of the Lithuanian Uhlans, in which Durova served from 1811 to 1816, collected materials and souvenirs for the regimental museum and published a well-documented biography that verifies Durova's account in

every respect (*Kavalerist-devitsa* [St. Petersburg, 1912]). It was not until 1983 that *The Cavalry Maiden* was reprinted in full for the first time in the Soviet Union (*Izbrannye sochineniia kavalerist-devitsy N. A. Durovoi* [Moscow, 1983]), and contemporary Russian critics have yet to publish any analysis of the text or of Durova's literary heritage.

3. Marina Warner analyzed Joan's legacy in *Joan of Arc: The Image of Female Heroism* (New York, NY: Alfred A. Knopf, 1981). Another recently rediscovered woman warrior whose exploits were recorded at an ecclesiastic trial was the runaway Spanish nun Catalina de Erauso, who served as a mule-driver and soldier in the New World in the early seventeenth century; see Mary Elizabeth Perry, " 'The Manly Woman': A Historical Case Study," *American Behavorial Scientist,* vol. 31, no. 1 (1987), pp. 86–100. Thérèse Figueur ("Sans-Gêne") fought in the French cavalry during the Napoleonic era with little pretense of being a man; her reminiscences were published as *Un ancien du 15e dragons* ([Paris] 1936). Marilyn Yalom has republished the dictated account of Renée Bordereau, a French peasant who fought for six years disguised as a man in the counter-revolutionary wars, in *Le Temps des Orages* (Paris: Maren Sell, 1989). Estelle Jelinek has retrieved and analyzed a series of autobiographies and picaresque first-person tales by English and American women who disguised themselves as men, usually in military uniform, from the late 1700s through the nineteenth century ("Disguise Autobiographies: Women Masquerading as Men," *Women's Studies International Forum,* vol. 10, no. 1 [1987], pp. 53–62).

4. " 'Divnyi phenomen nravstennogo mira . . . ' " ('A Miraculous Phenomenon of the Moral World . . . ') in N. A. Durova, *Izbrannoe* (Moscow, 1984), p. 17. (The title quotation, which suggests the impact Durova's journals made on sensitive contemporaries, is from a review by the famous critic V. G. Belinsky.)

5. By the 1920s the paradigm had been partially reversed; in "bohemian" circles at least Western women were accepted as honorary men by conforming to traditional male norms of promiscuity.

6. I am grateful to Kenneth Craven of Providence, NJ, for the formulation and much good advice on this paper in its formative stages.

7. Of the accounts that had appeared in print by the mid-1850s, *The Cavalry Maiden* most closely resembles Fedor Glinka's *Letters of a Russian Officer* (Moscow, 1815), which was also cast in the form of journals addressed to familiars. For others, see John L. H. Keep, "From the Pistol to the Pen: The military memoir as a source on the social history of pre-Reform Russia," *Cahiers du Monde russe et soviétique* 21: 3–4 (1980), pp. 295–320. Faddej Bulgarin's *Reminiscences: Excerpts from Things Seen, Heard and Experienced in Life,* 6 vols. (St. Petersburg, 1846–1849) is the prime example of a memoir influenced by Durova's journals, which Bulgarin reviewed enthusiastically in 1839.

8. Over 100 years later, in "My First Goose," Isaak Babel's bespectacled Jewish propagandist, another outsider, kills a goose to win acceptance from the rough Cossacks of his regiment *(Red Cavalry)*.

9. Durova did not deceive Alexander I; in official documents she is described as "by marriage Chernova."

10. Durova turns this incident into a long, semi-fictionalized tale, "Love," in the 1839 *Notes.*

11. The article is preserved in the archives of M. P. Pogodin in the Lenin Library, Moscow.

12. E. Men'shov, "Vesti iz Elabugi: Moe znakomstvo c devitseiu-kavaleristom Nad. Andr. Durovoi—otstavnym shtabs-rotmistrom Aleksandrovym," *Peterburgskii vestnik,* 1861, no. 3, pp. 64–65. In *The Cavalry Maiden* Durova wrote that on bachelor evenings in the cavalry she always danced the woman's part.

Chapter Four

1. Marilyn Yalom, "Women's Autobiography in French, 1793–1939: A Selected Bibliography" in *Autobiography in French Literature,* French Literature Series, Vol. XII (Columbia, SC: The University of South Carolina, 1985), pp. 197–205.

2. Charlotte Robespierre, *Mémoires de Charlotte Robespierre sur ses deux frères* (Paris: Au dépôt central, Faubourg St.-Denis, No. 16, 1835); Madame Martelet, *Dix Ans Chez Alfred de Musset* (Paris: Chamuel, 1899); Adèle Hugo, *Victor Hugo raconté par un témoin de sa vie* (Paris: Librairie internationale, 1863), 2 Vols. Reprinted as *Victor Hugo raconté par Adèle Hugo* (Paris: Librairie Plon, 1985). All citations are to the 1985 edition, henceforth referred to as *Victor Hugo raconté.* All translations are my own.

3. Françoise Basch, *Relative Creatures: Victorian Women in Society and the Novel* (New York, NY: Schocken Books, 1974).

4. Nancy K. Miller, "Women's Autobiography in France," *Women and Language in Literature and Society* (New York, NY: Praeger, 1980), p. 262.

5. Yves Gohin, "Portrait d'une Femme Quelconque," in *Victor Hugo raconté, op. cit.,* p. 33.

6. Ibid., citation from Adèle's letter of January 5, 1822.

7. Alain Decaux, *Victor Hugo* (Paris: Librairie Académique Perrin, 1985), p. 21. See also Irène Frain in "Une Voix dans le Demi-Jour," her preface to *Victor Hugo raconté* (pp. 11–28). This essay documents the full range of editorial control exercised over Adèle by Hugo, Vacquerie, and

others, as well as numerous other difficulties overcome by Adèle in ascending to authorship.

8. For a study of women's memoirs of the French Revolution, see Marilyn Yalom, *Le Temps des Orages: Aristocrates, Bourgeoises, et Paysannes Racontent* (Paris: Maren Sell, 1989).

9. Barbey d'Aurevilly, *Les Bas Bleus* (Paris: Victor Palme, 1878), p. xi.

10. *Victor Hugo raconté, op. cit.*, pp. 115–116.

11. This description of Jane Austen, undoubtedly from hearsay, is found in Harriet Martineau's *Autobiography* (London: Virago, 1983), Vol. 1, p. 100. Martineau reminds us that in her youth "it was not thought proper for young ladies to study very conspicuously; and especially with pen in hand." Despite her criticism of this attitude, Martineau, writing her memoirs in the eighteen-fifties, is, like Adèle Hugo, anxious to dissociate herself from the image of "being a literary lady who could not sew," p. 27.

12. Adèle Hugo, "La Dernière Année de Mme Dorval," in *Victor Hugo raconté, op. cit.*, p. 653.

13. *Victor Hugo raconté, op. cit.*, pp. 229–230.

14. Decaux, *op. cit.*, pp. 241–242.

15. *Victor Hugo raconté, op. cit.*, p. 87.

16. Ibid., p. 134.

17. Ibid., p. 698.

18. Ibid., p. 132.

19. Ibid., see examples pp. 333, 413, 485.

20. See, of course, Tillie Olsen, *Silences* (New York, NY: Delacorte Press/Seymour Lawrence, 1978).

21. Decaux, *op. cit.*, p. 545.

22. Joan Lidoff, "Autobiography in a Different Voice," in Shirley Lim, ed., *Approaches to Teaching Maxine Hong Kingston's "The Woman Warrior,"* forthcoming.

23. Nancy Chodorow, *The Reproduction of Mothering: Psychoanalysis and the Sociology of Gender* (Berkeley, CA: University of California Press, 1978); Carol Gilligan, *In a Different Voice: Psychological Theory and Women's Development* (Cambridge, MA: Harvard University Press, 1982).

24. Carolyn Heilbrun, *Writing a Woman's Life* (New York, NY: W. W. Norton & Company, 1988).

Chapter Five

1. Letter to Julian Sturgis, attributed to July 1894 by Hester Thackeray Ritchie in her edition of her mother's letters, *Thackeray and His Daughter* (New York, NY: Harper, 1924), p. 243; cited hereafter as *ATR Letters.* Winifred Gérin must date it to an earlier period, however, for she considers Julian's memoir of his father, Russell, as the subject of the full text of the letter and treats that book as the impetus to Ritchie's writing of her own memoirs. See Gérin, *Anne Thackeray Ritchie: A Biography* (Oxford: Oxford University Press, 1981), p. 229.

2. Estelle C. Jelinek discusses these and other aspects of women's autobiographical writings in her introductory chapter to her edited volume, *Women's Autobiography: Essays in Criticism* (Bloomington, IN: Indiana University Press, 1980), pp. 1–20. See also Judith Kegan Gardiner, "On Female Identity and Writing by Women," *Critical Inquiry* 8 (Winter 1981), pp. 347–61, and Susan Stanford Friedman, "Women's Autobiographical Selves: Theory and Practice," in Shari Benstock, ed., *The Private Self: Theory and Practice of Women's Autobiographical Writings* (Chapel Hill, NC: University of North Carolina Press, 1988).

3. Despite her criticism of certain "lady novelists," George Eliot valued this aspect of women writers—their "precious speciality, lying quite apart from masculine aptitude and experience." See "Silly Novels by Lady Novelists," *Westminster Review* 66 (October 1856), pp. 442–61; reprinted in Thomas Pinney, ed., *Essays of George Eliot* (New York, NY: Columbia University Press, 1963), p. 324. It is worth noting in this context that the 1919 essay by Virginia Woolf that restored Eliot to serious criticism cites her Aunt Anny's recollection of Eliot's conversation about how "we ought to respect our influence." See Woolf, "George Eliot," *The Times Literary Supplement,* 20 November 1920; reprinted in *The Common Reader* (New York: Harcourt, Brace, 1925), p. 167.

4. Avrom Fleishman, *Figures of Autobiography: The Language of Self-Writing* (Berkeley, CA: University of California Press, 1983), p. 37. For other examples of male critics who relegate the writing of memoirs to this lower status, see Roy Pascal, *Design and Truth in Autobiography* (London: Routledge and Kegan Paul, 1960), and A. O. J. Cockshut, *The Art of Autobiography in 19th and 20th Century England* (New Haven, CT: Yale University Press, 1984).

5. Thackeray actually uttered his famous proscription on numerous occasions, but one record of it occurs in his daughter's manuscript reminiscences written in the year following his death in 1863. See Gordon N. Ray, *Thackeray: The Uses of Adversity, 1811–1846* (New York, NY: McGraw-Hill, 1955), p. 2.

6. The first series appeared under the title *The Biographical Edition of the Works of William Makepeace Thackeray;* the second, occasioned by

the hundredth anniversary of his death and providing an opportunity for correction and expansion, was entitled *The Centenary Biographical Edition*. Both were published by the firm of Smith, Elder. AMS Press has just published a two-volume edition of Lady Ritchie's introductions, with a critical and historical introduction by Carol Hanbery MacKay and a bibliographic introduction by Peter L. Shillingsburg and Julia Maxey. I am grateful to AMS for permission to republish here a revised version of a portion of my introductory essay.

7. Fleishman summarizes and elaborates on the concept of "personal myth" as it has been advanced by Carl Jung, Charles Mauron, James Olney, William Empson, Kenneth Burke, and Northrop Frye; see especially pp. 22–27.

8. *Chapters from Some Memoirs* (London: Macmillan, 1894), p. 1.

9. *Chapters,* p. 12.

10. Gérin, p. 219.

11. *Chapters,* p. 4. Woolf picks up this view of her Aunt Anny when she recasts her as Mrs. Hilbery, the would-be biographer of her poet-father, in *Night and Day* (London: Hogarth Press, 1919), which was published in the year of Ritchie's death. See also MacKay. "The Thackeray Connection: Virginia Woolf's Aunt Anny," in Jane Marcus, ed., *Virginia Woolf and Bloomsbury: A Centennial Celebration* (Bloomington, IN: Indiana University Press and London: Macmillan, 1987), pp. 68–95.

12. *Records of Tennyson, Ruskin and Robert and Elizabeth Browning* (London: Macmillan, 1892), pp. 1–4.

13. Introd. to *Esmond,* The Centenary Biographical Edition (London: Smith, Elder, 1910–11), pp. xxxii–xxxvii. All subsequent references to Ritchie's biographical introductions will be to this edition.

14. "The Boyhood of Thackeray," *St. Nicholas* 17 (December 1889), p. 101.

15. Introd. to *Vanity Fair,* p. xv.

16. Introd. to *The English Humourists* and *The Four Georges,* p. xxii.

17. Ritchie is seeing at end-century what we of the twentieth century have come to realize more fully about the role and "creation" of childhood. For an extended discussion of this topic in relation to autobiography, see LuAnn Walther, "The Invention of Childhood in Victorian Autobiography," in George P. Landow, ed., *Approaches to Victorian Autobiography* (Athens, OH: Ohio University Press, 1979), pp. 64–83.

18. See her "Comment," *Harper's New Monthly Magazine* 82, no. 489 (February 1891), pp. 461–71; reprint Thackeray, *The Heroic Adventures of M. Boudin*, introd. and trans. Ray (Syracuse: Syracuse University Library Associates, 1980), pp. 17–20.

19. Introd. to *Vanity Fair*, p. xxvi.

20. Introd. to *Esmond*, p. xxii.

21. Introd. to *Newcomes*, pp. xxxi–xxxii.

22. Introd. to *Vanity Fair*, p. xl.

23. Introd. to *Miscellanies*, p. xlvi.

24. Introd. to *Esmond*, p. xxv.

25. Introd. to *Vanity Fair*, p. xxx.

26. Ritchie's own sketches, including self-portraits, pepper her letters, both published and unpublished. For Thackeray's portrait of eighteen-year-old Anny as "The Amanuensis," see the last volume of The Centenary Edition, facing p. xviii.

27. See MacKay, " 'Only Connect': The Multiple Roles of Anne Thackeray Ritchie," *The Library Chronicle*, n.s. 30 (1985), pp. 83–112.

28. Introd. to *Vanity Fair*, p. xxxvii.

29. Ibid., p. xxvi.

30. See William C. Spengemann, *The Forms of Autobiography: Episodes in the History of a Literary Genre* (New Haven, CT: Yale University Press, 1980).

31. Virginia Woolf, *The Times Literary Supplement*, 12 January 1922; reprinted in Mary Lyon, ed., *Books and Portraits* (New York, NY: Harcourt Brace Jovanovich, 1977), p. 112.

32. Letter of 7 July [1871] to James T. Fields, Huntington Library.

33. Note Ritchie's own wording at the head of her first introduction: "So much has been forgotten, so much that is ephemeral has been remembered, that it was my desire to mark down some of the truer chords to which [Thackeray's] life was habitually set" (Introd. to *Vanity Fair*, p. xiii).

34. Introd. to *Philip*, p. liii.

35. Letter of 12 May 1904, Fales Collection, New York University Library. The context of the letter reveals how difficult it still was for Ritchie to comment on her father's life: "having once for all written down what I wanted to say I am anxious to keep aloof & to express nothing more." Of course, she would go on to reexamine and recast what she just said in the

Biographical Edition when she took on the task of issuing the Centenary Edition. 36. See, for example, the discussion of immediate ancestry in the Introd. to *Vanity Fair,* pp. xviii–xix.

37. "The First Number of 'The Cornhill,' " *The Cornhill Magazine,* n.s. 1 (July 1896), pp. 15–16.

38. [Elizabeth] Gaskell, *Cranford,* introd. Anne Thackeray Ritchie (London: Macmillan, 1891), pp. v–vi and xxiv. Mrs. Gibson is a character in the novel.

39. See the undated letter by Ritchie's daughter Hester to Maude Frank about how Mme de Sévigné "was part of my mother's life, an intimate friend who[m] she quoted constantly; I should think she knew her letters almost by heart," Frank Collection, Columbia University Library.

40. *Madame de Sévigné* (Philadelphia, PA: J. B. Lippincott, 1881), pp. 116–117. Similarly, Howard Overing Sturgis cites two quotations by Ritchie on Elizabeth Gaskell "because they might have been written word for word about herself." See his tribute, "Anne Isabella Thackeray (Lady Ritchie)," *The Cornhill Magazine,* n.s. 47 (November 1919), p. 466.

41. *Madame de Sévigné,* p. 4. Ritchie then proceeds to note the added difficulty posed by translation: "but how impossible it is to translate her words!"

42. *The Times Literary Supplement,* 6 March 1919; reprint Gérin, pp. 279–84.

43. Virginia Woolf, "The Enchanted Organ," in Leonard Woolf, ed., *Collected Essays* (New York, NY: Harcourt, Brace & World, 1967), Vol. 4, p. 73.

44. See *ATR Letters,* pp. 284–88.

45. "Anne Thackeray Ritchie," review of *Thackeray's Daughter: Some Recollections of Anne Thackeray Ritchie,* compiled by Hester Thackeray Fuller and Violet Hammersley (Dublin: Euphorion, 1951), *The Times Literary Supplement,* 1 February 1952.

46. Gérin, p. 171.

47. [Seymour Vesey FitzGerald], "Sir Richmond Thackeray Willoughby Ritchie," *Dictionary of National Biography, 1912–1921* (London: Oxford University Press, 1927), pp. 462–63. Anne became "Lady Ritchie" in 1907 only because her husband was knighted in that year. Some six years later she would be granted her own honor: being elected President of the English Association.

Chapter Six

1. All references in parentheses are to John Stuart Mill, *Autobiography*, edited with an introduction and notes by Jack Stillinger (Boston, MA: Houghton Mifflin, 1969).

2. H. O. Pappe, *John Stuart Mill and the Harriet Taylor Myth* (London and New York: Cambridge University Press, 1960).

3. See for example, Bruce Mazlish, *James and John Stuart Mill, Father and Son in the Nineteenth Century* (New York, NY: Basic, 1975), pp. 284–288. (A new edition exists with a New Introduction: New Brunswick, NJ: Transaction Publishers, 1988.)

4. A. O. J. Cockshut, *The Art of Autobiography in 19th and 20th Century England* (New Haven, CT: Yale University Press, 1984), p. 9.

5. Jack Stillinger, ed., *The Early Draft of John Stuart Mill's "Autobiography"* (Urbana, IL: University of Illinois Press, 1961), p. 66.

6. Ibid., p. 184.

7. F. A. Hayek, *John Stuart Mill and Harriet Taylor: Their Correspondence and Subsequent Marriage* (Chicago, IL: University of Chicago Press, 1951).

8. Bruce Mazlish, *James and John Stuart Mill, passim.*

9. Hayek, pp. 32, 33.

10. Ibid., pp. 190, 194, 196.

11. Stillinger, *The Early Draft,* p. 171.

12. Leonore Davidoff and Catherine Hall, *Family Fortunes: Men and Women of the English Middle Class 1780–1850* (Chicago, IL: University of Chicago Press, 1987).

13. Sir Henry Maine and Johann Bachofen, Documents 101 and 102 in Susan Groag Bell and Karen Offen, eds., *Women, the Family and Freedom, The Debate in Documents 1750–1950,* 2 Vols. (Stanford, CA: Stanford University Press, 1983), Vol. 1.

14. Paul Broca, "Sur le volume et la forme du cerveau suivant les individus et suivant les races," *Bulletin Société d'Anthropologie,* Paris 2: (1861) p. 153.

15. Karl Christoph Vogt, *Lectures on Man, His Place in Creation and in the History of the Earth,* Anthropological Society of London, 1864, p. 183 f.

16. See, for example, Bell and Offen, Vol. 1, Document 105 *The Subjection of Women* (1869). Also Document 135 the *Speech* in the House of

222 *Notes*

Commons (1867), and Mill's correspondence with Auguste Comte, in L. Lévy-Bruhl, *Lettres inédites de John Stuart Mill à Auguste Comte* (Paris: Felix Alcan, 1899).

17. For example, William Wordsworth, "Tintern Abbey, 1798" in *Selected Poetry* (New York, NY: The Modern Library, 1950), p. 106.

18. Bell and Offen, Vol. 1, Doc. 10, pp. 43–49, Rousseau from *Émile*: "It is impossible for a woman who permits herself to be morally compromised ever to be considered virtuous . . . on the care of women depends the early education of men; and on women again, depend their mores, their passions, their tastes, their pleasures, and even their happiness."

19. Ibid., Doc. 28, p. 115 (Goethe from *Wilhelm Meister*).

20. Ibid., Doc. 63, pp. 226, Auguste Comte; and see also: Ibid., Doc. 43, p. 166 Louis Aimé-Martin: "On the maternal bosom the mind of nations reposes; their manners, prejudices, and virtues—in a word the civilization of the human race all depend upon maternal influence;" and p. 170, Joseph de Maistre: "Woman can accomplish anything by working through man's heart."

21. Ibid., Doc. 32, pp. 120–130 (Thompson/Wheeler).

22. Erna Hellerstein, Leslie Hume, and Karen M. Offen, eds., *Victorian Women, A Documentary Account of Women's Lives in Nineteenth-Century England, France and the United States* (Stanford, CA: Stanford University Press, 1981), p. 135.

23. Bell and Offen, Vol. 1, Doc. 97, p. 342 (Michelet, "Woman").

24. Ibid., Doc. 104, p. 389. (Ruskin, "Queens' Gardens").

25. Charles Fourier, *Théorie des quatre mouvements et des destinées générales* 3rd ed. (1841–1848). Originally published in 1808. Tr. Karen Offen in Bell and Offen, Vol. 1, Doc. 9, p. 41. James Mill, *The History of British India*, 2nd ed. (London: Baldwin, Craddock and Joy, 1820) p. 293, originally published 1817.

26. Cited in Mazlish, p. 329 from a letter to a Russian correspondent in 1868, from the Mill Taylor Collection 45/85; and see Bell and Offen, Vol. 1, Doc. 135, pp. 482–88 (Mill's speech from the debate in the House of Commons, 1867).

27. Bell and Offen, Vol. 1, Doc. 11, p. 53 (Catharine Macaulay), and Doc. 12, pp. 57, 59 (Mary Wollstonecraft).

28. *The Subjection of Women*, reprinted in Alice Rossi, ed., *John Stuart Mill and Harriet Taylor Mill, Essays in Sex Equality* (Chicago, IL and London: University of Chicago Press, 1970), p. 185.

29. Bell and Offen, Vol. 1, Doc. 135, pp. 485–486 (Mill's speech to the Commons).

30. Francis E. Mineka, ed., *The Earlier Letters of John Stuart Mill, 1812–1848* (Toronto: University of Toronto Press, 1962), p. 184. (This letter was written three years after falling in love with Harriet Taylor, when Mill was twenty-seven years old.)

Chapter Seven

1. I am very grateful to the Stanford Humanities Center and Pew Memorial Trust for supporting the research for this essay; to Susan Groag Bell and Marilyn Yalom for inviting me to participate in the conference where it was first presented; and to the Institute for Research on Women and Gender at Stanford University, for being there.

2. Lillian S. Robinson, "Working/Women/Writing," *Sex, Class, and Culture* (New York and London: Methuen, 1986), p. 226.

3. Adria Taylor Hourwich and Gladys L. Palmer, eds., *Women in America* Series (New York, NY: Arno Press, 1974).

4. "Three Women's Texts and a Critique of Imperialism," in Henry Louis Gates, Jr., ed., *"Race," Writing, and Difference* (Chicago, IL: University of Chicago Press, 1986), p. 265.

5. There are many works on the history of individual professions and the crucial periods of professional consolidation, such as the nineteenth century. The one I have found most useful is Magali Sarfatti Larson, *The Rise of Professionalism: A Sociological Analysis* (Berkeley, CA: University of California Press, 1979).

6. My edition of Disraeli is B. Disraeli, ed., *The Literary Character of Men of Genius* (New York, NY: Crowell, 1881).

7. Mary Jean Corbett, "Producing the Professional: Wordsworth, Carlyle, and the Authorial Self" in *Representing Femininity: Middle-Class Subjectivity in Women's Autobiographies, 1805–1914*, Ph.D. Dissertation, English Department, Stanford University, 1989, pp. 14–76.

8. Mary Poovey argued this in " 'The-Man-of-Letters Hero': Literary Labor and the Representation of Women," paper presented at a conference on "Dickens, Women, and Victorian Culture," University of California at Santa Cruz, August 6–9, 1987. The paper, in altered form, is included as chapter 4 in Poovey's *Uneven Developments: The Ideological Work of Gender* (Chicago, IL: University of Chicago Press, 1988).

9. Charles Dickens, *David Copperfield* (Middlesex: Penguin, 1986), pp. 279–80.

10. See also Alexander Welsh, *From Copyright to Copperfield* (Cambridge, MA: Harvard University Press, 1987).

11. Nora Barlow, ed., *The Autobiography of Charles Darwin 1809–1882* (New York, NY: Norton, 1969), pp. 232–234.

12. Ibid.

13. Florence Nightingale, *Cassandra* (New York, NY: Feminist Press, 1979), p. 34.

14. See however Martha Vicinus, *The Industrial Muse: A Study of Nineteenth Century British Working-Class Literature* (London: Croom Helm, 1974) and Nan Hackett, *XIX Century British Working-Class Autobiographies: An Annotated Bibliography* (New York, NY: AMS, 1985).

15. Margaret Llewelyn Davies, ed., *Life As We Have Known It: By Co-Operative Working Women* (1931; New York, NY: Norton, 1975). Further page references will be included in the text.

16. Pierre Bourdieu, *Distinction: A Social Critique of the Judgement of Taste* (Cambridge, MA: Harvard University Press, 1984).

17. For full discussion of the philosophical concepts of normative dualism, liberal rationality, and abstract individualism, see Alison M. Jaggar, *Feminist Politics and Human Nature* (Sussex: Harvester Press, 1983).

18. "Women's Strategies, 1890–1940" in Jane Lewis, ed., *Labour and Love: Women's Experience of Home and Family, 1850–1940* (Oxford: Basil Blackwell, 1986), pp. 243–244.

19. Ibid., "Marital Status, Work and Kinship, 1850–1930," p. 265.

20. William Tayler in John Burnett, ed., *Annals of Labour: Autobiographies of British Working-Class People 1820–1920* (Bloomington, IN: Indiana University Press, 1974), p. 175.

21. Georges Gusdorf, "Conditions and Limits of Autobiography," James Olney, ed., reprinted in *Autobiography: Essays Theoretical and Critical* (Princeton, NJ: Princeton University Press, 1980); Roy Pascal, *Design and Truth in Autobiography* (Cambridge, MA: Harvard University Press, 1960), p. 148; James Olney, *Metaphors of Self* (Princeton, NJ: Princeton University Press, 1972).

22. Paul Jay, *Being in the Text, Self-Representation from Wordsworth to Roland Barthes* (Ithaca, NY: Cornell University Press, 1984); Avrom Fleishman, *Figures of Autobiography: The Language of Self-Writing in Victorian and Modern England* (Berkeley, CA: University of California Press, 1983); Michael Sprinker, "Fictions of the Self: The End of Autobiography" in James Olney, ed., *Autobiography: Essays Theoretical and Critical* (Princeton, NJ: Princeton University Press, 1980). Also on the possible end of "autobiography" as individualist project see Elizabeth Bruss, *Autobiographical Acts: The Changing Situation of a Literary Genre* (Baltimore, MD: Johns Hopkins University Press, 1976). Although his interest re-

mains with the canonical literary writers who write from "some imperative authorial necessity" and want "to work through something for themselves" (p. 236), Paul John Eakin provides a balanced discussion of the cultural limits of literary autobiography. See *Fictions in Autobiography: Studies in the Act of Self-Invention* (Princeton, NJ: Princeton University Press, 1988), especially Eakin's judicious account of recent theoretical approaches to autobiography in chapter four, "Self-Invention in Autobiography: The Moment of Language," pp. 181–279.

23. Estelle C. Jelinek, ed., *Women's Autobiographies: Essays in Criticism* (Bloomington, IN: Indiana University Press, 1980); Sidonie Smith, *A Poetics of Women's Autobiography: Marginality and the Fictions of Self-Representation* (Bloomington, IN: Indiana University Press, 1987); Shari Benstock, ed., *The Private Self: Theory and Practice of Women's Autobiographical Writings* (Chapel Hill, NC: University of North Carolina Press, 1988); Bella Brodzki and Celeste Schenck, *Life/Lines: Theorizing Women's Autobiography* (Ithaca, NY: Cornell University Press, 1988).

24. This formulation is influenced by the work of Ernesto Laclau and Chantal Mouffe, *Hegemony and Socialist Strategy: Towards a Radical Democratic Politics* (London: Verso, 1985); J-F Lyotard, *The Postmodern Condition* (Minneapolis, MN: University of Minnesota, 1984); and Michel Foucault, *The History of Sexuality*. 3 vols. Translated by Robert Hurley (New York, NY: Pantheon, 1980, 1985, 1986).

25. See Roberto Mangabeira Unger, *Knowledge and Politics* (New York, NY: The Free Press, 1975) and *Passion: An Essay on Personality* (New York, NY: The Free Press, 1986).

26. See Chaim Perelman, *The New Rhetoric* (Notre Dame, IN: University of Notre Dame, 1969) and Thomas Nagel, *The View From Nowhere* (New York, NY: Oxford University Press, 1986).

27. For cyborg society see Donna Haraway, "A Manifesto for Cyborgs: Science, Technology, and Socialist Feminism in the 1980s," *Socialist Review* 80 (March-April, 1985), pp. 65–107. Roughly, Haraway intends "cyborg" to represent the collapse of the distinction between organic and mechanical.

28. See John Burnett, David Mayall, and David Vincent, eds., *The Autobiography of the Working Class: An Annotated Critical Bibliography, Volume 1, 1790–1900* (Brighton: Harvester, 1984); Gagnier, "Social Atoms: Working-Class Autobiography, Subjectivity and Gender," *Victorian Studies* (Spring 1987), p. 335–63. For the culmination of my comparative studies of autobiography, see Gagnier, *Subjectivities: A History of Self-Representation in Britain 1832–1920* (New York, NY: Oxford University Press, 1990). Also see Hackett (1985).

29. Louise Jermy, *The Memories of a Working Woman* (Norwich: Goose and Son, 1934); Peter Paterson [James Glass Bertram], *Behind the*

Scenes: Being the Confessions of a Strolling Player (London: Henry Lea, 1859); William Dodd, *Narrative of the Experience and Sufferings of William Dodd, A Factory Cripple, Written by Himself* (1841; rpt. ed. London: Cass, 1968); Rose Gibbs, *In Service: Rose Gibbs Remembers* (Cambridge, UK: Archives for Bassingbourn and Comberton Village Colleges, 1981); Anon., *The Autobiography of a Private Soldier, Showing the Danger of Rashly Enlisting* (Sunderland: Williams and Binns, 1838).

30. For statistics see P. Bairoch, *The Working Population and its Structure* (New York, NY: Gordon and Breach, 1968), p. 99. For detailed explanation see Burnett's Introductory essays to the following sections of *Annals of Labour:* "The Labouring Classes," "Domestic Servants," and "Skilled Workers."

31. William Adams, *Memoirs of a Social Atom* (1903; rpt. ed. New York, NY: Augustus M. Kelley, 1968), p. xiii.

32. Charles Shaw, *When I Was A Child* (1893; rpt. East Ardsley, Wakefield: SR Publishers, 1969), p. 97.

33. *Life As We Have Known It,* p. 60.

34. For a cultural critique of the narratives of English public school boys, see Gagnier, " 'From Fag to Monitor; Or, Fighting to the Front': Art and Power in Public School Memoirs," Robert Viscusi, ed., *Browning Institute Studies* 16 (1988), special volume on Victorian Learning, pp. 15–38. Also see Gagnier, *Subjectivities* (1990).

35. Emma Smith (pseud.), *A Cornish Waif's Story: An Autobiography* (London: Odhams, 1954), p. 154.

36. For the two modes see *Life As We Have Known It* and David Vincent, ed., *Testaments of Radicalism: Memoirs of Working Class Politicians 1790–1885* (London: Europa, 1977). The fact that these primarily political and polemical documents represent a wide historical distance is less significant when it is realized that the gender difference alluded to is borne out by many "genres" of working-class autobiography throughout the period: e.g., conversion and gallows narratives as well commemorative storytelling.

37. In *Victorian Writing and Working Women: The Other Side of Silence* (Cambridge: Polity Press, 1985), Julia Swindells also analyzes some working women's autobiographies in "Part 2: Working Women's Autobiographies" (pp. 115–207) in terms of what she calls "the literary." I see such "literary" effects controlling one kind of working-class writing, produced by men and women; whereas Swindells appears to find it characteristic of working women's writing exclusively and as a whole.

38. James Dawson Burn, *The Autobiography of a Beggar Boy* (1855) David Vincent, ed. (London: Europa, 1978), p. 78.

39. See Vincent's Introduction, p. 28.

40. John Burnett, ed., *Annals of Labour,* p. 52; Jermy (Norwich: Goose and Son, 1934).

41. Mayhew cited in John R. Gillis, *For Better or Worse: British Marriage, 1600 to the Present* (Oxford: Oxford University Press, 1985), p. 244.

42. Ellen Johnston, *The Autobiography, Poems, and Songs of "The Factory Girl"* (Glasgow: William Love, 1867), pp. 5, 62.

Chapter Eight

1. This and each of the personal narratives to which I refer is housed in the Bancroft Library, University of California, Berkeley. Unless otherwise indicated, references to the manuscripts will be cited by manuscript page (e.g., Lorenzana, p. 5) within the essay. All translations are mine, except those specified in the text.

2. Bancroft's opening comments in *California Pastoral* (San Francisco, CA: The History Co., 1888) should suffice to make my point here: "Before penetrating into the mysteries of our modern lotus-land, or entering upon a description of the golden age of California, if indeed any age characterized by ignorance and laziness can be called golden. . . ." (p. 1). The text, comprising some 800 pages of ethnographic information on Mexican society before and shortly after 1848, is saturated by this form of ethnocentric consciousness.

3. *Literary Industries: A Memoir* (San Francisco, CA: The History Co., 1891), p. 285. It should be pointed out that Bancroft hired numerous assistants to collect the personal narratives. Enrique Cerruti and Thomas Savage were two of the principle collectors who, during a six-year period from 1863–1870, traveled a wide circuit from San Francisco to San Diego transcribing the lives of the Californios. See Savage's "Report on Labors and Archives and Procuring Material for the History of California, 1876–79," and Cerruti's more autobiographical "Ramblings in California" (1874), both in the Manuscript Collection, Bancroft Library, University of California, Berkeley.

4. For useful accounts of the Mexican–American War, as well as the social, political, and cultural transformations that resulted, see: Rodolfo Acuna, *Occupied America: A History of Chicanos* (New York, NY: Harper & Row, 1981); Albert Camarillo, *Chicanos in a Changing Society: From Mexican Pueblos to American Barrios in Santa Barbara and Southern California, 1848–1930* (Cambridge, MA: Harvard University Press, 1979); Richard Griswold del Castillo, *The Los Angeles Barrio, 1850–1890: A Social History* (Berkeley, CA: University of California Press, 1979); John R.

Chavez, *The Lost Land: The Chicano Image in the Southwest* (Albuquerque, NM: University of New Mexico Press, 1984); Leonard Pitt, *The Decline of the Californios: A Social History of the Spanish-Speaking Californians, 1846–1980* (Los Angeles, CA: University of California Press, 1966); Carey McWilliams, *North from Mexico: The Spanish-Speaking People of the United States* (New York, NY: Greenwood, 1968).

5. In *California Pastoral,* Bancroft wishes to appear as a champion of the women, but given his ethnocentric proclivities and his own patriarchal bent, his sentiments are again immediately suspect. For example, Chapter 10, "Woman and Her Sphere," opens thus: "Women were not treated with the greatest respect: in Latin and in savage countries they seldom are . . ." (p. 305); and then adds: "It was a happy day for the California bride whose husband was American, and happier still for the California husband whose bride was Yankee" (p. 312). Later he delights in comparing Mexican women and their more *beautiful* American sisters, to the merit of neither: "The beauty of women is of shorter duration in Spanish countries than in the United States; but the monster Time behaves differently in the two places. In the states, the sere and yellow leaf of beauty shrivels into scragginess in the extremes of the type; but in Spanish-speaking countries it is not the withering of the gourd of beauty that those have to deplore who sit beneath its shadow with so great delight, but it is the broadening of that shadow. Without altogether endorsing sylph-like forms, it is yet safe to affirm that degrees of beauty in women are not in direct ratio to the degrees of the latitude of their circumference" (p. 324). Otherwise, Bancroft asserts that "among the married women of the common class, there was looseness—not remarkably so, but they were less strict than American women in this respect" (p. 321).

6. The "Recuerdos," unlike the Franklinian autobiographical text which charts the rise of the individual from poverty and obscurity, is a history of the individual's fall from power, loss of wealth, and social displacement. For all its troubling class attitudes and contradictions, it is also a consciously subversive narrative which was, by Vallejo's own reckoning, a staunchly revisionist counter-discourse. In a letter to his son, Platon, Vallejo writes: "I shall not stop moistening my pen in the blood of our unfounded detractors, certain accursed writers who have insulted us . . . to contradict those who slander 'tis not vengeance, it is regaining a loss." Madie Brown Emparan, *The Vallejos of California* (San Francisco, CA: University of San Francisco Press, 1968), p. 182.

7. The Bear Flag rebellion, which initiated the Mexican American War in California, commenced when a group of Americans took Mariano Vallejo, and his brother Salvador, Jacobo Leese, and other Californios prisoner, raised a flag with a bear insignia, and proclaimed their liberation from Mexican rule. Rosalia Vallejo de Leese describes these Americans as "a large group of rough-looking men, some wearing caps made

with the skins of coyotes or wolves, some wearing slouched hats full of holes, some wearing straw hats as black as coal. The majority of this marauding band wore buckskin pants . . . several had no shirts, shoes were only to be seen on the feet of the fifteen or twenty among the whole lot." And like Angustias de la Guerra she describes having resisted the Americans, by saving a seventeen-year-old girl from being sexually assaulted by Fremont and his officers. She also bitterly remembers being forced to write a letter to a Captain Padilla, who was riding toward Sonoma with troops, requesting him to return to San Jose; she says "I consented, not for the purpose of saving my life, but being then in the family way I had no right to endanger the life of my unborn baby; moreover, I judged that a man who had gone so far would not stop at anything [Fremont told me he would burn our houses with us inside them] . . . and being desirous of saving trouble to my countrywomen I wrote the fatal letter." "History of the Bear Flag Party," Manuscript Collection, Bancroft Library, p. 5.

8. Rosalia Vallejo de Leese's narrative "History of the Bear Flag Party" is only some six pages long. A note in the manuscript vaguely mentions that it was recorded by her daughter Rosalia, but it was probably transcribed by Enrique Cerruti, who was the chief collector in the Sonoma area, and whose transcription of Salvador Vallejo's narrative is also recorded in English.

9. As it turned out, Doña Perez was actually about 104 years old when she narrated her life. Her repute as an "ancient woman," however, had circulated sufficiently to make her an item of wide curiosity. In fact, at the very end of the narrative, her daughter, María de Rosario, was worried that a member of the family would try to capitalize on her mother's reputed age: "In June of the year 1876 my sister Maria Antonia . . . wanted to make some money by capitalizing on my mother for six weeks, exhibiting her in San Francisco for $5,000 in Woodward Gardens, and afterwards taking her to the exposition in Philadelphia. Fortunately, she had already been taken secretly to Los Angeles." "Una vieja y sus recuerdos," Manuscript Collection, Bancroft Library, p. 34.

Chapter Nine

1. Clara Shortridge Foltz, "The Struggles and Triumphs of a Woman Lawyer," *The New American Woman,* (March, 1918) [Hereinafter "Struggles."]

With its focus on her early career, "Struggles" is a major source for this article. Its value, however, is somewhat diminished because the columns bear the disorganized mark of haste. Many of them were written late at night, when Foltz was tired and sad. Others are, as she acknowledged, "embroidered with flowers of fancy," as well as embellished with pieces of past lectures and bits of poetry. Nevertheless, used with caution and subjected to factual confirmation, "Struggles" is an invaluable reference, both for her feelings and for her actions during the years 1878–1879.

2. In the only extensive law review article about Clara Foltz, the authors cite a telephone interview with the housekeeper of Virginia Foltz Catron, the only child to survive Foltz. The housekeeper asserted that after Foltz's death, Virginia sold her mother's furniture and destroyed her papers because "Virginia was never a saver." Schwartz, Brandt and Milrod, "Clara Shortridge Foltz: Pioneer in the Law," 27 *Hastings Law Review*, 545, n. 150 (1976). This is an excellent article, which saved Foltz from the historical oblivion into which she had fallen.

In March 1988, investigators in my employ interviewed a man who was Foltz's neighbor in Los Angeles, and who helped to clean out the house when she died in 1934. He reported that there was a big auction of her furniture and that "tons of papers," including letters, pictures, scrapbooks, and portfolios of oil stocks, were "chucked out."

3. Foltz was a publisher four times. In 1887–1888, she put out a daily newspaper, *The San Diego Bee*. It offers a wealth of information about her activities and interests, and reflects her thought in editorials.

In 1898–1899, she practiced in Denver, as well as New York, and helped start a weekly magazine, *The Mecca* (because Colorado, having accorded women suffrage in 1895, was a "mecca for all civilized men and women"). My research to date indicates that she did not stay with this enterprise long enough for it to be a major source of information about her.

Returning to San Francisco around the turn of the century, Foltz became an oil and gas lawyer and published the monthly magazine *Oil Fields and Furnaces*. Amidst advertisments and engineering reports of promising oil fields are lively accounts of Foltz's visits to sites, and her opinions on other people in the industry.

Finally, she published *The New American Woman* in Los Angeles from 1916–1918. It started as a newsletter to her friends but almost immediately grew into a monthly magazine, crammed with Foltz's opinions on everything from Wilson's war policies to the future of moving pictures.

4. Newspapers are a major source of biographical information about Clara Foltz. There were hundreds of newspapers in her day and she was a famous person who appeared in print regularly. The nineteenth-century newspapers did not espouse objectivity, or demarcate reporting and commentary. Many insights into the newswriters', the public's and Foltz's own assessment of events can be found in the numerous stories about her activities.

5. Many of Foltz's friends, colleagues, associates, and allies were well documented people. Because she was a lawyer, court papers, bar listings, and biographical indexes, transcripts of trials and reported appellate

opinions record factual data and enable an assessment of her professional reputation and the nature and quality of her practice.

6. "A Sketch of Clara Shortridge Foltz," *West Coast Magazine* 13 (October 1912), pp. 43–44.

7. "Struggles" (August 1916).

8. *San Jose Mercury* (reprinted from the *San Francisco Post*), (20 August 1882), p. 5.

9. Ella Sterling Cummins, "Clara Shortridge Foltz," *San Franciscan Magazine* (ca 1883). A reprint of the Cummins article, undated and without a source for the reprint, is in a "Foltz Biographical" file at the California State Library, Sacramento. The ages of her children, mentioned in the article, place it at about 1883. Cummins, one of the leading women journalists of the West Coast, seems to have inspired Foltz's confidence and reports details of her marriage and divorce that are not included in later interviews and official biographical entries. Parts of the Cummins story about Foltz were widely reprinted in newspapers.

10. "Struggles" (August, 1916). For the full context of the quotation, see text at footnote 28.

11. Cummins, *supra* n. 9.

12. Ibid.

13. Wells Drury to Governor H. H. Markham, April 10, 1891 (on file in the archives of the California Secretary of State, Sacramento).

14. California Constitution, Article 9, Section 9 (education clause); Article 20, Section 18, (employment clause) (1879).

15. *Foltz v. Hoge,* 54 Cal. Rep. 28 (1879).

16. *San Jose Times Mercury,* (1 January 1885), p. 1.

17. *Bradwell v. Illinois,* 83 U.S. (16 Wall) 130, (1873) (Justice Bradley concurring).

18. There are explanations, other than giving a more acceptable rationale for her career, for her lie about being a widow. Perhaps she grew to dislike the position of deserted wife, and felt that the title of widow was more dignified, or required less explanation. Perhaps she lied for social-status reasons, although divorce was not as socially unacceptable in the West as elsewhere in the country.

Laura Gordon also once referred to herself as a "widow" shortly after her divorce. (Laura Gordon to un-named friend, 16 February 1877. Papers of Laura DeForce Gordon, Stein Collection, Bancroft Library, University of California at Berkeley). Perhaps it was customary to treat divorce like death, at least in its immediate aftermath.

19. "A Prominent Woman Lawyer of New York," *The New York Times Illustrated Magazine* (11 July 1897), p. 4.

20. *San Jose Mercury* (14 March 1878), p. 4. "Mrs. Clara Foltz and her daughter, Trella E." went to Oregon "to visit their husband and father at Portland, and Mrs. Foltz to attend the Oregon State Woman Suffrage Convention . . ." She also "addressed large audiences in Albany, Salem, and Portland; and the press generally speak in the highest terms of her efforts in behalf of the cause of woman's enfranchisement."

The City Directory of San Jose for 1878 lists Clara Foltz as a widow. She may have assumed this designation after her trip to Portland, although she did not file for divorce until July, 1879.

21. *New Northwest* (1 March 1878), p. 1. "We learn that she expects to return to Oregon in the Autumn to practice her chosen profession."

22. "Mrs. Foltz as a Lawyer," *New Northwest* (reprinted in part from the *San Francisco Chronicle*), (6 February 1879), p. 2.

23. Sarah Wallis to Laura Gordon (7 March 1879), Gordon papers, *supra* n. 18. Wallis also said of Jeremiah Foltz: "he will be no benefit to her in her noble efforts to place her sex upon an equal plane with men politically and civilly."

24. "Correspondence of the Record Union," *Sacramento Record Union* (25 February 1879), p. 1, emphasis supplied.

25. "Finding her burdens heavier than she could bear, [Clara Foltz] applied for and received a divorce and the custody of her children. In two weeks time, Mr. Foltz had married again." Cummins, *supra* n. 9.

26. Josephine Woolcott to Laura Gordon (19 April 1879), Gordon papers, *supra* n. 18.

27. *San Francisco Post, supra* n. 8.

28. "Struggles" (August 1916).

29. *New York World* (ca 1897). (This clipping was in an undated batch of newspaper clippings on Foltz in the San Diego Law Library.)

30. "Struggles" (August 1916).

31. "Women at the Bar: Clara Foltz of San Francisco," *The Students Helper*, 1 (October 1893), pp. 263–265. Repeatedly, press accounts and interviews stress Foltz's feminine virtues: her home's tasteful decor, her beautiful dress, her womanly manner. This happens so often that she, rather than many different interviewers, must have placed this emphasis. The story quoted in the text was written in 1893, just after she returned from speaking at the Chicago World's Fair on the subject of Public Defenders. The article concludes:

But, after all, it is as hostess that Mrs. Foltz is at her best, which is demonstrated to all who call on her at her beautiful home on Van Ness Avenue, in San Francisco. Here, with her mother and two daughters still at home, she lives, a standing demonstration that a woman may be a lawyer, an orator, may take an active and earnest interest in her country and the welfare of her people, and not for a moment lose the graces, or sweetness, or beauty that crowns and glorifies woman in the home.

Chapter Ten

1. Cid Corman, ed., *The Granite Pail: The Selected Poems of Lorine Niedecker* (San Francisco, CA: North Point Press, 1985). Robert Bertholf, ed., *From This Condensery: The Complete Writing of Lorine Niedecker* (Highlands, NC: Jargon Society Press, 1985). This edition of Niedecker's work is used throughout.

2. Niedecker to Kenneth Cox, 10 December 1966, "Extracts from Letters to Kenneth Cox," in Peter Dent, ed., *The Full Note: Lorine Niedecker* (Devon: Interim Press, 1983), p. 36.

3. *From This Condensery*, p. 93.

4. Ibid.

5. For a more detailed analysis of the correspondence, tracing Zukofsky's influence on Niedecker's poems, see my essay "Lorine Niedecker and Louis Zukofsky," *Pacific Coast Philology* 20, 1–2 (November 1985), pp. 25–32. The text of Niedecker's postcard to Zukofsky, given on page 30 of my essay, makes clear that she thought of marriage as enslavement for the husband as well as the wife.

6. *From This Condensery*, p. 104.

7. Ibid., p. 91.

8. Cid Corman reports Niedecker's recollection in "With Lorine," *Truck*, No. 16 (Summer 1975), p. 5. Letters and manuscripts exchanged by Niedecker and Zukofsky are in the Louis Zukofsky Collection of the Humanities Research Center at the University of Texas, Austin. In the collection are four folders of letters from Zukofsky to Niedecker, dating from 1933–1970. Niedecker cut up many of Zukofsky's letters, then arranged and mounted the fragments on sheets of paper, as preparation for her edition of his letters. The collection includes 323 cards and letters by Niedecker to Zukofsky, dating from 1937–1966.

9. Niedecker to Cox, 10 December 1966.

10. Niedecker to Cox, 11 June 1969.

11. Niedecker to Cid Corman, 28 May 1969, in Lisa Pater Faranda, ed., *"Between Your House and Mine": The Letters of Lorine Niedecker to Cid Corman, 1960 to 1970* (Durham, NC: Duke University Press, 1986). All subsequent references to Niedecker's letters to Corman are to this text.

12. My information about Niedecker's stay with Zukofsky comes from interviews with two people who have requested anonymity. According to one of my sources, the abortion revealed twin fetuses, which Niedecker referred to as "Lost and Found." Her "joke" reveals her bitterness and dismay.

13. Niedecker to Zukofsky, 12 January 1947. Unpublished letter in the Louis Zukofsky Collection, Humanities Research Center, University of Texas, Austin. Niedecker's letter is an enthusiastic response to Zukofsky's essay, "Poetry: For My Son When He Can Read." The sentence immediately preceding the quotation reads: "The first moments of reading essay I was so excited and carried back to years ago when I first saw your writing in the Poetry issue."

14. Niedecker to Corman, 28 July 1965.

15. Niedecker's review appeared in August Derleth's "Books of Today" section of *Capital Times* (Madison, WI), 18 December 1948. Her essay, "The Poetry of Louis Zukofsky," was published in *Quarterly Review of Literature*, 8, 3 (1956): 198–210.

16. Niedecker to Williams, 29 December 1956. Unpublished letter in The Poetry/Rare Books Collection, The University at Buffalo, State University of New York. The manuscript was tentatively titled "For Paul and Other Poems."

17. Niedecker to Corman, 9 February 1966.

18. Interview with Carl Rakosi, San Francisco, CA, 30 April 1986.

19. Niedecker to Corman, 8 June 1965.

20. Niedecker to Corman, 8 June 1965 and 7 October 1965.

21. Niedecker to Corman, 7 October 1965.

22. Niedecker to Cox, 2 May 1969.

23. Niedecker to Cox, 2 February 1970.

24. Niedecker to Gail Roub, June 1970, quoted by Lisa Faranda in *"Between Your House and Mine,"* p. 229.

25. "Paean to Place," *From This Condensery*, p. 222.

26. Niedecker to Corman, 15 May 1969. She is quoting from a letter to her from Kenneth Cox.

27. Niedecker to Jonathan Williams, 20 August 1965. (The letter is dated 22 August, but the postmark is 20 August.) Unpublished letter, The Poetry/Rare Books Collection, The University at Buffalo, State University of New York.

28. *From This Condensery*, p. 211.

29. Darwin to Watkins, 18 August 1832, in Francis Darwin, ed., *The Life and Letters of Charles Darwin*, 2 Vols. (New York, NY: Basic Books, 1959), Vol. I, p. 214.

30. Darwin to Hooker, quoted by Alan Moorehead in *Darwin and "The Beagle"* (New York, NY: Harper & Row, 1969), p. 261. I believe this was Niedecker's source for the quotation.

31. Darwin to Gray, 22 May 1865, in *The Life and Letters*, Vol. II, p. 105.

32. *From This Condensery*, p. 215.

33. Ibid., p. 106.

34. In her 1831 introduction to *Frankenstein*, Mary Shelley concludes, "And now, once again, I bid my hideous progeny go forth and prosper." Like many readers of Shelley's novel, Niedecker has given Frankenstein's monster his creator's name. Her syntax in this third stanza creates additional mergings of identity: "his yellow eye" seems to belong to the monster, his creator Frankenstein and their creator Mary Shelley. In this poem about identity, such confusions must be deliberate.

Chapter Eleven

1. Ian Hamilton, *Robert Lowell, A Biography* (New York, NY: Random House, 1982), p. 3.

2. Peter Manso, *Mailer: His Life and Times* (New York, NY: Simon and Schuster, 1985), p. 11.

3. Elinor Langer, *Josephine Herbst: The Story She Could Never Tell* (Boston, MA: Atlantic–Little, Brown, 1984), p. 3.

Chapter Twelve

1. Paul Celan, "Ansprache anlässlich der Entgegennahme des Literaturpreises der freien Hansestadt Bremen" (Bremen speech, 1958), in Beda Allemann & Stefan Reichert, eds. with Rolf Bücher, *Gesammelte Werke* (Frankfurt: Suhrkamp, 1983), Vol. III, p. 185. This collected

edition, in five volumes, is hereafter referred to as *GW*. All translations in this essay are mine.

2. Robert Hass, "Meditation at Lagunitas," in *Praise* (New York, NY: Ecco, 1979), p. 4.

3. *GW*, Vol. I, p. 111.

4. George Steiner, *Language and Silence: Essays on Language, Literature, and the Inhuman* (New York, NY: Atheneum, 1967).

5. *GW*, Vol. III, p. 186.

6. *GW*, Vol. III, p. 185.

7. *GW*, Vol. I, p. 129.

8. *GW*, Vol. I, p. 222.

9. *GW*, Vol. III, p. 95. H. N. Bialik, *Kol Shirei* (Tel Aviv: Davir, 1961), p. 182.

10. *GW*, Vol. I, p. 66.

11. For material on Celan's early years, see Israel Chalfen, *Paul Celan: Eine Biographie seiner Jugend* (Frankfurt: Insel, 1979), the first two chapters of which have been translated by Robert de Beaugrande in *Dimension* 7, 3 (1974), pp. 324–35. See also John Felstiner, "Paul Celan: The Strain of Jewishness," *Commentary* (April 1985), pp. 44–55.

12. Chalfen, pp. 40, 31.

13. Otto Pöggeler, "Kontroverses zur Asthetik Paul Celans (1920–1970)," *Zeitschrift für Asthetik und allgemeine Kunstwissenschaft* 25, 2 (1980), p. 226.

14. Clarence Brown, ed., *The Prose of Osip Mandelstam* (Princeton, NJ: Princeton University Press, 1965), pp. 81, 90.

15. Paul Celan, *Gedichte 1938–1944* (Frankfurt: Suhrkamp, 1985), p. 16.

16. *Gedichte,* p. 17.

17. Chalfen, p. 119.

18. *Gedichte,* p. 88.

19. *GW*, Vol. III, p. 25.

20. Chalfen, p. 127 and Ruth Rubin, *Voices of a People: The Story of Yiddish Folksong* (Philadelphia, PA: Jewish Publication Society, 1979), pp. 371–72.

21. *GW*, Vol. III, p. 20.

22. Chalfen, p. 148.

23. *Literatur und Kritik* 125 (June, 1978), pp. 273–4.

24. *GW,* Vol. III, pp. 192–3.

25. George Steiner, *After Babel: Aspects of Language and Translation* (New York, NY: Oxford University Press, 1975), chapter 5.

26. *GW,* Vol. I, p. 110.

27. *GW,* Vol. I, p. 239.

Chapter Thirteen

I would like to thank the director and staff of the Joods Historisch Museum in Amsterdam for the use of the Charlotte Salomon collection; and Marilyn Yalom, Susan Bell, and John Felstiner for their advice and tireless assistance.

1. Reproductions of Charlotte Salomon's work and information about her life are available in the following publications. *Charlotte: Life or Theater? An Autobiographical Play by Charlotte Salomon,* translated by Leila Vennewitz (New York, NY: Viking Press in association with Gary Schwartz, 1981). In German this book appeared as Charlotte Salomon, *Leben oder Theater? Ein autobiographisches Singspiel in 769 Bildern* (Cologne: Kiepenheuer & Witsch, 1981). Page numbers are the same in English and German editions. Translations from Charlotte Salomon's German texts are my own. Hereafter, the autobiography is referred to as *Leben oder Theater?*

An earlier selection of eighty reproductions was published as Charlotte Salomon, *Ein Tagebuch in Bildern, 1917–1943* (Hamburg: Rowohlt, 1963), and in English as *Charlotte: A Diary in Pictures* (New York, NY: Harcourt, Brace, and World, 1963). Written material on Charlotte Salomon appears in prefaces and introductions by Judith Belinfante, Gary Schwartz, Judith Herzberg in *Charlotte: Life or Theater?;* by Emil Straus in *Charlotte: A Diary in Pictures;* and in an exhibition catalogue compiled by Christine Fischer-Defoy, published as *Charlotte Salomon—Leben oder Theater?* (Berlin: Das Arsenal, 1986). Charlotte Salomon's work has been exhibited in museums in the Netherlands, the United States, Israel, Japan, and Germany.

2. See, for example, Estelle Jelinek, ed., *Women's Autobiography: Essays in Criticism* (Bloomington, IN: Indiana University Press, 1980), pp. 1–20; Domna Stanton, ed., *The Female Autograph* (New York, NY: New York Literary Forum, 1984). On transmission from mother to daughter and women's identification with others, see Nancy Chodorow, *The Repro-*

duction of Mothering: Psychoanalysis and the Sociology of Gender (Berkeley, CA: University of California Press, 1978) and Dorothy Dinnerstein, *The Mermaid and the Minotaur: Sexual Arrangement and Human Malaise* (New York, NY: Harper, 1977).

3. Emil Straus, Introduction, Charlotte Salomon, *Charlotte: Ein Tagebuch in Bildern,* p. 9.

4. Charlotte Salomon, *Leben oder Theater?*, pp. 637, 639, 643, 688.

5. See Mary Felstiner, "Taking Her Life/History: The Autobiography of Charlotte Salomon," in Bella Brodzki and Celeste Schenck, eds., *Life/ Lines: Theorizing Women's Autobiographies* (Ithaca, NY: Cornell University Press, 1988), pp. 320–337.

6. *Leben oder Theater,* p. 711.

7. Ibid., pp. 640–641.

8. Ibid., pp. 685–686.

9. Ibid., p. 687.

10. Emil Straus, *op. cit.,* p. 11.

11. *Leben oder Theater?,* p. 693.

12. Statistics from Gilbert Badia, *Les Barbelés de l'exil: Études sur l'émigration allemande et autrichienne, 1938–1940* (Grenoble: Presses universitaires, 1979), pp. 15, 17, 21.

13. *Leben oder Theater?,* p. 695–697.

14. Ibid., pp. 698–700.

15. Ibid., pp. 702–05.

16. Ibid., pp. 706–13.

17. Ibid., pp. 722–23.

18. Ibid., pp. 744–45.

19. Ibid., pp. 746–53.

20. Ibid., p. 755.

21. Ibid., p. 777.

22. Ibid., p. 781.

23. Ibid., pp. 722, 729.

24. Ibid., pp. vii, 781.

25. Ibid., pp. 722–723.

26. Unnumbered paintings #808, 810, 811, 807. Aside from the paintings Charlotte Salomon chose and ordered by number for "Life or Theater?," she saved hundreds of painted studies and texts, which are archived as unnumbered paintings in the Amsterdam Jewish Historical Museum.

27. *Leben oder Theater?*, p. 636.

28. Ibid., pp. 781–82.

29. Ibid., p. 782–783.

30. Phrase recalled by the Villefranche doctor's wife, Madame Moridis, quoted in "Foreword" by Judith Herzberg, Ibid., vii, xii. Auschwitz was the deathcamp in Poland where most of those deported from France lost their lives.

Chapter Fourteen

1. Among the many father-memoirs not dealt with individually here are Peter Henisch, *Die kleine Figur meines Vaters. Erzählung* (Frankfurt am Main: S. Fischer, 1975); Elisabeth Plessen, *Mitteilung an den Adel. Roman* (Zurich: Benziger, 1976); Bernward Vesper, *Die Reise. Romanessay* (Berlin: Marz, 1977); Paul Kersten, *Der alltägliche Tod meines Vaters*, (Cologne: Kiepenheuer & Wietsch, 1978); E. A. Rauter, *Brief an meine Erzieher* (Munich, Weismann, 1979); Heinrich Wiesner, *Der Riese am Tisch* (Basel: Lenos, 1979); Barbara Bronnen, *Die Tochter. Roman* (Munich: Piper, 1980); Christoph Meckel, *Suchbild. Über meinen Vater* (Dusseldorf: Claassen, 1980); Jutta Schutting, *Der Vater. Erzählung* (Salzburg: Residenz, 1980); Brigitte Schwaiger, *Lange Abwesenheit* (Vienna: Paul Zsolnay, 1980); Günter Seuren, *Abschied von einem Mörder* (Reinbeck: Rowohlt, 1980); Herrad Schenk, *Die Unkündbarkeit der Verheissung. Roman* (Dusseldorf: Claassen, 1984); and most recently Niklas Frank, *Der Vater. Eine Abrechnung* (Munich: Bertelsmann, 1987).

My work on this material has been greatly assisted by the 1984 NEH Summer Seminar on The Woman Question: 1750–1950, conducted at Stanford University by Susan Groag Bell and Karen Offen, and by a sabbatical leave and a Henry Luce Fellowship from The College of Wooster.

2. *Der Mann auf der Kanzel: Fragen an einen Vater* (Munich: Hanser, 1977). The translation of the title and of all quotations from the text are mine.

3. *Nachgetragene Liebe* (Darmstadt: Luchterhand, 1980). The translation of title and of all quotations from the text are mine.

4. Klaus Theweleit provides a provocative if controversial survey of the psychological and cultural mechanisms at work in the Nazi ideology of masculinity in *Männerphantasien*, 2 vols. (Reinbeck bei Hamburg:

Rowohlt, 1977). Volume I recently appeared in English as *Male Fantasies: Women, Floods, Bodies, History,* translated by Stephen Conway et al., vol. 22 of *Theory and History of Literature* (Minneapolis, MN: University of Minnesota Press, 1987).

5. A particularly good discussion of the psycho-pathology of the postwar family can be found in Michael Schneider, "Väter und Söhne posthum. Das beschädigte Verhältnis zweier Generationen," *Den Kopf verkehrt aufgesetzt oder die melancholische Linke. Aspekte des Kulturzerfalls in den siebziger Jahren* (Darmstadt: Luchterhand, 1981).

6. Alexander und Margarete Mitscherlich, *Die Unfähigkeit zu trauern. Grundlagen kollektiven Verhaltens,* 2nd ed. (Munich: R. Piper, 1980), especially pp. 1–84.

7. *Vaterspuren. Eine Erzählung* (Frankfurt am Main: Suhrkamp, 1982), originally published by Athenaum Verlag, Konigstein/Ts, 1979.

8. *Ghost Waltz: A Memoir* (New York, NY: Viking, 1980). Published in German as *Geisterwalzer,* translated by Ingeborg Day and Ulrich Fries (Salzburg: Residenz, 1983).

9. "Gespräch zwischen Sigfrid Gauch und Jürgen Serke," *Deutsche Väter. Über das Vaterbild in der deutschsprachigen Gegenwartsliteratur,* vol. 6 of *Loccumer Protokolle* (Loccum: Evangelische Akademie Loccum, 1981), p. 74.

10. Gauch and Serke, "Gesprach," p. 73.

11. In this connection Susan Lanser speaks of "the relationship of the writer to the act of producing and transmitting the literary work. Such a relationship is essentially ideological as well as aesthetic, for the act of writing, indeed the act of using language, is defined, contained and conventionalized according to a system of values, norm, and perspectives of the world." *The Narrative Act: Point of View in Prose Fiction* (Princeton, NJ: Princeton University Press, 1981), p. 65. The father's relationship to his literary work is very different from that of the son's to his.

12. Wolfgang Neuber understands the daughters' radical critique of the fathers as a consequence of their inability as women to identify with their fathers' authority and power. I cannot agree however with his conclusion that in the father books male means of coming to terms with the father are overly rationalized and that female means are irrational and aggressive. "Fremderfahrungen von den kleinen Herrscherfiguren der Väter," *Amsterdamer Beitrage zur neueren Germanistik* 14 (1982), p. 271.

13. Although Day's memoir was published in English in the United States, I discuss it here because it suggests that the European interest in fathers is strong enough to span the Atlantic, because it is accessible to those who do not read German, and because its treatment of father-controlled language and narrative is particularly interesting.

14. The inadequacy of scholarly historical research and writing for understanding the past is a theme implicit in the father books by daughters, especially Ruth Rehmann, Herrad Schenk, and Barbara Bronnen.

15. See for example most recently Reinhard Baumgart, "Das Leben— kein Traum? Vom Nutzen und Nachteil einer autobiographischen Literatur," in Herbert Heckmann, ed., *Literatur aus dem Leben. Autobiographische Tendenzen in der deutschsprachigen Gegenwartsdichtung. Beobachtungen, Erfahrungen, Belege* (Munich: Hanser, 1984) pp. 20–22. I have found in newspaper reviews of the father literature a reluctance to accept the validity of individual stories for historical interpretation; a strongly defined set of gender expectations about daughterly piety and duty; concerns about what can appropriately be made public; and occasionally, especially by 1980, accusations of opportunism, of riding a popular literary wave.

16. An example of this kind of history on the recent German cultural scene are the family chronicles by Walter Kempowski, immensely popular as books and in their later television versions.

17. Ursula Mahlendorf suggests ways in which literature about the German past identifies or denies the importance of the family as a source of fascist mentality. "Confronting the Fascist Past and Coming to Terms With It," *World Literature Today* 55 (1981), pp. 556–558.

18. The political implications of narrative structure in the literary project of coming to terms with the German past are discussed by Judith Ryan in *The Uncompleted Past, Postwar German Novels and the Third Reich* (Detroit, MI: Wayne State University Press, 1983), p. 21 and passim.

Contributors

Jane Aaron is a lecturer in English at the University of Leicester, England, where she teaches courses on Romanticism, women's writing, and feminist theory. She has just finished a book on Charles and Mary Lamb, to be published by Oxford University Press, and is currently engaged in a more general study of gender and Romanticism for the Open University Press.

Barbara Allen Babcock, like her subject Clara Foltz, has often been "the first woman"—first to be a professor at the Stanford Law School, first to hold an endowed chair, first to direct the public defender service in Washington, D.C. She is the Ernest E. McFarland Professor of Law at Stanford University.

Susan Groag Bell is a historian and Senior Research Associate at the Institute for Research on Women and Gender at Stanford University. She has published *Women from the Greeks to the French Revolution* and *Women, the Family and Freedom: The Debate in Documents 1750–1950* (the latter with Karen Offen). She has written numerous articles on various aspects of women's history, including medieval women bookowners and women's relationship to the garden. At present she is working on an NEH-funded analysis of two thousand British women's autobiographies.

Glenna Breslin is Professor of English at Saint Mary's College at Moraga, California. She is writing a biography of Lorine Niedecker.

John Felstiner is the author of *The Lies of Art: Max Beerbohm's Parody and Caricature* and *Translating Neruda: The Way to Macchu Picchu.* He has written on Paul Celan for numerous journals and is tentatively entitling his new book *Translating Celan: The Strain of Jewishness.* He is Professor of English at Stanford University.

Mary Lowenthal Felstiner is Professor of History at San Francisco State University. She has published articles on the history of women, Latin America, and the Holocaust, and is writing a book about Charlotte Salomon.

Susan Figge is Associate Professor of German and Women's Studies at The College of Wooster in Ohio. She has written on the East German poet Sarah Kirsch and on German "father literature."

Regenia Gagnier, Associate Professor of English at Stanford University, is the author of *Subjectivities: The Pragmatics of Self-Representation* (Oxford, 1990), *Idylls of the Marketplace: Oscar Wilde and the Victorian Public* (Stanford, 1986), and many articles on feminist and social theory. At Stanford, she is also on the policy board of the Institute for Research on Women and Gender and a founding member of the Cultural Studies Group.

Anna Kuhn is Professor of German at the University of California at Davis. She is the author of *Christa Wolf's Utopian Vision: From Marxism to Feminism* and *Dialog bei Frank Wedekind.* She has also written on film and numerous German writers.

Carol Hanbery MacKay, Associate Professor of English at the University of Texas at Austin, specializes in Victorian fiction and Women's Studies. She is the author of *Soliloquy in Nineteenth-Century Fiction* as well as the editor of *The Two Thackerays* and *Dramatic Dickens.* Her current work in progress is a study of Victorian novelists and the Cult of the Actress.

Diane Wood Middlebrook is the Howard H. and Jessie T. Watkins University Professor and Professor of English at Stanford University. She is the author of *Walt Whitman and Wallace Stevens,* and *Worlds into Words: Understanding Modern Poems,* and the co-editor of *Coming to Light: American Women Poets in the Twentieth Century.* Her biography of Anne Sexton is forthcoming from Houghton Mifflin Company.

Genaro Padilla has taught English and Chicano Studies at the University of Utah and the University of California at Berkeley. He has published *The Stories of Fray Angelico Chavez* and several articles on Chicano literature.

Marilyn Yalom is the Senior Scholar at the Institute for Research on Women and Gender at Stanford University, where she has been since 1976. She was Professor of French at California State University, Hayward from 1963 to 1976. She is the author of *Maternity, Mortality, and the Literature of Madness* and *Le Temps des Orages: Aristocrates, Bourgeoises, et Paysannes Racontent*. She is the editor of *Women Writers of the West Coast,* co-editor of *Coming to Light: American Women Poets in the Twentieth Century,* and one of the associate editors of *Victorian Women: A Documentary Account of Women's Lives in Nineteenth-Century England, France and the United States.*

Mary Fleming Zirin is a freelance translator from Altadena, California and the founder-editor of *Women East—West,* a newsletter of Slavic women's studies. She is the translator and editor of *The Cavalry Maiden: Journals of a Russian Officer in the Napoleonic Wars.* She is currently at work on a comprehensive bio-bibliographic dictionary of Russian women writers to 1900.

Index